FOUNDATIONS IN RITUAL STUDIES

Liturgical

FOUNDATIONS IN RITUAL STUDIES

A reader for students of Christian worship

Edited by
PAUL BRADSHAW
and
JOHN MELLOH

Baker Academic
Grand Rapids, Michigan

© 2007 by Paul Bradshaw and John Melloh

Published in the United States by Baker Academic
a division of Baker Publishing Group
P.O. Box 6287, Grand Rapids, MI 49516-6287
www.bakeracademic.com

Library of Congress Cataloging-in-Publication Data is on file at the Library of Congress, Washington, DC

ISBN 10: 0-8010-3499-X
ISBN 978-0-8010-3499-2

Contents

Contents

Part 4
METHOD

Preface

Traditionally, the study of liturgy was understood as being the study of liturgical history: in order to understand what we do today, we need to know the origin and development of each particular liturgical practice and unit. It was only in the second half of the twentieth century that the horizons of the discipline began to be extended to include other dimensions, and in particular those of liturgical theology and ritual studies. The latter utilizes methods that had long been developed by the human sciences – especially cultural anthropology, psychology, sociology, linguistics and performative language theory, communications studies, semiotics, and phenomenology – but had previously been ignored by the theorists and practitioners of Christian liturgy.

The starting point for ritual studies is, as far as possible, the empirical observation and recording of the totality of an act of worship, since what is printed in liturgical texts and what is happening in the actual event are quite different things. In this process it is especially attentive to that often overlooked dimension of the phenomenon of worship – the people who are involved in the activity. Their attitudes, outlooks, lifestyles and behaviour, their understanding of what liturgy is for, their motives for participating in it, and the accounts they give of its place in their lives, all these are open to empirical research and constitute relevant data. In particular, this approach facilitates the possibility of a comparison between the theological claims which are made for liturgy and the actual experience and perception of its participants. Once the data has been collected, it must then be analysed. Among the many questions which may be addressed to the material are: How do signs and symbols operate within the liturgical event? What are they intended to communicate and how effective are they in this aim? How does a believer enter into a rite and become engaged by it? In what respects does a gathering of people for worship constitute a community and how does it function as such? How does the liturgical realm relate to and interact with the 'real world' within which the worshippers necessarily exist, and how does it affect their social and cultural identity in that world?

Although still in its infancy as far as liturgical scholars and teachers are concerned, ritual studies obviously has huge potential for helping worship leaders to understand better the activity in which they are engaged and the effect that their innovations can have on congregations.

It thus deserves a significant place in any curriculum of liturgical study. So far, however, it has been slow to receive that. In part, this is because those who teach have received little, if any, grounding in this aspect of the discipline, and even where they do feel prepared to tackle it in the courses that they give, they lack convenient access to written resources to support their work. This is where the genesis of this particular volume occurred. Collaboration between a liturgical historian, who is not an expert in the field of ritual studies but who recognizes its vital importance in the training of competent liturgical practitioners, and a teacher who focuses much of his work in this particular area has given rise to a series of carefully chosen extracts from previously published material, which it is hoped will assist both the individual student who wants to know more and also those responsible for giving instruction in liturgy to become better acquainted with some of its key scholars and theories.

Paul Bradshaw
John Melloh

Acknowledgements

The editors acknowledge with gratitude permission to reproduce these extracts granted by their authors and publishers:

Aldine Transaction, a division of Transaction Publishers, for 'Liminality and Communitas' by Victor Turner, copyright © 1969 by Aldine Publishers; and for Chapter 1 of *The Forest of Symbols* by Victor Turner, first published in *Closed Systems and Open Minds*, ed. Max Gluckman, copyright © 1964 by Aldine Publishers.

Catherine Bell, for 'Ritual, Change, and Changing Rituals'.

Mary Douglas and Taylor & Francis Books UK, for extracts from *Purity and Danger*, copyright © 1966 by Routledge & Kegan Paul, and from *Natural Symbols*, copyright © 1970 by Barrie & Rockliff.

The Editors of *The Study of Liturgy*, for 'Ritual' by Mark Searle.

Ronald L. Grimes, for 'Modes of Ritual Sensibility'.

The International African Institute for Chapter 2 of *The Forest of Symbols* by Victor Turner, first published in *African Systems of Thought*, ed. M. Fortes and G. Dieterlen (London: Oxford University Press 1965).

Margaret Mary Kelleher, for 'Liturgical Theology: A Task and a Method'.

Nathan D. Mitchell and The Liturgical Press, Collegeville, Minnesota, for 'New Directions in Ritual Research'.

The Notre Dame Center for Pastoral Liturgy, for 'The Authority of Ritual Experts' by Catherine Bell; 'Liturgical Supinity, Liturgical Erectitude: On the Embodiment of Ritual Authority' by Ronald L. Grimes; and 'For Our Own Purposes: The Appropriation of the Social Sciences in Liturgical Studies' by John Witvliet.

Part 1
CONTEXT

1

Romano Guardini

Introduction

No doubt there is nothing more morbid in itself, more inimical to nature, than *to see things as they are*... O Socrates, the universe cannot for one instant endure only to be what it is... The mistakes, the appearances, the play of the dioptrics of the mind deepen and quicken the world's miserable mass... The [imagined] idea introduces into what is, the leaven of what is not. (Paul Valéry, *Dance and the Soul*, in *The Collected Works of Paul Valéry*, ed. Jackson Mathews [New York: Pantheon Books 1954], 4: 52)

The Italian-born German theologian Romano Guardini (1885–1968) is generally regarded as the father of the German liturgical movement. In his short 'Open Letter' to Mgr Wagner, the organizer of the Third German Liturgical Congress, originally published in *Herder Correspondence* (Special Issue 1964), 24–26, he raises significant questions concerning the nature of the liturgical act in the wake of individualism, asking whether it is possible for twentieth-century Christians really to engage in worship. Is it possible to 'relearn a forgotten way of doing things and recapture lost attitudes', so as to enter into the liturgical experience?

For further reading

Ray Bradbury, *Dandelion Wine* (New York: Bantam 1976, 1981), 26–32, and 'Just This Side of Byzantium, An Introduction', vii–xiii.
Henri Nouwen, *Clowning in Rome* (New York: Doubleday 1979, 2000), Chapter 4, 'Contemplation and Caring'.

★★★

An open letter

Dear Friend,

I had very much wanted to take part in the Liturgical Congress at Mainz; I should have been glad of the opportunity to raise a point that seems important to me.

This is, unfortunately, impossible; I must be content to tell you my thoughts in a letter and hope that you will find a way to pass them on.

3

Essence of the liturgical act

Liturgical work, as we all know, has reached an important juncture. The Council has laid the foundations for the future – and the way this came to pass and truth became manifest will remain a classical example of the way the Spirit guides the Church. But now the question arises how we are to set about our task, so that truth may become reality.

A mass of ritual and textual problems will, of course, present themselves – and long experience has shown how much scope there is for a right and a wrong approach. But the central problem seems to me to be something else: the problem of the cult act or, to be more precise, the liturgical act.

As I see it, typical nineteenth-century man was no longer able to perform this act; in fact he was unaware of its existence. Religious conduct was to him an individual inward matter which in the 'liturgy' took on the character of an official, public ceremonial. But the sense of the liturgical action was thereby lost. The faithful did not perform a proper liturgical act at all, it was simply a private and inward act, surrounded by ceremonial and not infrequently accompanied by a feeling that the ceremonial was really a disturbing factor. From that point of view the efforts of those who concerned themselves with the liturgy must have appeared as peculiarities of aesthetes who lacked Christian sincerity.

The intensity of the Council discussions could not fail to bring home to anyone actively interested in the Church that here was a matter of fundamental importance. Anyone who did not become too engrossed in secondary problems such as the advisability of using the mother tongue must have found himself wondering what it was about the liturgy that caused such fierce arguments. The conclusion was inescapable that the religious act underlying the liturgy was something singular and important.

Further consideration of the nature of this singularity would lead to the conclusion that the liturgical act was performed by individuals who did, however, insofar as they were a sociological entity, form a *corpus*: the congregation, or rather the Church present therein. The act embraced not only a spiritual inwardness, but the whole man, body as well as spirit. Therefore the external action was in itself a 'prayer', a religious act; the times, places, and things included in the action were not merely external decorations, but elements of the whole act and would have to be practised as such, and so forth.

The usual discussion generally brings out only the sociological, ethnological aspect: participation by the congregation and use of the vernacular. There is, of course, far more to it than that; the act as a whole needs to be considered, in fact a whole world of acts which have become atrophied and are now to take on new life. But they must first be noticed and recognized as essential – and the danger is great that everything that is said will be dismissed as artificial and officious, especially by those whose inclinations are individualistic, rationalistic and above all, attached to traditions.

The question is whether the wonderful opportunities now open to the liturgy will achieve their full realization; whether we shall be satisfied with just removing anomalies, taking new situations into account, giving better instruction on the meaning of ceremonies and liturgical vessels or whether we shall relearn a forgotten way of doing things and recapture lost attitudes.

Liturgical crisis

The question will, of course, arise whether our present liturgy contains parts which cannot mean much to modern man. I remember a conversation with the late Abbot Ildefons Herwegen of Maria Laach, the great champion of liturgical renewal. We had been considering various aspects and I said a sign that the work for the liturgy was really coming to life would be a liturgical crisis, and Abbot Herwegen thoughtfully agreed. As long as liturgical actions are merely 'celebrated' objectively and texts are merely 'got through', everything will go smoothly because there is no question of an integrated religious act. But once serious prayer is joined to the action, the parts that have no living appeal become apparent.

But those whose task it is to teach and educate will have to ask themselves – and this is all-decisive – whether they themselves desire the liturgical act or, to put it plainly, whether they know of its existence and what exactly it consists of and that it is neither a luxury nor an oddity, but a matter of fundamental importance. Or does it, basically, mean the same to them as to the parish priest of the late nineteenth century who said, 'We must organize the procession better; we must see to it that the praying and singing is done better.' He did not realize that he should have asked himself quite a different question: how can the act of walking become a religious act, a retinue for the Lord progressing through his land, so that an 'epiphany' may take place.

Participation through looking

The basic question then is this: of what does the integrated liturgical act consist?

This becomes clearest when it is a matter of 'doing', for instance, the offertory procession, where this is customary. It makes all the difference whether the faithful look on this procession as a mere means to an end which could have been achieved equally well by someone coming round with a collection-plate, or whether they know that the act of bringing their gifts is a 'prayer' in itself, a readiness towards God.

The act of 'doing' can also incorporate a thing, in this case a coin; or holy water for the sign of the cross; and the celebrant has the bread and the chalice with the wine. There is no need for words to give the 'meaning', for it is realized in the act itself. The same is true of localities and special places, times, days, and hours.

The liturgical act can be realized by looking. This does not merely mean that the sense of vision takes note of what is going on in front, but it is in itself a living participation in the act. I once experienced this in Palermo Cathedral when I could sense the attention with which the people were following the blessings on Holy Saturday for hours on end without books or any words of 'explanation'. Much of this was, of course, an external 'gazing', but basically it was far more. The looking by the people was an act in itself; by looking they participated in the various actions. However, cinema, radio, and television – not to forget the flood of tourists – will have destroyed this remainder of old contemplative forces.

Only regarded in this way can the liturgical-symbolical action be properly understood, for instance the washing of hands by the celebrant, but also liturgical gestures, like the stretching out of hands over the chalice. It should not be necessary to have to add in words of thought, 'this means such and such', but the symbol should be 'done' by the celebrant as a religious act and the faithful should 'read' it by an analogous act; they should see the inner sense in the outward sign. Without this everything would be a waste of time and energy and it would be better simply to 'say' what was meant. But the 'symbol' is in itself something corporal-spiritual, an expression of the inward through the outward, and must as such be co-performed through the act of looking.

The communal act

Of particular importance for the liturgical act is the active and full participation of the congregation as a body. The act is done by every individual, not as an isolated individual, but as a member of a body in which the Church is present. It is this body which is the 'we' of the prayers. Its structure is different from that of any other collection of people meeting for a common purpose. It is that of a *corpus*, an objective whole. In the liturgical act the celebrating individual becomes part of this body and he incorporates the *circumstantes* in his self-expression. This is not so simple if it is to be genuine and honest. Much that divides men must be overcome, dislikes, indifference towards the many who are 'no concern of mine', but who are really members of the same body; lethargy, etc. In the act the individual becomes conscious of the meaning of the words 'congregation' and 'Church'.

Learning the liturgical act

If the intentions of the Council are to be realized, proper instruction will be needed, but real education will be needed too; practice will be necessary in order to learn the act. The active presence of the people of Palermo was based on the fact that they did not merely look up in the book what the various actions 'meant', but they actually 'read' them by simply looking – an after-effect of antique influences, probably paid for by a lack of primary education. Our problem is to rise above reading and writing and learn really to look with understanding.

This is the present task of liturgical education. If it is not taken in hand, reforms of rites and texts will not help much. It may even happen that people with a genuine concern for real piety come to feel that a misfortune is happening – like the venerable old parish priest who said, 'Before they started all this business with the liturgy my people were able to pray. Now there is a lot of talking and running around.'

A great deal of thought and experiment will, of course, be needed to get modern man to 'perform' the act without being theatrical and fussy. Nor must we forget that many who should be teachers and leaders are quite inexperienced in this field themselves; some even resist because they are inclined towards an individualistic way of devotion, regard these new demands as unreasonable and think in their hearts that it is just a question of waiting for the 'fashion' to pass – 'no doubt in the end everything will remain as it has always been'.

Phases of the liturgical movement

The liturgical movement has passed through various phases. It would be useful and interesting to trace them not only in their chronological order, but also in their progressively changing inner sense. If I may make a very summary sketch, I would describe the first phase, which started at Solesmes, as restorative and in some ways politically restorative. (It was connected with efforts to overcome Gallicanism and sought closer ties with Rome.) The second originated in Belgian Benedictine monasteries and was of a strongly academic nature. The third, which was centred on the Austrian monastery of Klosterneuburg and various centres of the German Catholic youth movements, had a practical, realistic character: it tried to reach and interest the congregation as it was and thus came up primarily against the problem of the vernacular.

Now, as a result of the impulse given by the Council, a fourth phase must begin, one infusing new life into the liturgy. It will be raising a number of questions: What is the nature of the genuine liturgical action as opposed to other religious actions, such as individual devotions or the loose communal act of popular devotions? How is the basic liturgical act constituted? What forms can it take? What might go wrong with it? How are its demands related to the make-up of modern man? What must be done so that he can really and truly learn it?

There are plenty of problems and tasks ahead. But perhaps one should for the sake of clarification put a preliminary question: Is not the liturgical act and, with it, all that goes under the name of 'liturgy' so bound up with the historical background – antique or medieval or baroque – that it would be more honest to give it up altogether? Would it not be better to admit that man in this industrial and scientific age, with its new sociological structure, is no longer capable of a liturgical act? And instead of talking of renewal ought we not to consider how best to celebrate the sacred mysteries so that modern man can grasp their meaning through his own approach to truth?

This seems a hard saying. But there are quite a number of people who think this way. We cannot simply dismiss them as people standing aloof, but we must ask how – if liturgy is indeed fundamental – we can best approach them.

There are indeed some promising and related developments. It is, for instance, no accident that the latest phase of the liturgical movement coincides with an awakening of a greater interest in the Church. At the same time the educational trend has been to present a far truer picture of man as a being whose body and spirit, outward and inner personality, form an integrated whole. The work for liturgical renewal has a lot to learn from these related developments. Some wise educationists have pointed out that modern man needs more than mere talk, intellectual explanations, and formal organizing. The faculties of looking, doing, and shaping must be fostered and included in the formative act; the musical element is more than merely decorative; the communal body of the congregation more than a mere sitting together, but rather a solidarity of existence, and so forth.

There is a great deal to be said on this subject, but perhaps I had better close, or else my letter will turn into an epistle . . .

Romano Guardini

2

Mark Searle

Introduction

[T]his study brings a particular perspective . . . , namely the position that 'ritual' is not an intrinsic, universal category or feature of human behavior – not yet, anyway. It is a cultural and historical construction that has been heavily used to help differentiate various styles and degrees of religiosity, rationality, and cultural determinism. (Catherine Bell, *Ritual: Perspectives and Dimensions* [New York: Oxford University Press 1997], ix)

Until his untimely death, Mark Searle taught liturgical studies in the Department of Theology at the University of Notre Dame, Notre Dame, Indiana, USA. In this short overview entitled 'Ritual', from *The Study of Liturgy*, ed. Cheslyn Jones, Geoffrey Wainwright, Edward Yarnold and Paul Bradshaw (revised edn; London: SPCK 1992), 51–58, he situates ritual within the orbit of liturgical studies, describing the emergence of this relatively new field of exploration. He raises, in seminal form, some important issues under discussion today.

***

Ritual

Study of liturgy as ritual

To study liturgy as ritual is to study liturgy, whether in history or in the present, in its empirical reality as a species of significant human behaviour. This is an approach to liturgical studies that has remained largely unexplored until very recent times, perhaps because the very idea of ritual was somewhat suspect. Among Roman Catholics, the Council of Trent confirmed a long-established dichotomy between the sacramental kernel of the rite, seen as an act of God, and the rest of the liturgy regarded as 'mere ceremony', useful for the edification of the faithful but generally relegated to the rubricists. Among Protestants, it has invariably proven difficult to evade the Puritan criticism of any preoccupation with 'externals' as a degenerate form of religion. In a sense, the whole Reformation was a protest against the way the word had been eclipsed by ritual in medieval Christianity, so that any concern with ritual was adjudged at best a distraction to religious seriousness, at worst a relapse into paganism.

Such Protestant disparagement of ritual carried over into late nineteenth- and early twentieth-century anthropology, where studies of 'primitive societies' focused on social organization, kinship, economic structures, and even mythology, but tended to disregard ritual behaviour as either childish and meaningless or as an obviously inadequate technology. This attitude is most manifest in the invention of the convenient distinction between 'religion' (where communication with the deity takes place rationally through the word) and 'magic' (regarded as an irrational belief in the power of human beings to coerce the powers believed to rule the world).

Later, with Durkheim, the distinction between 'religion' and 'magic' was recast in terms of whether public or private interests were being served, but Durkheim's identification of the transcendent object of ritual with society itself was not likely to commend itself to those who studied liturgy as believers. Similarly, when Freud drew attention to religious ritual as a public counterpart of private obsessive practices, this seemed more like an attack on the liturgy of church and synagogue than a stimulus to studying it as ritual.

Since the 1960s, however, there has been a new interest in ritual both among liturgists and in the human sciences. For liturgists, the mixed results of the reforms introduced by the Second Vatican Council prompted new attention to the human dynamics of the liturgy. By 1968, it was becoming apparent that the implementation of the reform was raising problems to which historical and theological studies alone could give no answer: problems raised by negative reaction to the reforms, and even more by the rash of radical 'experiments' that they unwittingly unleashed. What was needed, it seemed, was a more profound understanding of the human dynamics of liturgy as ritual behaviour.

In the same decade, new interest in ritual was stirring among a number of British anthropologists. Monica Wilson and Victor Turner both went so far as to claim that a society's ritual is the key to how that society understands itself and its world. In the United States, Clifford Geertz has made a similar claim for the role of ritual in creating and sustaining the identity and ethos of religious systems. In psychology, Erik Erikson has moved beyond Freud's view of ritual as being a disguised compensation for repressed drives, and developed an 'ontology of ritualization' which sees it as an essential and central component of the emotional development of every individual. Most recently, the new field of 'ritual studies' emerged from the American Academy of Religion under the leadership of Ronald Grimes and gave birth in 1986 to the *Journal of Ritual Studies*. Ritual studies remain more of a field than a discipline, since they must draw on a wide variety of related disciplines ranging from experimental theatre through linguistic philosophy and semiotics to anthropology, psychology, and religious studies.

Defining ritual

Each of these disciplines brings its own agenda to the study of ritual, with the result that ritual studies have long been handicapped by the problem of how to determine what counts as ritual behaviour. Since definitions of ritual differ, the application of any given definition to liturgy needs to be made with adequate recognition of the particular values with which the definition may be freighted. Beyond that, three broad approaches to the definition of ritual may be identified.

Formal definitions of ritual work seek to differentiate ritual activity from other forms of behaviour in terms of its distinctive features, usually identified as repetitive, prescribed, rigid, stereotyped, and so on. Thus Rappaport defines ritual as 'the performance of more or less invariant sequences of formal acts and utterances not encoded by the performers'. One problem with such a definition is that it is so broad as to encompass everything from the nesting habits of the weaver bird to the coronation of the emperor of Japan. Not surprisingly, there is an ongoing argument about whether the term 'ritual' should be used as a generic term for all kinds of pre-patterned behaviour, or whether it should be used more specifically (in opposition, say, to 'ceremony') for religious behaviour. Zuesse is one who opts for the more specific usage: 'We shall understand as "ritual" those conscious and voluntary, repetitious and stylized symbolic bodily actions that are centered on cosmic structures and/or sacred presences.'

Functionalist definitions approach ritual in terms of the purposes it serves in human life. Psychologists will focus on ritual behaviour as it serves the needs (usually unconscious) of the individual. One influential example might be the definition given by Erik Erikson: 'an agreed upon interplay between at least two people who repeat it at meaningful intervals and in recurring contexts, this interplay having adaptive value for both participants'. Sociologists and anthropologists, on the other hand, look at the way ritual serves collective needs. Here a whole range of functions has been identified: the maintenance of group solidarity, the rehearsal of group values and *Weltanschauung*, the maintenance of social distinctions and categories, the containing of social conflict, the facilitating of transitions between categories or states of life. Functionalist views of ritual often portray it as maintaining social cohesion and cultural coherence in the face of various kinds of threats. Religious ritual, particularly, is said to enable people, collectively as well as individually, to face the boundary situations of human existence. In religious ritual, the world of faith and the world of experience are recognized as one and the same (Geertz).

Symbolic approaches to the definition of ritual look at it in terms of communication: it is an activity that conveys meaning. Again, we are left with a concept so broad as to be almost unusable, since all verbal and most non-verbal activity is liable to be interpreted as having some meaning. It becomes important, then, to determine what kinds of communication are included. If the term be restricted to human communication, it is necessary to differentiate public from private meanings; meanings recognized by experts, such as theologians, from meanings identified by ordinary practitioners; meanings consciously recognized or intended from meanings beyond the conscious grasp of participants. It is also important to recognize the essential polyvalence of ritual: the fact that it carries different meanings for different people, and that it operates at several different levels and in several different fields simultaneously. Thus a liturgical rite may explicitly mediate contact with the divine while simultaneously rehearsing the participants in the community's value system, covering over potential sources of conflict in the community, and consolidating the power structure operative in the community by associating it with the sacred and thus with the unquestionable.

Ritual modes

Because of its essential polyvalence, it seems more discreet not to attempt a single definition of ritual, but to acknowledge that there are different kinds of ritual and that the liturgy of the Church will often employ several of them in a single celebration. This is what Ronald Grimes does in proposing that 'ritual' be used as a generic term covering six 'modes' of ritual or 'ritual sensibilities'. *Ritualization* refers to the rooting of symbolic activity in patterns of gesturing or posturing, or in stylized forms of behaviour, as found in both humans and animals. Closest to this on the ritual scale is *decorum*, the stylized behaviour governing personal interactions. In public life this merges into *ceremony*, which displays and respects status and power. *Liturgy*, as Grimes defines it, is any ritual action with an ultimate frame of reference. It is closely related to *magic*, on the one hand, when participants are attempting to manipulate the transcendent, and to *celebration*, on the other, when participants focus more on the encounter with the transcendent than on the outcome.

The difficulty with defining ritual lies in trying to distinguish it from (while relating it to) ceremony, parade, etiquette, habit, routine, and so on. The advantage of Grimes's taxonomy is that it shows how what we call 'liturgy' is composed of a broad range of ritual 'modes', not all of which are 'liturgy' in his sense of the term, and not all of whose meanings are religious. In any given liturgy there may be elements of celebration and elements of magic. There will certainly be elements of decorum and ceremony, and some elements that are reducible to idiosyncratic 'ritualization' on the part of one or more of the participants. This, in turn, opens the way for a certain 'hermeneutics of suspicion' in liturgical studies, particularly for the purposes of identifying the ways in which, for example, 'ceremony' (display of social power) may be masquerading as 'liturgy' or even 'celebration'.

Ritual and the body

Although liturgy is essentially something that is done, an event, the study of liturgy has for the most part been the study of liturgical texts. And since these texts tend to provide a much more complete record of what is said than of what is done, liturgical studies are all too often restricted to the verbal dimension of the rite, with only a nod at fragments of the non-verbal dimensions.

This is unfortunate, since what differentiates liturgy from other faith-expressions, such as preaching, poetry, iconography, and so on, is that it is essentially something that is what it is when it is *carried out* (Rappaport). It requires the physical presence of living bodies inter-acting in the same general space at the same time and passing through a series of prescribed motions. Liturgy is uniquely a matter of the body: both the individual body and the collective body. From the viewpoint of the individual, liturgy requires bodily presence and a bodily engagement that includes, but is by no means confined to, verbal utterances. Even these utterances, it should be noted, are rarely 'statements', almost invariably ritual 'performances', that is to say, pre-formulated acts of praise, petition, repentance, which the individual assumes and, if they are to be sincere, owns. Through such ritual acts, verbal and non-verbal, the collective body acts corporately and affirms its corporate identity, while the individual participants temporarily sub-ordinate their individuality to the constraints of the joint undertaking.

This says something important about the nature of ritual and thus about the nature of liturgy. The Puritan preference for word to the exclusion of rite was based on an anthropology that granted priority to the individual over the community, to mind over body, and to the conscious over the unconscious. Ritual best makes sense, however, in an anthropology that sees the community as prior to the individual, and sees the mind coming to self-consciousness only in interaction with the external world: *nihil in intellectu nisi prius fuerit in sensu.*[1] In liturgy, the world is encountered *in sensu*, and reveals itself as sacrament through an almost experimental acting out of the ritual, through an exploratory assumption of the prescribed words and gestures, whose meaning is revealed in the doing. That is perhaps why liturgy has survived – in the case of the Roman liturgy, for centuries – in a hieratic language unintelligible to most participants, and why neither in the sixteenth nor in the twentieth century did translation into the vernacular have the immediate hoped-for effect. While ritual is subject to discursive analysis and theological evaluation, it is always more than words can tell.

Some would argue, indeed, that there is a real opposition between ritual and language, between the bodiliness of the rite and the discursive character of other faith expressions. Claude Lévi-Strauss, for example, argues that ritual gestures and objects short-circuit the process of verbalization. Language, he suggests, characteristically divides up the world. Discourse distinguishes, introducing distinctions and discontinuities into life. Ritual, on the contrary, tries to reassert the connectedness of things and the continuities in life; it is less an expression of thought than an experiment in living. It is where we lead with the body and the mind follows, discovering the revelation it is given along the way. 'Ritual condenses into a concrete and unitary form procedures which otherwise would have to be discursive . . . ritual uses gestures and things to replace their analytic expression' (Lévi-Strauss). To this way of thinking, the priority given to the spoken texts of the rite, and to their (implicit) doctrinal contents, by both Catholics and Protestants is quite mistaken. While it is possible to reconstruct the beliefs of a community on the basis of their fragmentary verbal expression in the rite, it is more important to trace the trajectory of the ritual *doing* and to ask, not what is being said, but what is being done. In Ricoeur's phrase, the symbol gives rise to thought. But the ritual symbol is an enacted symbol: it is an embodied parable, whose meaning is not so much conceptualized and then expressed in gesture, as something that dawns upon those who carry it out. For that reason, ritual will always be more than doctrine-in-action, as encounter will always be more than its description.

Issues in ritual studies

One of the problems of drawing conclusions about our present liturgical experience from the studies of anthropologists like Lévi-Strauss or Victor Turner, is that the post-modern Western world is so

---

[1] Nothing is in the intellect unless it has first been in the senses.

different from that of pre-modern cultures. Indeed, it may be that anthropological studies could better help us understand how our liturgy used to work than how it works today. Today a ritual studies approach to liturgical practice has continually to bear in mind the question raised by Romano Guardini in the 1960s about modern people's capacity for symbolic activity (*Liturgiefähigkeit*). Moreover, this question of the modern capacity for symbolic modes of thought and thus for ritual cannot be dealt with apart from broader questions about the nature of modern society as this affects ritualization (Bocock, Douglas). Conversely, the study of ritual will prove important to pastoral work in so far as it can help to identify the subjective and objective conditions under which people today might still be able to participate fruitfully in the liturgy. These conditions include appropriate forms of social life and ecclesial structure, as well as personal dispositions. In both instances, a ritual studies approach to liturgy will find itself ceasing to be purely descriptive and moving instead into the properly theological realms of ecclesiology, sacramental theory, and moral theology. Conversely, understanding how ritual works and under what conditions must be considered an indispensable prolegomenon to any theology of liturgy.

References

Frederick Bird, 'The Contemporary Ritual Milieu', in Ray B. Brown, ed., *Rituals and Ceremonies in Popular Culture* (Bowling Green, OH: Bowling Green University Popular Press 1980), 19–35.

Robert Bocock, *Ritual in Industrial Society: A Sociological Analysis of Ritualism in Modern England* (London: George Allen & Unwin 1974).

Mary Douglas, *Natural Symbols* (London: Barrie & Rockliff 1970).

Emile Durkheim, *The Elementary Forms of the Religious Life* (London: George Allen & Unwin 1915).

Erik Erikson, 'The Development of Ritualization', *The World Yearbook of Religion* 1 (1969), 711–32.

Erik Erikson, *Toys and Reasons* (New York: Norton 1977).

Sigmund Freud, 'Obsessive Actions and Religious Practices', *Standard Edition of the Complete Psychological Works of Sigmund Freud* 9 (London: Hogarth Press 1950), 115–28.

Clifford Geertz, 'Religion as a Cultural System', in M. Banton, ed., *Anthropological Approaches to the Study of Religion* (New York: Praeger 1965), 1–46.

Jack Goody, 'Religion and Ritual: The Definitional Problem', *British Journal of Sociology* 12 (1961), 142–64.

Roger Grainger, *The Language of the Rite* (London: Darton, Longman & Todd 1974).

Ronald Grimes, *Beginnings in Ritual Studies* (Lanham, MD: University Press of America 1982).

Ronald Grimes, *Ritual Criticism* (Columbia, SC: University of South Carolina Press 1990).

E. Leach, 'Ritual', in D. Sills, ed., *International Encyclopedia of the Social Sciences* 13 (New York: Macmillan 1968).

Claude Lévi-Strauss, 'Finale', in *The Naked Man* (New York: Harper & Row 1981), 625–95.

Roy Rappaport, *Ecology, Meaning and Religion* (Richmond, CA: North Atlantic Books 1979), 173–222.

Victor Turner, *Image and Pilgrimage* (New York: Columbia University Press 1978), esp. Appendix A, 243–55.

Victor Turner, *The Ritual Process* (London: Routledge & Kegan Paul 1969).

Monica Wilson, *Religion and the Transformation of Society* (London/New York: Cambridge University Press 1971), 52–75.

E. Zuesse, 'Ritual', in Mircea Eliade, ed., *The Encyclopedia of Religion* 12 (New York: Macmillan 1987).

3

John D. Witvliet

Introduction

> We must begin to look at the liturgy as it is experienced by the man or woman in the pew and try to understand the effect that it has upon them during the performance of the rite itself and throughout their lives, also the way in which this effect is being achieved. (Martin Stringer, 'Liturgy and Anthropology: The History of a Relationship', *Worship* 63 [1989], 517)

How pastoral and academic liturgists have appropriated social science methods is the topic examined by John Witvliet, Director of the Institute of Christian Worship at Calvin College in Holland, Michigan, USA, in his essay, 'For Our Own Purposes: The Appropriation of the Social Sciences in Liturgical Studies', *Liturgy Digest* 2/2 (Spring/Summer 1995), 6–35. By probing frequently discussed conceptual problems in social-scientific theories, he leads the reader through significant issues which must be engaged. Beginning from a quotation from Geoffrey Wainwright's address to the North American Academy of Liturgy, Witvliet offers an extended commentary on how 'we [liturgists] must retain our freedom to use borrowed tools in our own ways and for our own purposes'. Liturgists of whatever stripe, the author argues, have a task that is both descriptive and prescriptive. The human sciences can be especially useful in the descriptive task. Yet these methodological approaches need to be approached with caution. In the end Witvliet wisely notes that liturgists need awareness of both their own goals and the implications of their own faith commitments when exploring the weighty issues of contemporary epistemology, metaphysics, and the social sciences.

For further reading

Talal Asad, 'Religion as an Anthropological Category', in *Genealogies of Religion* (Baltimore: The Johns Hopkins University Press 1993), 27–54.

Lawrence A. Hoffman, 'Reconstructing Ritual as Identity and Culture', in Paul F. Bradshaw and Lawrence A. Hoffman, eds, *The Making of Jewish and Christian Worship* (Notre Dame: University of Notre Dame Press 1991), 22–41.

Johnathan Lieberson, 'Interpreting the Interpreter: Clifford Geertz and Anthropology', *Theology Today* 41 (1985), 383–89.

Timothy Radcliffe, 'Relativizing the Relativizers: A Theologian's Assessment of the Role of Sociological Explanations of Religious Phenomena and Theology

Today', in David Martin, John Orme-Mills and W. S. F. Pickering, eds,
Sociology and Theology: Alliance or Conflict (New York: St Martin's Press 1980),
151–62.
Martin Stringer, 'Liturgy and Anthropology: The History of a Relationship',
Worship 63 (1989), 503–21.

***

For our own purposes: the appropriation of the social sciences in liturgical studies

Christian liturgy, if nothing else, is a robustly human activity. Whether
gathering in a small roadside chapel in rural Alabama, in a stately
Gothic cathedral, in a mud hut in the African bush, or in a lush South
American rain forest, worshippers bring with them their particular
ways of construing the world, their distinctive patterns of interaction,
and their idiosyncratic styles of expressing their deepest yearnings,
hopes, and fears. It is no surprise, then, that the human sciences –
psychology, sociology, and anthropology among them – have so much
to teach us about the inner dynamics and the outer patterns of liturgical action. It is also no surprise that in the past generation, students of Christian liturgy have embraced these disciplines and begun
a variety of conversations with social scientists that share a great deal
of promise for generating insight into the dynamics of Christian
communities at worship (see Martin D. Stringer, 'Liturgy and
Anthropology: The History of a Relationship', *Worship* 63/6 [Novem-
ber 1989], 503–21). Nevertheless, liturgists, typically, are not trained
in the social sciences, serving rather as historians, theologians, artists,
and pastors, and devoting special attention to the spiritual and theological dimensions of the liturgical assembly. When using methodologies imported from the social sciences, however, liturgists often set
aside theological questions and claims to focus on the *human* aspects
of liturgical experience. Perhaps the greatest challenge for liturgists
today is the integration of social-scientific and theological perspectives
on liturgical action. This task is particularly daunting, especially in
light of the guiding assumptions which drive the most prevalent social
scientific theories and methods. As Wolfhart Pannenberg has observed,
'A disregard of the theological questions concerning the human person is, then, implicitly, even if more or less unreflectively, at work in
most contributions to modern anthropology' (Wolfhart Pannenberg,
Anthropology in Theological Perspective, trans. Matthew J. O'Connell
[Philadelphia: Westminster Press 1985], 18). This disregard is evident
in recent social-scientific studies of liturgy that attempt to understand
human ritual actions through relentless anthropological field work,

analysis according to the strictures of semiotic analysis, or explanation along biogenetic lines, while eschewing the theological dimensions of the same rites. The task of integrating theological and humanistic perspectives has only rarely, if ever, been achieved.

With this in mind, a variety of voices have called theologians and pastoral liturgists to approach the social sciences with caution. In an article that generally commended the interdisciplinary dialogue between ritual studies and liturgical theology, Theodore W. Jennings nevertheless cautioned that 'liturgical theology will do well to avoid the uncritical importation of notions, categories and theoretical formulations generated by attention to ritual and cultic phenomena generally' (Theodore W. Jennings, 'Ritual Studies and Liturgical Theology: An Invitation to Dialogue', *Journal of Ritual Studies* 1 [1987], 51). From outside the liturgical academy, Catherine Bell has wondered about the 'faith liturgical studies has in social science'. She asks, 'Why is it [liturgical studies] so willing to take social scientific expertise at its word and believe that social science really has a clue as to which cultural forms express what?' (Catherine Bell, 'The Authority of the Ritual Experts', *Studia Liturgica* 23 [1993], 114). Speaking to the North American Academy of Liturgy, Geoffrey Wainwright similarly advised that 'It may well be that we have to borrow tools from the religionists although I hope we realize that 'value-free' in sociological language often means 'reductionist' from a theological viewpoint; and *we must retain our freedom to use borrowed tools in our own ways and for our own purposes*' ('A Language in Which We Speak to God', *Worship* 57 [1983], 313; emphasis added). Taking its cue from these cautionary words, this report attempts to discern exactly what '*in our own ways and for our own purposes*' might mean. To accomplish this, it will summarily probe a number of frequently discussed conceptual problems in social-scientific theory, particularly concerning the study of religious phenomena, reviewing recent contributions that are especially relevant to the issue of how liturgists might appropriate the social sciences. This report is a brief catalogue of significant issues that are addressed in current discussions. A rather dizzying variety of arguments and sources are presented, not with the intention of solving the problems presented, nor even of arguing for one monolithic strategy, but rather with the goal of challenging liturgists to appreciate the far-reaching consequences of their methodological choices. Importantly, this essay does not intend to discount the value of the social sciences for liturgists, but rather calls for rigorous self-consciousness about why and how they are used (such suspicions are outlined in Mark Kline Taylor, 'What Has Anthropology to Do With Theology', *Theology Today* 41 [1985], 379–82).

Social-scientific data and worldviews

A first – and foundational – question concerns the nature of evidence used by the social sciences both to describe a given social reality and to support a given conceptualization or theory of reality. Whether observing a Ndembu ritual or crafting a complex statistical analysis of American religious life, social scientists – like all scientists – gather and analyze empirical data. Understanding the nature and limits of these data is necessary for any interdisciplinary exchange.

Three approaches

The nature of empirical data, however, is not unambiguous, nor is it constant among the social sciences. So-called empirical data ranges widely from qualitative narrative descriptions of a ritual event to quantitative demographics of a given community. For the purposes of analyzing the diversity and nature of social-scientific data, it is instructive to compare at least three types of theories of such data that are evident in twentieth-century scholarship: a *value-free approach*, a *value-aware approach*, and a *value-committed approach*. (This typology is freely borrowed from Richard Perkins, 'Values, Alienation, and Christian Sociology', *Christian Scholar's Review* 15 [1985], 8–27.)

The *'value-free'* approach argues that social-scientific data is not coloured or shaped by human thought, judgment, or values, but is instead objective scientific observation. By this way of thinking, all observation is merely empirical and all data can be straightforwardly quantified, digitalized, and analyzed. Whether listing the sequence of events in a tribal ritual or a Mennonite footwashing or counting the offspring of hundreds of fruitflies in a high school biology lab, what is generated is *'hard', quantifiable data that are simply descriptive.*

In contrast, the *'value-aware'* approach emphasizes the role of human subjectivity in shaping both the perception and conceptualization of empirical data. This view acknowledges that the implicit cultural framework of the scientist may influence the way in which data are gathered and analyzed. This approach argues that *both perception and theorizing are functions of interpretation*, as can be seen in many recent studies in cultural anthropology, where the researcher's own culturally informed ideas about social control, the distribution of power, or gender roles influence what types of cultural artefacts and patterns of behaviour she notices and reports. In liturgical studies, these values are apparent when liturgists apply the categories and norms from their own particular tradition to the study of another, as when a liturgist formed by the *Book of Common Prayer* applies its categories to the study of Southern Baptist child dedications, for example. This approach argues that *what the observer perceives as being present or absent in a given rite is irrevocably shaped by his own formation.*

Third, the *'value-committed'* approach posits that empirical observation is a function of the scientist's inevitably value-laden worldview. Like the 'value-aware' approach, this theory notices the significance of cultural values in shaping scientific perceptions. In contrast, this approach argues that these values are often the products of religiously held beliefs. By this way of thinking, *the scientist's value commitments provide spectacles through which data are analyzed, predisposing the scientist to construe data in a certain way.* This pattern can be observed in many varieties of recent scholarship. Feminist scholars, for example, are especially sensitized to any unwitting manipulations of data by theories or methods that are needlessly masculine or hierarchical. Their commitment to a feminist hermeneutic opens their eyes to certain dimensions of the data that might otherwise have gone unnoticed; it also leads them to question any data that violate a feminist canon of assumptions and values. Another example can be observed in the controversy over Charles Murray and Richard Herrnstein's *The Bell Curve* (New York: Free Press 1994). In this case, the scientific community's tenacious commitment to the value and ideal of racial equality led to the challenge of *The Bell Curve's* conclusions. The reason Murray and Herrnstein's arguments were given such close scrutiny was not so much that the scientific community discovered poor scientific groundwork, but rather that they discovered conclusions that violated certain religiously held values. Without the functioning of these beliefs, this study would likely have been lost in the sea of social-scientific studies produced each year. (I do not intend here to defend or promote the validity of *The Bell Curve's* arguments or conclusions, only to observe how value judgments have influenced the debate about it.) The influence of such values is also evidenced when beliefs are explicitly religious. For example, the belief that God exists and stands in relationship to humanity leads the scientist who holds that belief to approach methods and theories that are explicitly a- or anti-theistic with caution. This 'value-committed' approach does not itself argue about whether this is good or bad, but simply that it is inevitable.

As scholarship has developed throughout the twentieth century, the first approach, with its positivistic overtones, has – generally speaking – been abandoned, while the second and third options have been widely adopted. (See, for example, M. Elaine Botha, 'Objectivity Under Attack: Rethinking Paradigms in Social Theory – A Survey', in *Social Science in Christian Perspective*, Paul A. Marshall and Robert F. Vander Vennen, eds [Lanham, MD: University Press of America 1988], 33–62.) This movement away from positivistic empiricism is symbolically represented by Thomas Kuhn's influential work on scientific paradigms (Thomas S. Kuhn, *The Structure of Scientific Revolutions* [Chicago: University of Chicago Press 1962, 1973]). Kuhn's basic premise is very familiar, and largely assumed, in contemporary academic discourse: observation is theory-laden; meanings are theory-relative; facts are theory-dependent. What is interesting about Kuhn's analysis is the religious nature of what he calls a paradigm, featuring, in Botha's words, 'symbolic generalizations, shared commitments to beliefs, values that provide natural scientists with a sense of community . . .' (Botha, 46). Even Emile Durkheim, a classic exemplar of empiricist sociology, came to his empirical work with prior commitments. In Robert Nisbet's words, Durkheim generated theories more like an artist than a data processor (Robert A. Nisbet, *The Sociological Tradition* [New York: Basic Books 1966], 19). Thus, it is now largely assumed that the scientist's work is guided by some larger framework or worldview. As Christopher Harris puts it,

> [A]ll scientific enterprises are only possible on the basis of metaphysical assumptions about the nature of the phenomena which they study, and that these assumptions, being metaphysical, are not open to investigation by the same sort of methods as those which are conventional in the physical sciences, and consequently has no more 'scientific' warrant than the metaphysical assumptions which ground theological investigation. (Christopher Harris, 'The Sociological Mode and the Theological Vocabulary', in *Sociology and Theology. Alliance or Conflict*, David Martin, John Orme Mills, and W. S. F. Pickering, eds [New York: St. Martin's Press 1980], 27)

Even mundane tasks are guided and shaped by one's worldview; even 'expressing something in a quantitative form is always and inevitably a classification' – which, in turn, implies a worldview (see Paul A. Marshall, 'Reflections on Quantitative Methods', in *Social Science in Christian Perspective*, 98).

Three cautions

These observations suggest a series of important cautions for liturgists as they approach the social sciences. For one, liturgists may be tempted to hold an unwitting commitment to empiricism or positivism, that is, to wrongly and naively assume that a given body of liturgical data is somehow value-free, ideologically neutral, or purely empirical. This error has been addressed by a variety of ritual scholars and liturgists who have acknowledged the value-laden nature of any cultural observation. Clifford Geertz, for example, claims that the anthropologist's

> personal relationship to this object of study is . . . inevitably problematic. Know what he thinks a savage is and you have the key to his work. You know what he thinks he himself is and . . . you know in general what sort

of thing he is going to say . . . All ethnography is part philosophy, and a good deal of the rest is confession. (Clifford Geertz, *The Interpretation of Cultures: Selected Essays* [New York: Basic Books 1973], 345–46)

For this reason, Ronald Grimes has developed a highly nuanced participant-observer framework by which ritual observers can take account of both the rites they observe and their own reaction to these rites (Ronald Grimes, *Beginnings in Ritual Studies* [Lanham, MD: University Press of America 1981], 4ff.). Margaret Mary Kelleher has indicated several levels of hermeneutical awareness to which the liturgical observer must be attentive (Margaret Mary Kelleher, 'Hermeneutics in the Study of Liturgical Performance', *Worship* 67 [1993], 292–318). Catherine Bell offers perhaps the most nuanced argument as she proposes a pattern of theorizing in which 'the dichotomy underlying a thinking theorist and an acting actor is simultaneously affirmed and resolved' (Catherine Bell, *Ritual Theory, Ritual Practice* [New York: Oxford University Press 1992], 31). Each of these approaches represents a necessary warning and corrective to liturgists who might otherwise needlessly read their own aesthetic preferences and ideological commitments into the rites they observe. They represent a rigorous academic self-consciousness (reflexivity, self-awareness) to which liturgists must aspire.

A second temptation for liturgists is that of 'bracketing' or even unwittingly denying a fundamental value commitment in the effort to embrace a wide range of social scientific methodologies. It would be self-defeating for a feminist scholar to adopt uncritically a particular methodology that was dripping with patriarchal assumptions (thus the sturdy feminist critique of classical social theories by Victoria Lee Erickson, *Where Silence Speaks: Feminism, Social Theory, and Religion* [Minneapolis: Fortress Press 1993]). Similarly, it is questionable for Christian scholars to adopt uncritically theories and methods that are inherently anti-theistic. As Yale theologian and philosopher Nicholas Wolterstorff has argued, 'The Christian scholar ought to allow the belief-content of his [/her] authentic Christian commitment to function as a control within his [/her] devising and weighing of theories' (*Reason within the Bounds of Religion*, second edition [Grand Rapids: Eerdmans 1984], 76). Just as one's commitment to racial equality will suggest questioning the conclusions of *The Bell Curve*, so too one's commitment to a theistic worldview argues for questioning theoretical approaches that deny God's existence. If, as John Milbank has argued, ' "scientific" social theories are themselves theologies or anti-theologies in disguise' (*Theology and Social Theory: Beyond Secular Reason* [Oxford: Basil Blackwell 1990], 3), then the least that Christian liturgists (who themselves hold Christian beliefs) can do is to compare and contrast the implicit theological implications of these theories with their own.

A third and final danger for liturgists to avoid is that of glib unawareness of their own liturgical preferences and theological commitments. For example, a Christian observer of a Christian liturgical event will likely be more attuned to the biblical themes explored or reflected than a non-Christian observer might be. Knowledge of scripture, or lack thereof, is already a hermeneutical lens which shapes how one might experience the event. Likewise, a liturgist from a highly sacramental tradition will be more aware of implicit signals that worshipers believe God to be acting in their midst than would another. A liturgist with a high view of ordination and the hierarchy of church structures might be tempted to observe and analyze only the movement, gestures, and words of the clergy in the liturgical assembly, ignoring the complex dance of gathering and dispersing enacted by the laity. (Studying clergy is no mistake, but assuming that it is the only thing to study is.) Working with the social sciences demands that liturgists be rigorously self-aware of their own biases, lest the social sciences be turned into a means for propaganda. As Peter Berger once observed, 'the moment the discipline [the social sciences or sociology] ceases to be value-free in principle, it ceases to be a science, and becomes nothing but ideology, propaganda, a part of the instrumentarium of political manipulation' (*Facing Up to Modernity: Excursions in Society, Politics, and Religion* [New York: Basic Books 1977], vii–ix).

Distinguishing and integrating the social sciences and liturgical studies

Yet Berger's point presents certain tensions for liturgists. For liturgists, far more so than anthropologists, approach their work with a vested interest in promoting certain ideals. Anthropologists observe a ritual to understand what is going on and to learn what it teaches about human culture. As Catherine Bell observes, 'a social scientist should not even pretend to offer more than a particular analysis, certainly no prescriptions or suggestions on how to do ritual or even what to think about ritual' ('The Authority of Ritual Experts', 120). *In contrast, liturgists who aspire to a pastoral function in an ecclesial community intend not only to describe existing ritual practice but also to envision a liturgical ideal, to diagnose ritual pathology, to discern exemplary ritual improvisations, and to prescribe appropriate ritual adaptation.* Even if Grimes is correct that 'prescription must follow, not precede, sensitive observation and description' (Grimes, *Beginnings in Ritual Studies*, 4), liturgists are ultimately about the business of *prescription*, of carrying out *an essentially normative discipline.* This distinction clarifies roles of the pastoral liturgist *vis-à-vis* the social scientist: *the social scientist only describes and analyzes; the liturgist not only describes and analyzes, but also prescribes.*

This suggests that pastoral liturgists need to master two distinct, yet ongoing tasks. The first is simply to describe liturgical events. More specifically, liturgists observe religious rites with the goal of describing and interpreting what is going on and, eventually, of hypothesizing about the relationships the rites express and the theological commitments they imply. Like anthropologists observing the fertility rites of a third-world tribe, liturgists observe Christian ritual, describing not what they believe *should* be done, but rather what is being done, and then interpreting that action in terms of the theological commitments it reflects. Particular attention is given to nonverbal communication, to meanings not self-consciously promoted. What is revealed may be the true theology, the lived theology of the community. It is in this particular activity that liturgists must master the art of self-consciousness, so that the descriptions they generate arise as much as possible from the given liturgical event and not from the liturgist's own ideals. It is in the performance of *this* task that liturgists can profit most from the social sciences.

The second task, however, is more properly theological. This is the normative or prescriptive task, one that envisions a liturgical praxis that more fully embodies the Christian faith and more meaningfully expresses that faith in terms of human ritual capacity. To use the social sciences in this task is to deny the very principles on which they operate, turning them, as Berger suggests, into agents of propaganda. But to shy away from the second task would be in effect to subsume liturgy under the social sciences. This theological task is necessary and important. It simply must be distinguished from the former.

To the extent that liturgists engage in both descriptive and prescriptive work, they are, in the terms described above, value-laden practitioners. Like Marx – perhaps the most famous value-committed theorist – pastoral liturgists might well 'agree that the goal of value-committed sociology [or ritual studies] is praxis: the conjoining of empirical theory and social action based on value commitments' (Perkins, 13–14). Like Marx, liturgists find that 'the goal is not to describe the world but to change it' (quoted in Nicholas Wolterstorff, *Until Justice and Peace Embrace* [Grand Rapids: Eerdmans 1983], 164. Wolterstorff develops a more nuanced version of this idea, suggesting ways in which scholarship can serve praxis-oriented renewal without violating the 'canons of rationality').

But once these tasks are distinguished, what then? Is there not a temptation to separate them, to abort the conversation between them? Or is there a forum where liturgists and social scientists might enrich each others' efforts? Can descriptive and prescriptive tasks be carried out in a mutually enriching way? Without attempting an exhaustive answer to these questions, several positive areas for rapprochement can be identified. The task of description can and must serve the task of prescription, and *vice versa*.

For its part, the descriptive task, and the social scientists who are proficient at it, help liturgists arrive at what might be called an accurate 'ritual diagnosis'. Just as an appropriate medical prescription is dependent upon a correct diagnosis, so too helpful suggestions for liturgical reform and renewal are dependent upon a careful and accurate assessment of current liturgical practice. And accurate description of a worshiping community, with its complex patterns of communication and structures of power, is far more complex than might be first imagined. The social sciences are useful precisely because they acknowledge this complexity. They constantly strive to sharpen our powers of perception regarding what may be happening 'underneath' or 'behind' a given behaviour. They recognize, for example, the role of a collective memory, nonverbal communication, and patterns of social control in shaping ritual practice. Such insights are invaluable to liturgists in describing liturgical events and for identifying the audience to which liturgists address their claims.

Conversely, the prescriptive task can aid the descriptive task by recommending subjects for study. The literal explosion of data in our 'information age' demands that scholars, like consumers, make careful choices about what they will study and how they will study it. Just as the computer technician is prevented from ever keeping abreast of all recent developments in computer technology by the sheer quantity of published materials, so too the liturgical scholar and social scientist are forced to choose among the hundreds of options of communities and rites that could be helpfully observed and analyzed. Having a clear sense about what is important and valuable, as is possible only through a carefully considered notion of an ideal or norm, provides a guide to these choices.

The turn to the subject

An even more fundamental issue in interdisciplinary exchange is essentially epistemological, arising out of twentieth-century debates about the genesis and nature of human knowledge. In fact, the central issue behind much of the mutual exchange between the social sciences and theology in the past generation concerns the epistemological implications of twentieth-century subjectivism. Ever since Immanuel Kant's *Critique of Pure Reason*, the assumption that the very structure of reality is conferred by human conceptual activity has been widely adopted. In Kant's words: 'The intellect does not derive its laws (*a priori*) from nature but prescribes them to nature' ('Prolegomena to Every Future Metaphysics That May Be Presented as a Science', trans. Carl J. Friedrich, *The Philosophy of Kant* [New York: Modern Library 1949], 91). Kant's dictum has particular significance for how religious experience is construed and raises a variety of fundamental questions about traditional 'objective' theological formulations. To what extent are religious experiences and divine presence objective? Are there such things as objective divine actions? Does the Holy Spirit really move about in the world? Is God's providence active? Is God properly considered an agent of sacramental efficacy?

Liturgists may be tempted to assume that such questions remain outside the scope of their inquiry, falling squarely in the domain of systematic and philosophical theology. Yet while liturgists may avoid theologizing in light of these questions, the appropriation of social-scientific methods and theories introduces subtle, but potent versions of subjectivism into liturgical discourse. It is true that social scientists generally do not concern themselves with the technical arguments of Kant and his intellectual progeny. Nevertheless, it is striking to observe the extent to which the subjectivist worldview has influenced the development of the social sciences. These sciences, by definition, seek to discern ways in which the social dimension of human life is a formative agent for human communication, behaviour, and belief. A particular subjectivist twist is evidenced any time the social causes and forms are taken to be structuring elements on which a given reality depends. In such instances, reality is believed to be either governed by or dependent upon human subjectivity, here understood in a collective, not individual sense. This assumption is ever-present in the current literature, and is reported as a matter of course, for example, by David Kertzer: 'people are not generally aware that they themselves endow the world with their own symbolically constructed version of reality. On the contrary, people believe the world simply presents itself in the form in which it is perceived' (*Ritual, Politics, and Power* [New Haven: Yale University Press 1988], 4). Taken to its logical extreme, this approach suggests that nothing (including, in most cases, God) has positive metaphysical status outside of human subjectivity. The famous German philosopher T. W. Adorno warned of this tendency in his indictment that 'isolated social research becomes false as soon as it conceives the wish to eradicate totality as a crypto-metaphysical superstition, simply because that totality systematically eludes its methodology' (T. W. Adorno, 'Sociology and Empirical Research', in P. Connerton, ed., *Critical Sociology* [Harmondsworth 1976], 249; quoted in John Orme Mills, 'Introduction: Of Two

Minds', in *Sociology and Theology: Alliance or Conflict*, 8). This approach 'denies any ontological reality beyond the knowing subject' (Eileen Barker, 'The Limits of Displacement: Two Disciplines Face Each Other', in *Sociology and Theology: Alliance or Conflict*, 20). In this way of thinking, God does not exist, except as a property of cognitive functioning or societal myths.

If a first-level subjectivist impulse seeks to 'eradicate reality', perhaps a second-level, or somewhat diluted, impulse entails not so much a denial of objectivity, but a heightened sense of cultural relativism. In this way of thinking, 'Reality' is admitted, but our own cultural bias and framework for understanding it are emphasized to the point where human knowledge can only approximate that 'Reality'. No doubt the most famous parable to convey this notion is that offered by John Hick:

> An elephant was brought to a group of blind men who had never encoun-
> tered such an animal before. One felt a leg and reported that an elephant
> is a great living pillar. Another felt the trunk and reported that an elephant
> is a great snake. Another felt a tusk and reported that an elephant is like a
> sharp plough-share . . . Of course, they were all true, but each referring only
> to one aspect of the total reality and all expressed in very imperfect analogies.
> (John Hick, *God and the Universe of Faiths* [London: Macmillan 1977])

As Hick argues, all humans have a limited ability to make claims about 'Reality': for both the scope of reality to which they have access and the analogies used to describe it present limitations that render all knowledge contingent. The social sciences operate nearly entirely on the assumption of such a contingency (see Elvin Hatch, *Culture and Morality: The Relativity of Values in Anthropology* [New York: Columbia University Press 1983]; Ernest Gellner, *Relativism and the Social Sciences* [Cambridge: Cambridge University Press 1985]; and Marcelo Dascal, ed., *Cultural Relativism and Philosophy: North and Latin American Per-spectives* [Leiden: E. J. Brill 1991]). For example, the functionalism of Claude Lévi-Strauss 'implies a cultural relativism which in turn implies an epistemological relativism' (Allen Brent, *Cultural Episcopacy and Ecumenism* [Leiden: Brill 1992], 41). In this way of thinking, God may be thought to exist, but any notion that we can really know anything about God with certainty is considered naive.

Generally, liturgists have worked with social scientific theories that avoid full-blown metaphysical subjectivism. In the words of Martin Stringer, 'liturgists . . . assume that the fundamental meaning of a rite must be theological and not sociological at all' (Stringer, 514). One such balanced approach would be that of Mary Douglas. Douglas does suggest that 'the religious beliefs of a society reflect (and perhaps are reflected by) the kind of social organization which the society has' (Barker, 17). Yet Douglas also argues that anthropological explanation 'does not exhaust the meaning of the Eucharist. Its full meaning involves . . . sacramental efficacy . . . The crux of the doctrine is that a real, invisible transformation has taken place' (Mary Douglas, *Natural Symbols* [New York 1970], 47–48). Her approach acknowledges that society shapes belief, but denies that any social actuality can ultimately define the Reality which belief professes. Similarly, Clifford Geertz contends that 'anthropology does not seek to understand "the basis of belief" but rather belief's manifestations. The task of analyzing and systematizing the "basis of belief" resides squarely in the lap of theologians and philosophers' (John H. Morgan, 'Clifford Geertz: An Interfacing of Anthropology and Religious Studies', in *Understanding Religion and Culture: Anthropological and Theological Perspectives* [Washington, DC: University Press of America 1979], 10). Liturgists need to be aware of the metaphysical baggage they may be unwittingly bringing to their discussion about liturgy. Knowing only the first half of Mary Douglas's claims, for example, could easily tempt one to objectify her sociological explanation of reality in ways that she never intends. Similarly, reading Durkheim's theories without realizing their positivistic overtones could lead liturgists down a path of theoretical syncretism.

Subjectivism itself is approached in two ways by liturgists. Some fuse the tasks of social scientific and theological analysis, rendering social explanations for what occurs in liturgy as a means of founding its theological significance, only to bracket this knowledge and return to a 'second naiveté' (after terminology established by Paul Ricoeur; see John Shea, 'Second Naiveté: Response to a Pastoral Problem', in *The Persistence of Religion*, ed. Andrew Greeley and Gregory Baum, *Concilium* 81 [New York: Herder & Herder], 1973). This approach seeks to use a 'complex blend of science, psychology, sociology, and history' to understand the nature of religious symbols, while attempting to 'recover a sensitivity' to their 'transcendent dimension' (Shea, 116). Ultimately, this solution assumes a subjectivist framework, resolutely maintaining belief and liturgy in the face of it.

Another approach admits, and even celebrates the objective nature of liturgical action, all the while realizing that our subjective appropriation of that objectivity is irrevocably shaped by our cultural milieu. Timothy Radcliffe, for example, observes that 'it is commonly assumed that sociology and theology provide alternative explanations of religious phenomena. Sociology explains what happens by reference to patterns of social interaction; theology by reference to God's intervention.' He further argues that

theological references to divine intervention are not, or should not be, understood as explanatory at all. Rather, they are claiming that the events in

> question are, in some sense, revelatory . . . The theological claim that it was
> God who caused the Exodus does not explain how the event happened; it
> is the recognition of the event as revelatory of God and his purposes.

Thus, theologians should not rule out all sociological explanations, but rather should question those which imply that God does not or could not exist or act (Timothy Radcliffe, 'Relativizing the Relativizers: A Theologian's Assessment of the Role of Sociological Explanations of Religious Phenomena and Theology Today', in *Sociology and Theology: Alliance or Conflict*, 151–62). A similar distinction is made by philosopher Richard Swinburne, who maintains that the sciences and theology maintain unique and different modes of explanation. The sciences, for Swinburne, discuss the physical objects and social constructs as the instrumental causes for a given event or phenomenon. In contrast, a 'personal explanation' may be offered for a variety of events and phenomena, where one sees a rational intentionality of a person as the instrumental cause (which, by extension, may be applied to God) (Richard Swinburne, *The Existence of God* [Oxford: Clarendon Press 1979]). According to this approach, ritual studies for liturgists would be viewed as a means by which to sharpen our understanding of subjectivity and to ascertain strategies for deepening our ability to appropriate the profundity of objective reality. In other words, social scientific theories 'will be seen as relative to their assumptive framework and fragmentary with respect to the whole of reality' (S. D. Gaede, *Where Gods May Dwell: On Understanding the Human Condition* [Grand Rapids: Zondervan 1985], 160).

Sacrality

A related question concerns the nature of and language for discussing sacrality. The notion of the sacred, quite naturally, has long been a central category in religious studies. Already in 1898, Henri Hubert and Marcel Mauss theorized that ritual activities 'effectively sacralize things' (Bell, 15. See Henri Hubert and Marcel Mauss, *Sacrifice: Its Nature and Function*, trans. W. D. Hall [Chicago: University of Chicago Press 1981]; originally published in 1898). Perhaps the most famous discussions of sacrality have been the widely influential works of Rudolf Otto and Mircea Eliade (see Rudolf Otto, *The Idea of the Holy* [London: Oxford University Press 1923]; Mircea Eliade, *The Sacred and the Profane: The Nature of Religion* [New York: Harper 1957]).

Of particular interest for our purposes is the notion that sacrality is a function of human activity. By this principle, often assumed in the field of religious studies, ritual brings about sacrality; or, to put it more dispassionately, ritual is 'planned or improvised performance that effects a transition from everyday life to an alternative framework within which the everyday is transformed.' (This definition is proposed by Bobby C. Alexander, *Pentecostal Possession* [unpublished Ph.D. dissertation, Columbia University 1985], 21; quoted in Tom F. Driver, *The Magic of Ritual* [San Francisco: Harper 1991], 238.) Similarly, Roy Rappaport proposes that the sacred is 'the quality of unquestionableness imputed by congregations to postulates in their nature absolutely unfalsifiable and objectively unverifiable' ('Veracity, Verity, and *Verum* in Liturgy', *Studia Liturgica* 23 [1993], 44). In each case, it is human ritual that is understood as bringing about the sacrality of the space or event. It is significant here that a very value-charged term, 'sacrality', is used to describe a given space, time, or action. (One would think that anthropologists might prefer a neutral term, such as Alexander's 'alternative framework', to the value-charged term 'sacred'.)

For Christian liturgists, however, the use of the term 'sacrality' is problematic. In fact, for Christians in some theological traditions, the language of sacrality radically violates some basic theological commitments. The notion that sacrality is effected by human cognition or ritual, for example, stands in contradiction to a belief that sacrality is conferred by God's presence, the action of the Holy Spirit, or by sacramental efficacy. This contradiction is especially poignant when the very same people who argue against understanding sacramental efficacy in terms of human, priestly action employ the term 'sacred' in a way that implies that sacrality is conferred by human activity.

Further, the very notion of sacred/non-sacred dualism (the notion that some space is sacred and other space is not) contradicts many traditional understandings of the nature of God and the cosmos God created. A full-orbed theology of creation would reject the secular/sacred dichotomy (see Hendrick Hart, 'The Idea of An Inner Reformation of the Sciences', in *Christian Science in Social Perspective*, 23). By this way of thinking, nothing is outside of God's domain. All space is God's space. All time is God's time. This is not to say that there is no dichotomy between good and evil, rather, this dichotomy is understood in terms of eschatological and not spatial or temporal categories. The dualism of this tradition is the already/not yet of the kingdom of God, which is fundamentally different from any distinction between the sacred and the secular. No Christian worldview is without its dualism. But the nature of that dualism, whether it is conceived along geographical, temporal, or eschatological lines, has profound implications for theology proper, sacramental theology, ethics, and liturgy. Liturgists may find helpful the insights of social scientists who use the language of sacrality. However, liturgists should be wary of allowing that language to dictate how a given dualism will function in their theologizing.

The human person

Finally, the use of the social sciences by pastoral liturgists raises questions about how the fundamental nature of the human person is understood and conceptualized. The very fact that there are a constellation of distinct disciplines that claim the title 'anthropology' – including disciplines in the natural and social sciences, as well as in philosophy and theology – suggests that there are very different notions about humanity that may surface in interdisciplinary interchanges. Observing points of similarity and difference in how human beings are understood in the various disciplines is essential for meaningful interdisciplinary discourse.

Humans and animals; humans and God

A first anthropological question concerns the basic or fundamental nature of the human being. 'Man [*sic*],' wrote Reinhold Niebuhr, 'has always been an enigma to himself... The finiteness of human life, contrasted with the limitless quality of the human spirit, presents us with a profound mystery' (see Reinhold Niebuhr, *Nature and Destiny of Man*, vol. 1: *Human Nature* [New York: Charles Scribners' Sons 1964], 1–4). On one hand, the human species resembles other animal species in profound and shocking ways, in anatomy, psychology, and even in the structure of community. On the other hand, humans are profoundly unlike animal species, in the manipulation of symbols, the development of ethical norms, and the persistent and irreducible quest for knowledge of God. How can humans be at once so much like animals and so much like gods? Niebuhr set out to find a coherent theory to account for this paradoxical ambiguity. His analysis, however dated, provides a useful structure for comparing anthropological theories. Three secular contenders took their turn in Niebuhr's court. All three – naturalism, idealism, and romanticism – failed to persuade him, because they overemphasized a particular aspect of human nature. These same emphases surface as theologians appropriate the social sciences today, warranting a closer examination (see C. Stephen Evans, *Preserving the Person: A Look at the Human Sciences* [Downers Grove, IL: InterVarsity Press 1977]).

A first contender, *naturalism*, attempts to account for humanity as one of many animal species, observing the significant points of resemblance between human beings and other animal species. This portrait of humanity is painted with data assembled from comparative biology, animal psychology, and evolutionary theory. This theory is prevalent in the natural and social sciences alike, and has shaped the work of many ritual studies scholars who are influential among liturgists. Ronald Grimes, for example, observes that 'If we forget our kinship with beasts and plants, we are likely to become in a perverse way what we deny' (Grimes, *Beginnings in Ritual Studies*, 36). Similarly, Tom Driver argues that rituals are 'created in the course of time on the basis of ritualizations evolved by many species, not least our own, to cope with danger, to communicate, and to celebrate' (Driver, 15; see also his Chapter 2, 'Ritualizing: The Animals Do It and So Do We'). Finally, recent efforts have attempted to come to terms with the biogenetic roots of ritual behaviour (see the summary of this activity in 'What Biogeneticists Are Saying About Ritual', *Liturgy Digest* 1 [1993], 38–67). Not all of these approaches evidence thorough-going naturalism. These authors may be quite self-consciously looking at the only animal-like qualities of human persons, saving their examination of ways in which humans resemble or reflect the 'image of God' for another time or place. But liturgists who read them will need to realize that this is only one part of a complete portrait of humanity, at least as traditional Christianity has understood it (for a study of how Clifford Geertz balanced his analysis of the animal-like and god-like characteristics of humanity, see Jonathan Lieberson, 'Interpreting the Interpreter: Clifford Geertz and Anthropology', *Theology Today* 61 [1985], 383–89).

A second contender, *idealism*, is based on the idea that 'human beings, in some deep and important way, are ourselves responsible for the structure and nature of the world' (Alvin Plantinga, *The Twin Pillars of Christian Scholarship* [Grand Rapids: Calvin College and Seminary 1990], 14). This picture of humanity coheres with the post-Kantian subjective view of reality and knowledge discussed earlier in this review. Unlike naturalism, this view emphasizes the god-like qualities of human beings. In Niebuhr's words, it 'appreciates the depth of the human spirit', identifying it with 'an aspect of the universal mind' (Niebuhr, 75). The anthropology of idealism has been prominently featured in many strands of twentieth-century theology, perhaps most prominently in liberal Protestant theology, such as that of Gordon Kaufman. It is perhaps less prominent in recent liturgical work, but is not altogether absent either. For one example, some liturgists have been heavily influenced by the theology of Bernard Lonergan (for example, Margaret Mary Kelleher, 'Liturgical Theology: A Task and Method', *Worship* 62/1 [1988], 2–25). Although Lonergan is no thoroughgoing idealist like Kaufman, his emphasis on a 'public world of meaning' nevertheless resembles idealist themes. Another more telling example of latent idealism is the reticence of some liturgists to acknowledge the embodied character of liturgical experience. This is reflected when liturgical studies focus only on the *ideas* communicated in liturgy to the exclusion of the physical dimensions of the liturgical event. This tendency is also evidenced in sociological and anthropological theories that fail to acknowledge the embodied character of *all* human existence. (The need to account for the body in sociology is presented by Bryan S. Turner, *The Body and Society: Explorations in Social Theory* [Oxford: Basil Blackwell 1984].)

A third contender, which Niebuhr defines as *romanticism*, like idealism, recognizes the spiritedness of humanity, but ascribes this spirit to purely internal and natural agency, rather than to an entity that transcends the individual human subject (Niebuhr, 81). This ideology celebrates the spirit of the individual person and revels in individual human achievement. Of the three theories presented here, this is the least reflected in recent liturgical writings. Nevertheless, a tendency in this direction may be observed in recent work on new and emerging forms of ritual, which have been 'characterized by a distinctive individualism that focuses on the body and speaks the language of the self' (*Liturgy Digest* 1:1; 24). The ascription of ritual ingenuity to the human spirit reflects a vocabulary that is ultimately indebted to a Romantic heritage.

Niebuhr rejects all three of these views of humanity, finding each of them unsatisfying because of their inability to account for the simultaneous animal-like and god-like characteristics of humans. He then looks to a biblical view of humanity as one that gives an adequate explanation. Biblical narratives portray humans as both earthy beings, created out of earth's dust, and god-like beings, formed in the likeness and image of God. Humans were created 'a little less than God', but sinned and were thus cursed, preventing them from realizing the full potential of the created order. Creation and fall, *imago Dei* and original sin, serve for Niebuhr (and for much of traditional Christianity) as the loci which both account for and interpret the fundamental character of the human person. Significantly, they are described in the biblical text in narrative form, one which serves as a fundamental point of orientation, a guiding *mythos* for the Christian worldview, and a framework for thinking Christianly about the human person.

Articulating the nuances and implications of this worldview is the proper function of *theological* anthropology. Theological anthropology is attuned to what biblical narratives, Christian experience in community, and the experience of Christian liturgy imply about humanity. In Mary Aquin O'Neill's terms, 'While every faith tradition has an implicit or explicit theological anthropology, what distinguishes Christian anthropology is that it answers the question on the basis of the Christian revelation and on the experience of life in the Christian community of believers' ('The Mystery of Being Human Together', in Catherine Mowry LaCugna, ed., *Freeing Theology: The Essentials of Theology in Feminist Perspective* [San Francisco: Harper 1993]). Theological anthropology, for Niebuhr and for O'Neill, provides spectacles through which human beings are viewed in a new way.

These spectacles in turn provide a new point of departure for examining the latent conceptions of humanity in various social-scientific theories and methods. For certain social scientific theories and methods surface as being more successful in naming and describing the essential qualities of the human person. Importantly, it is not only theological anthropology that can offer a balanced description of the human being, for a variety of philosophical and cultural anthropologists have also contended that humanity is a complex mixture of animal and god-like qualities. Wolfhart Pannenberg's magisterial *Anthropology in Theological Perspective* is, in fact, primarily a reading of recent philosophical and cultural anthropological theory that argues this very point. What a whole cadre of thinkers have come to realize, according to Pannenberg, is that unlike animals, *humans show a remarkable ability for self-transcendence*, which he defines as 'exocentricity'. Thus, 'the concept of self-transcendence . . . summarizes a broad consensus among contemporary anthropologists in their effort to define the special character of the human' (Pannenberg, 63). Pannenberg's unabashedly theological orientation provided him with a lens for seeing the theological implications of recent social-scientific theories and for negotiating their nuances in a way that preserves and even highlights their theological significance.

Among social theorists, Gotthard Booth is only one of many who have argued for the intimate relationship between the natural and the ideal, arguing that the human experience is shaped by the convergence of a complex matrix of factors, including biology, heredity, social environment, symbols, and value commitments (see description by Grimes, *Beginnings in Ritual Studies*, Chapter 8). Although Booth does not develop the theological implications that Pannenberg does, his argument can be understood as a refusal to limit the horizon of scientific inquiry with respect to human beings to either the natural or ideal realms.

In sum, Niebuhr's tripartite analysis provides a useful heuristic device for conceptualizing the views espoused about human beings in recent social-scientific theory and ritual studies and the view of humanity commended by a faith-committed reading of scripture. What is especially significant is that every anthropology – whether biological, sociological, or philosophical – contains some implicit judgment about the nature of the human person. Sorting them out is a necessary and ongoing task for those concerned with interdisciplinary research and for those concerned with preserving the integrity of what it means to be human in relationship to God.

Constitutive dimensions of humanity and the relationship of human faculties

A second question about humanity concerns the identification of what is taken to be the constitutive aspect or activity of human beings. The past century has witnessed a long line of anthropological theories that claim to have identified the single dimension of the humanity on which all others are founded. Thus, some would see humans as being defined or constituted by work: *homo faber* – humans, the makers. Others, following Freud, would define humans according to their sexual nature. Others, like Marx, would see humans most fundamentally as economic beings. Still others, like Jean-Paul Sartre or Albert Camus, would see humans as hapless pawns in a meaningless universe. Johan Huizinga even proposed that humans are primarily beings that play (Johan Huizinga, *Homo Ludens. A Study of the Play-Element in Culture* [Boston: Beacon Press 1950]). These theorists do not naively assume that the particular characteristics they discuss are the only interesting ones to examine. Rather, these traits, in all cases, are taken to be prior to or explanatory of other dimensions of human existence in some sense.

Not surprisingly, students of ritual, including some liturgists, have emphasized the ritual dimension of human activity. At the very least, the field of ritual studies has suggested that rituals are inevitable accompaniments of human life: 'The human choice is not whether to ritualize but when, how, where, and why' (Driver, 6). Ritual is considered of central importance, as it is for Roy Rappaport, who takes 'ritual to be *the* basic social act' (Roy A. Rappaport, *Ecology, Meaning, and Religion* [Richmond, CA: North Atlantic Books 1979], 174). In the extreme versions of this view, ritual is seen as *the* defining or constitutive element of human personhood. The temptation of practitioners in the field is to take this theory to an extreme, much like the followers of Freud, Marx, or Camus have. The temptation to shrink our concept of human beings to fit one given theory is always present. Ritual activity is an important dimension of being human; it need not be assumed to be *the* constitutive dimension.

A related question concerns how various human faculties and activities should be properly conceptualized and related. We humans perform a dizzying array of tasks and functions: we think, speak, and act; we remember, enact, and dramatize; we tell stories, create concepts, and generate images; we pray, believe, and worship. Many anthropological theories suggest how these faculties and activities are related. Narrative theory, to mention only one example, argues that the act of telling stories is in some sense prior to other activities, such that human conceptualizing can never ultimately transcend the narrative structure of the human mind and human societies. For liturgists, this task of relating human faculties has immediate and far-reaching implications. Consider the questions: What is the relation of thinking to doing? Of ritualizing to knowing? Of praying to believing? Most liturgical reform is based on implicit understandings of the answers to these questions.

Perhaps the most common tendency in recent literature has been that of identifying human ritualizing as the root of many human activities, including knowing. Grimes, for example, speaks of 'the epistemological primacy of the body' (Ronald Grimes, *Research in Ritual Studies* [Metuchen, NJ: ATLA Bibliography Series. The Scarecrow Press 1985], 17–18). In another place, he notes that 'ritual studies asserts the priority of persons-in-actions and interprets words and cultural objects in light of this acting' (Grimes, *Beginnings in Ritual Studies*, preface). Tom Driver provides a model that integrates ritual activity, cognition, and action, speaking of a triumvirate of ritual, confessional, and ethical performance (Driver, 79–130). What is common to these and other related theories is the idea of a ritual mode of knowing, where humans come to intuit and comprehend both ideas and emotion by means of ritualization (see also Theodore Jennings, 'On Ritual Knowledge', *Journal of Religion* 62 [1982], 111–27; Mark Johnson, *The Body in the Mind* [Chicago: University of Chicago Press 1987]). One immediately thinks of Romano Guardini's heightened awareness of the importance of looking and doing in liturgy ('A Letter from Romano Guardini', *Herder Correspondence* [Special Issue 1964], 24).

Particularly interesting for Christian liturgists and students of ritual is the relationship perceived between believing and ritualizing. Every invocation of the maxim *lex orandi, lex credendi* implies that human activity is always prior to human cognition or belief. Emile Durkheim, in his seminal work, *The Elementary Forms of the Religious Life*, argued that ritual not only leads humans to intuit and comprehend ideas and affections, but also leads them to accept them as true and to live by them. Durkheim's argument was, of course, not entirely new. Theologians and spiritual directors (as well as psychologists) have long acknowledged the formative role that action plays in forming belief. Blaise Pascal firmly believed that habit was the surest way to beget faith: 'proofs only convince the mind; habit provides the strongest proofs and those that are most believed' (Blaise Pascal, *Pensées* [New York: Penguin Books 1966], 274). Even John Calvin acknowledged that 'genuine piety begets genuine confession' (*De fugiedis*, quoted in Carlos M. N. Eire, *War Against the Idols: The Reformation of Worship from Erasmus to Calvin* [Cambridge University Press 1986], 199). If this is so, then it sheds new light on the nature of *lex orandi*.

(See Thomas John Fisch, *The Liturgical Lex: A Preliminary Theological Statement Utilizing the thought of Gregory Bateson* [Ph.D. Dissertation, University of Notre Dame 1988].) As Driver summarizes, 'theology comes *after* and not *before* religion's rituals' (Driver, 42).

But again the question of reductionism rears its head. Is this the only way that human activity works? Do not beliefs, in fact, function to shape ritual and ritualizations? Could not the 'renewing of our minds' be the genesis of ritual reform? History suggests that it could. While most humans may hold certain beliefs because they participate in certain rituals, movements of liturgical reform evidence a reversal in this process, featuring an unusually high role for human cognition in the reshaping rites. (The two-way influence of ritual and belief is described by Geoffrey Wainwright in *Doxology* [New York: Oxford University Press 1980], 218–86.) Certainly much of the Reformation must be understood as the self-conscious adoption of a platform of ideas. The emerging rituals of the Reformation churches were largely shaped by a two-step process that began with the articulation of given theological suppositions and only then attempted to craft corporate worship to reflect and promote them. Thus, Calvin also spoke, for example, of 'pure doctrine, which alone can guide us to true worship' (John Calvin, *De necessitate*, quoted in Eire, 198). Luther also advised: 'Do not begin with innovations in rites . . . Put first and foremost what is fundamental in our teaching . . . Reform of impious rites will come of itself when what is fundamental in our teaching has been effectively presented, has taken root in our pious hearts' (text quoted in J. G. Davies, *Worship and Mission* [New York: Association Press 1967], 142). At best, ritual activity and rational theology must be viewed as partners in an ongoing dialogue. Consider Catherine Bell's recent observations about the prevalence of ritual experts who 'devise' rituals in part, at least, *based on criteria outside the ritual itself* (see Bell, 'The Authority of the Ritual Experts', 102). The conceptualization of ritual activity as being prior to knowledge poses an unnecessary and fruitless dichotomy between ritual behaviour and cognition. Bell has observed that, 'theoretical descriptions of ritual generally regard it as action and thus automatically distinguish it from the conceptual aspects of religion, such as beliefs, symbols, and myths' (Bell, *Ritual Theory, Ritual Practice*, 19). Perhaps this dichotomy is simply false, perhaps mind and body cannot be so easily separated, as Grimes seems to suggest (see Ronald Grimes, 'Reinventing Ritual', *Soundings* 75/1 [Spring 1992], 31–32). Perhaps theologians and liturgists need to speak of the complex interrelations of cult, conduct, and creed, avoiding the temptation to elevate one over the other as far as an epistemology of the sacred is concerned.

The social character of the human person

A third and final question regarding our conception of humanity concerns the place of the individual within society. Do individual humans act on society? Do individuals retain any influence over society? Or are they irrevocably and one-sidedly moulded by society? The functionalism of Claude Lévi-Strauss, for example, emphasizes the role of society in shaping the experience of the individual human person. According to Stephen Evans, functionalism tends to view 'a society as a working system which can be analyzed independently of the beliefs of the members of the society', leading to the 'concept of a person as a valuing, rational agent has suffered a severe setback' (Evans, 63; 66). Lévi-Strauss is only one of many who emphasize that humans are primarily highly socialized animals.

In recent theological discourse, the decisively formative role of culture on the individual is reflected in the theory of religion proposed by George Lindbeck. For Lindbeck, religions are 'comprehensive interpretive schemes, usually embodied in myths or narratives and heavily ritualized, which structure experience and understanding of self and world' (*The Nature of Doctrine* [Philadelphia: Westminster Press 1984], 33). Other approaches emphasize the ingenuity of the human person in improvising within a given cultural framework. One critique of Lindbeck, for example, questions his emphasis on the formative nature of culture, arguing instead that individual religious experience and cultural norms mediated through linguistic structures stand in a dialectical relationship of mutual influence (Antonio Gualtieri, 'Doctrines, Implicit Beliefs, and Cosmologies in Recent Religious Studies', in *Religious Studies*, ed. Klaus Klostermaier and Larry Hurtado [Atlanta: Scholars Press 1991], 228).

In general, liturgists have emphasized the social aspects of human activity, in part, as a response to the individualism that is perceived as a threat to liturgical ideals. But not every ritual theorist espouses such a view. In fact, the recently identified 'supine' school of ritual studies stands almost by definition against such claims (Ronald Grimes, 'Liturgical Supinity, Liturgical Erectitude: On the Embodiment of Ritual Authority', *Studia Liturgica* 23 [1993], 51–69). Grimes, in his defence of an individual perspective in ritual studies, admits that ritual 'is necessarily collective', that 'nothing escapes socialization', and that 'the body is always – no matter how closeted or private – socially inscribed' (Grimes, 'Reinventing Ritual', 27). More fundamentally, Victor Turner's emphasis on the processual character of ritual (the ways in which liminality generates rituals which move and change a particular social structure) calls attention to the ways in which the individual or subgroup within a society can move beyond its socialized station to actually alter the shape of the community (see Turner's *The Ritual Process: Structure and Anti-Structure* [Chicago: Aldine 1969]). Thus, Grimes and Turner balance an awareness of the ways in which societal structures dictate human behaviour and belief, while also acknowledging that individuals or subgroups are capable of improvising within and upon these structures. Similarly, the challenge for Christian liturgists is a dual one: both to appreciate the power and pervasiveness of socialization and to retain a respect for the human individual. To fail at the first task is to wander naively into liturgical planning without appreciating the central process by which people have and will come to appreciate liturgy. To fail at the second is, among other dangers, to limit unnecessarily the potential for individual conversion.

★★★

This report has attempted to ask how pastoral liturgists should appropriate the social sciences in their work, advancing the thesis that liturgists should freely draw from the insights of the social sciences, *but only for their own purposes.* To do this liturgists must understand both their own goals and the implications of their own faith commitments for epistemology, metaphysics, and anthropology. In addition, there are undoubtedly other areas that could have been addressed, such as the political dimension involved in the use and selection of theories and methods (see Bell, *Ritual Theory, Ritual Practice*, 197).

There is some risk, of course, in the kind of self-consciousness that this essay promotes. For in efforts to be self-conscious about the use of a given methodology or theory, liturgists may never actually get around to using them. The danger is that of expending so much energy in learning to use a given methodology that one never distils the knowledge about Christian liturgy that a methodology could give. This is the reason that some ritual analyses end up being more about a particular ritual theory than they are about the community or ritual that is being studied.

Despite this risk, the importance of a Christian self-consciousness about the use of the social sciences must be a high priority. The social sciences have a great deal to contribute to liturgical understanding. In Eileen Barker's memorable words, the social sciences provide 'a positive challenge to the manner in which that faith is held and the way in which it is lived' such that 'religion, not God, is challenged' (Barker, 15; see also the essays in Thomas A. Idinopulos and Edward Y. Yonan, eds, *Religion and Reductionism: Essays on Eliade, Segal, and the Challenge of the Social Sciences for the Study of Religion* [Leiden: E. J. Brill 1994]). May pastoral liturgists consider it their goal that this be so!

Part 2

CLASSICAL VIEWS

4

Mary Douglas

Introduction

> Reflection on dirt involves reflection on the relation of order to disorder, being to non-being, form to formlessness, life to death. Wherever ideas of dirt are highly structured their analysis discloses a play upon such profound themes. (Mary Douglas, *Purity and Danger*, 5–6)

Mary Douglas's *Purity and Danger* (London: Routledge & Kegan Paul 1966) treats the twinned concepts of pollution and taboo. Selections from two chapters are included (pp. 29, 32–33, 34–40, 94–99, 112–13) because the pregnant ideas which Douglas develops can fruitfully be mined for ecclesiological insights. Dirt, as she notes, is merely matter out of place; it is a violation of established order. Thus, dirt implies system and system leads to categorization, e.g. who is 'in' and who is 'out'. Contemporary questions regarding the ecclesiastical status of divorced and remarried couples or of gay, lesbian and trans-gendered men and women can be framed using some of Douglas's insights. Her treatment of those 'on the margins' and their need for protection may, for instance, prove to be a sociological support for the age-old practice of assigning a sponsor to catechumens. Explorations of the anomalous, too, can relate to ecclesial life. Might the hour of dusk – an anomalous time – be viewed by people as an appropriate time to gather for prayer to pray for protection?

> [T]he bodily movements of ritually knowledgeable agents actually define the special qualities of the environment, yet the agents understand themselves as reacting or responding to this environment. They do not see how they have created the environment that is impressing itself on them but assume, simply in how things are done, that forces from beyond the immediate situation are shaping the environment and its activities in fundamental ways. (Catherine Bell, *Ritual: Perspectives and Dimensions* [New York: Oxford University Press 1997], 82)

Mary Douglas's *Natural Symbols: Explorations in Cosmology* (London: Barrie & Rockliff 1970) teems with insights concerning ritual. The selections here, taken from that first edition of the book (pp. 54–58, 59–66, 67–68, 69, 70–72, 73–74, 80–81; she made considerable changes in the second edition), treat two main ideas, viz., her theory of 'group and grid' and her reflections on the interrelation of the human body and the social body. Whether or not her group/grid theory has been generally accepted by sociologists, it has proven useful in various theological disciplines. For instance, Jerome Neyrey, SJ, and Bruce Malina, to name but two biblical scholars, have fruitfully used her theory. Liturgists may note that her theory does suggest that ritual malaise may find its roots not in the rite, but rather in differing views of group and grid within a specific ecclesial entity.

The late Karl Rahner, SJ, asserted that the basis for sacramental symbolism is first of all the human body. Douglas would offer support for his insight from her field of expertise; her interests, however, extend to considerations of how social constraint and bodily restraint play out. Her insights relate to, for example, matters of 'style' in worship.

Mary Douglas was professor at University College, London until her retirement in 1977, when she lectured widely in the United States. She died in 2007.

For further reading

Daniel E. Albrecht, 'Pentecostal Spirituality: Looking Through the Lens of Ritual', *Pneuma: The Journal of the Society for Pentecostal Studies* 14 (1992), 107–25.

Nathan Mitchell, *Liturgy and the Social Sciences* (Collegeville, MN: The Liturgical Press 1999), Chapter 1, 'Search for Ritual's Roots in Anthropology'; Chapter 2, 'Critiquing the "Classical" Consensus'.

James V. Spickard, 'A Guide to Mary Douglas's Three Versions of Grid/Group Theory', *Sociological Analysis* 50/2 (1989), 151–70.

For viewing

The Dancing Church of the South Pacific: Liturgy and Culture in Polynesia and Melanesia, video recording by Thomas A. Kane, CSP (Mahwah, NJ: Paulist Press 1998).

The Dancing Church: Video Impressions of the Church in Africa, by Thomas A. Kane, CSP (Mahwah, NJ: Paulist Press 1991).

★★★

Purity and Danger

Chapter 2: Secular defilement

Comparative religion has always been bedevilled by medical materialism. Some argue that even the most exotic of ancient rites have a sound hygienic basis. Others, though agreeing that primitive ritual has hygiene for its object, take the opposite view of its soundness. For them a great gulf divides our sound ideas of hygiene from the primitive's erroneous fancies. But both these medical approaches to ritual are fruitless because of a failure to confront our own ideas of hygiene and dirt.

On the first approach it is implied that if we only knew all the circumstances we would find the rational basis of primitive ritual amply justified. As an interpretation this line of thought is deliberately prosaic. The importance of incense is not that it symbolises the ascending smoke of sacrifice, but it is a means of making tolerable the smells of unwashed humanity. Jewish and Islamic avoidance of pork is explained as due to the dangers of eating pig in hot climates.

It is true that there can be a marvellous correspondence between the avoidance of contagious disease and ritual avoidance. The washings and separations which serve the one practical purpose may be apt to express religious themes at the same time. So it has been argued that their rule of washing before eating may have given the Jews immunity in plagues. But it is one thing to point out the side benefits of ritual actions, and another thing to be content with using the by-products as a sufficient explanation. Even if some of Moses's dietary rules were hygienically beneficial it is a pity to treat him as an enlightened public health administrator, rather than as a spiritual leader.

. . .

So much for medical materialism, a term coined by William James for the tendency to account for religious experience in these terms: for instance, a vision or dream is explained as due to drugs or indigestion. There is no objection to this approach unless it excludes other interpretations. Most primitive peoples are medical materialists in an extended sense, in so far as they tend to justify their ritual actions in terms of aches and pains which would afflict them should the rites be neglected. I shall later show why ritual rules are so often supported with beliefs that specific dangers attend on their breach. By the time I have finished with ritual danger I think no one should be tempted to take such beliefs at face value.

As to the opposite view – that primitive ritual has nothing whatever in common with our ideas of cleanness – this I deplore as equally harmful to the understanding of ritual. On this view our washing, scrubbing, isolating and disinfecting has only a superficial resemblance with ritual purifications. Our practices are solidly based on hygiene; theirs are symbolic: we kill germs, they ward off spirits. This sounds straightforward enough as a contrast. Yet the resemblance between some of their symbolic rites and our hygiene is sometimes uncannily close. For example, Professor Harper summarises the frankly religious context of Havik Brahmin pollution rules. They recognise three degrees of religious purity. The highest is necessary for performing an act of worship; a middle degree is the expected normal condition, and finally there is a state of impurity. Contact with a person in the middle state will cause a person in the highest state to become impure, and contact with anyone in an impure state will make either higher categories impure. The highest state is only gained by a rite of bathing.

> A daily bath is absolutely essential to a Brahmin, for without it he cannot perform daily worship to his gods. Ideally, Haviks say, they should take three baths a day, one before each meal. But few do this. In practice all Haviks whom I have known rigidly observe the custom of a daily bath, which is taken before the main meal of the day and before the household gods are worshipped ... Havik males, who belong to a relatively wealthy caste and who have a fair amount of leisure time during certain seasons, nevertheless do a great deal of the work required to run their areca nut estates. Every attempt is made to finish work that is considered dirty or ritually defiling – for example, carrying manure to the garden or working with an untouchable servant – before the daily bath that precedes the main meal. If for any reason this work has to be done in the afternoon, another bath should be taken when the man returns home ... (p. 153).

A distinction is made between cooked and uncooked food as carriers of pollution. Cooked food is liable to pass on pollution, while uncooked food is not. So uncooked foods may be received from or handled by members of any caste – a necessary rule from the practical point of view in a society where the division of labour is correlated with degrees of inherited purity.

. . .

Food which can be tossed into the mouth is less liable to convey saliva pollution to the eater than food which is bitten into. A cook may not taste the food she is preparing, as by touching her fingers to her lips she would lose the condition of purity required for protecting food from pollution ... A Havik in a condition of grave impurity should be fed outside the house, and he is expected himself to remove the leaf-plate he fed from. No one else can touch it without being defiled. The only person who is not defiled by touch and by eating from the leaf of another is the wife who thus, as we have said, expresses her personal relation to her husband. And so the rules multiply. They discriminate in ever finer and finer divisions, prescribing ritual behaviour concerning menstruation, childbirth and death.

. . .

The more deeply we go into this and similar rules, the more obvious it becomes that we are studying symbolic systems. Is this then really the difference between ritual pollution and our ideas of dirt: Are our ideas hygienic where theirs are symbolic? Not a bit of it. I am going to argue that our ideas of dirt also express symbolic systems and that the difference between pollution behaviour in one part of the world and another is only a matter of detail.

Before we start to think about ritual pollution we must go down in sack-cloth and ashes and scrupulously re-examine our own ideas of dirt. Dividing them into their parts, we should distinguish any elements which we know to be the result of our recent history.

There are two notable differences between our contemporary European ideas of defilement and those, say, of primitive cultures. One is that dirt avoidance for us is a matter of hygiene or aesthetics and is not related to our religion . . . The second difference is that our idea of dirt is dominated by the knowledge of pathogenic organisms. The bacterial transmission of disease was a great nineteenth-century discovery. It produced the most radical revolution in the history of medicine. So much has it transformed our lives that it is difficult to think of dirt except in the context of pathogenicity. Yet obviously our ideas of dirt are not so recent. We must be able to make the effort to think back beyond the last 100 years and to analyse the bases of dirt-avoidance, before it was transformed by bacteriology; for example, before spitting deftly into a spittoon was counted unhygienic.

If we can abstract pathogenicity and hygiene from our notion of dirt, we are left with the old definition of dirt as matter out of place. This is a very suggestive approach. It implies two conditions: a set of ordered relations and a contravention of that order. Dirt then, is never a unique, isolated event. Where there is dirt there is system. Dirt is the by-product of a systematic ordering and classification of matter, in so far as ordering involves rejecting inappropriate elements. This idea of dirt takes us straight into the field of symbolism and promises a link-up with more obviously symbolic systems of purity.

We can recognise in our own notions of dirt that we are using a kind of omnibus compendium which includes all the rejected elements of ordered systems. It is a relative idea. Shoes are not dirty in themselves, but it is dirty to place them on the dining table; food is not dirty in itself, but it is dirty to leave cooking utensils in the bedroom, or food bespattered on clothing; similarly, bathroom equipment in the drawing room; clothing lying on chairs; out-door things indoors; upstairs things downstairs; under-clothing appearing where over-clothing should be, and so on. In short, our pollution behaviour is the reaction which condemns any object or idea likely to confuse or contradict cherished classifications.

We should now force ourselves to focus on dirt. Defined in this way it appears as a residual category, rejected from our normal scheme of classifications. In trying to focus on it we run against our strongest mental habit. For it seems that whatever we perceive is organised into patterns for which we, the perceivers, are largely responsible. Perceiving is not a matter of passively allowing an organ – say of sight or hearing – to receive a ready-made impression from without, like a palette receiving a spot of paint. Recognising and remembering are not matters of stirring up old images of past impressions. It is generally agreed that all our impressions are schematically determined from the start. As perceivers we select from all the stimuli falling on our senses only those which interest us, and our interests are governed by a pattern-making tendency, sometimes called *schema* (see Bartlett, 1932). In a chaos of shifting impressions, each of us constructs a stable world in which objects have recognisable shapes, are located in depth, and have permanence. In perceiving we are building, taking some cues and rejecting others. The most acceptable cues are those which fit most easily into the pattern that is being built up. Ambiguous ones tend to be treated as if they harmonised with the rest of the pattern. Discordant ones tend to be rejected. If they are accepted the structure of assumptions has to be modified. As learning proceeds objects are named. Their names then affect the way they are perceived next time: once labelled they are more speedily slotted into the pigeon-holes in future.

As time goes on and experiences pile up, we make a greater and greater investment in our system of labels. So a conservative bias is built in. It gives us confidence. At any time we may have to modify our structure of assumptions to accommodate new experience, but the more consistent experience is with the past, the more confidence we can have in our assumptions. Uncomfortable facts which refuse to be fitted in, we find ourselves ignoring or distorting so that they do not disturb these established assumptions. By and large anything we take note of is pre-selected and organised in the very act of perceiving. We share with other animals a kind of filtering mechanism which at first only lets in sensations we know how to use.

But what about the other ones? What about the possible experiences which do not pass the filter? Is it possible to force attention into less habitual tracks? Can we even examine the filtering mechanism itself?

. . .

But it is not always an unpleasant experience to confront ambiguity. Obviously it is more tolerable in some areas than in others. There is a whole gradient on which laughter, revulsion and shock belong at different points and intensities. The experience can be stimulating. The richness of poetry depends on the use of ambiguity, as Empson has shown. The possibility of seeing a sculpture equally well as a landscape or as a reclining nude enriches the work's interest. Ehrenzweig has even argued that we enjoy works of art because they enable us to go behind the explicit structures of our normal experience. Aesthetic pleasure arises from the perceiving of inarticulate forms.

I apologise for using anomaly and ambiguity as if they were synonymous. Strictly they are not: an anomaly is an element which does not fit a given set or series; ambiguity is a character of statements capable of two interpretations. But reflection on examples shows that there is very little advantage in distinguishing between these two terms in their practical application. Treacle is neither liquid nor solid; it could be said to give an ambiguous sense-impression. We can also say that treacle is anomalous in the classification of liquids and solids, being in neither one nor the other set.

Granted, then, that we are capable of confronting anomaly. When something is firmly classed as anomalous the outline of the set in which it is not a member is clarified. To illustrate this I quote from Sartre's essay on stickiness. Viscosity, he says, repels in its own right, as a primary experience. An infant, plunging its hands into a jar of honey, is instantly involved in contemplating the formal properties of solids and liquids and the essential relation between the subjective experiencing self and the experienced world (1943, p. 696 seq.). The viscous is a state half-way between solid and liquid. It is like a cross-section in a process of change. It is unstable, but it does not flow. It is soft, yielding and compressible. There is no gliding on its surface. Its stickiness is a trap, it clings like a leech; it attacks the boundary between myself and it.

. . .

So from these earliest tactile adventures we have always known that life does not conform to our most simple categories.

There are several ways of treating anomalies. Negatively, we can ignore, just not perceive them, or perceiving we can condemn. Positively we can deliberately confront the anomaly and try to create a new pattern of reality in which it has a place. It is not impossible for an individual to revise his own personal scheme of classifications. But no individual lives in isolation and his scheme will have been partly received from others.

Culture, in the sense of the public, standardised values of a community, mediates the experience of individuals. It provides in advance some basic categories, a positive pattern in which ideas and values are tidily ordered. And above all, it has authority, since each is induced to assent because of the assent of others. But its public character makes its categories more rigid. A private person may revise his pattern of assumptions or not. It is a private matter. But cultural categories are public matters. They cannot so easily be subject to revision. Yet they cannot neglect the challenge of aberrant forms. Any given system of classification must give rise to anomalies, and any given culture must confront events which seem to defy its assumptions. It cannot ignore the anomalies which its scheme produces, except at risk of forfeiting confidence. This is why, I suggest, we find in any culture worthy of the name various provisions for dealing with ambiguous or anomalous events.

First, by settling for one or other interpretation, ambiguity is often reduced. For example, when a monstrous birth occurs, the defining lines between humans and animals may be threatened. If a monstrous birth can be labelled an event of a peculiar kind the categories can be restored. So the Nuer treat monstrous births as baby hippopotamuses, accidentally born to humans and, with this labelling, the appropriate action is clear. They gently lay them in the river where they belong (Evans-Pritchard, 1956, p. 84).

Second, the existence of anomaly can be physically controlled. Thus in some West African tribes the rule that twins should be killed at birth eliminates a social anomaly, if it is held that two humans could not be born from the same womb at the same time. Or take night-crowing cocks. If their necks are promptly wrung, they do not live to contradict the definition of a cock as a bird that crows at dawn.

Third, a rule of avoiding anomalous things affirms and strengthens the definitions to which they do not conform. So where Leviticus abhors crawling things, we should see the abomination as the negative side of the pattern of things approved.

Fourth, anomalous events may be labelled dangerous. Admittedly individuals sometimes feel anxiety confronted with anomaly. But it would be a mistake to treat institutions as if they evolved in the same way as a person's spontaneous reactions. Such public beliefs are more likely to be produced in the course of reducing dissonance between individual and general interpretations. Following the work of Festinger it is obvious that a person when he finds his own convictions at variance with those of friends, either wavers or tries to convince the friends of their error. Attributing danger is one way of putting a subject above dispute. It also helps to enforce conformity . . .

Fifth, ambiguous symbols can be used in ritual for the same ends as they are used in poetry and mythology, to enrich meaning or to call attention to other levels of existence. We shall see . . . how ritual, by using symbols of anomaly, can incorporate evil and death along with life and goodness, into a single, grand, unifying pattern.

To conclude, if uncleanness is matter out of place, we must approach it through order. Uncleanness or dirt is that which must not be included if a pattern is to be maintained. To recognise this is the first step towards insight into pollution. It involves us in no clearcut distinction between sacred and secular. The same principle applies throughout. Furthermore, it involves no special distinction between primitives and moderns: we are all subject to the same rules. But in the primitive culture the rule of patterning works with greater force and more total comprehensiveness. With the moderns it applies to disjointed, separate areas of existence.

. . .

Chapter 6: Powers and dangers

Granted that disorder spoils pattern; it also provides the materials of pattern. Order implies restriction; from all possible materials, a limited selection has been made and from all possible relations a limited set has been used. So disorder by implication is unlimited, no pattern has been realised in it, but its potential for patterning is indefinite. This is why, though we seek to create order, we do not simply condemn disorder. We recognise that it is destructive to existing patterns; also that it has potentiality. It symbolises both danger and power.

Ritual recognises the potency of disorder. In the disorder of the mind, in dreams, faints and frenzies, ritual expects to find powers and truths which cannot be reached by conscious effort. Energy to command and special powers of healing come to those who can abandon rational control for a time. Sometimes an Andaman Islander leaves his band and wanders in the forest like a madman. When he returns to his senses and to human society he has gained occult power of healing (Radcliffe Brown, 1933, p. 139). This is a very common notion, widely attested. Webster in his chapter on the Making of a Magician (*The Sociological Study of Magic*), gives many examples. I also quote the Ehanzu, a tribe in the central region of Tanzania, where one of the recognised ways of acquiring a diviner's skill is by going mad in the bush. Virginia Adam, who worked among this tribe, tells me that their ritual cycle culminates in annual rain rituals. If at the expected time rain fails, people suspect sorcery. To undo the effects of sorcery they take a simpleton and send him wandering into the

51

bush. In the course of his wanderings he unknowingly destroys the sorcerer's work.

In these beliefs there is a double play on inarticulateness. First, there is a venture into the disordered regions of the mind. Second, there is the venture beyond the confines of society. The man who comes back from these inaccessible regions brings with him a power not available to those who have stayed in the control of themselves and of society.

This ritual play on articulate and inarticulate forms is crucial to understanding pollution. In ritual form it is treated as if it were quick with power to maintain itself in being, yet always liable to attack. Formlessness is also credited with powers, some dangerous, some good. We have seen how the abominations of Leviticus are the obscure unclassifiable elements which do not fit the pattern of the cosmos. They are incompatible with holiness and blessing. The play on form and formlessness is even more clear in the rituals of society.

First, consider beliefs about persons in a marginal state. These are people who are somehow left out in the patterning of society, who are placeless. They may be doing nothing morally wrong, but their status is indefinable. Take, for example, the unborn child. Its present position is ambiguous, its future equally. For no one can say what sex it will have or whether it will survive the hazards of infancy. It is often treated as both vulnerable and dangerous. The Lele regard the unborn child and its mother as in constant danger, but they also credit the unborn child with capricious ill-will which makes it a danger to others. When pregnant, a Lele woman tries to be considerate about not approaching sick persons lest the proximity of the child in her womb causes coughing or fever to increase.

. . .

Lévy-Bruhl noted that menstrual blood and miscarriage sometimes attract the same kind of belief. The Maoris regard menstrual blood as a sort of human being *manqué*. If the blood had not flowed it would have become a person, so it has the impossible status of a dead person that has never lived. He quoted a common belief that a foetus born prematurely has a malevolent spirit, dangerous to the living (pp. 390–96). Lévy-Bruhl did not generalise that danger lies in marginal states, but Van Gennep had more sociological insight. He saw society as a house with rooms and corridors in which passage from one to another is dangerous. Danger lies in transitional states, simply because transition is neither one state nor the next, it is undefinable. The person who must pass from one to another is himself in danger and emanates danger to others. The danger is controlled by ritual which precisely separates him from his old status, segregates him for a time and then publicly declares his entry to his new status. Not only is transition itself dangerous, but also the rituals of segregation are the most dangerous phase of the rites. So often do we read that boys die in initiation ceremonies, or that their sisters and mothers are told to fear for their safety, or that they used in the old days to die from hardship or fright, or by supernatural punishment for their misdeeds.

. . .

During the marginal period which separates ritual dying and ritual rebirth, the novices in initiation are temporarily outcast. For the duration of the rite they have no place in society. Sometimes they actually go to live far away outside it. Sometimes they live near enough for unplanned contacts to take place between full social beings and the outcasts. Then we find them behaving like dangerous criminal characters. They are licensed to waylay, steal, rape. This behaviour is even enjoined on them. To behave anti-socially is the proper expression of their marginal condition (Webster, 1908, chapter III). To have been in the margins is to have been in contact with danger, to have been at a source of power. It is consistent with the ideas about form and formlessness to treat initiands coming out of seclusion as if they were themselves charged with power, hot, dangerous, requiring insulation and a time for cooling down. Dirt, obscenity and lawlessness are as relevant symbolically to the rites of seclusion as other ritual expressions of their condition. They are not to be blamed for misconduct any more than the foetus in the womb for its spite and greed.

It seems that if a person has no place in the social system and is therefore a marginal being, all precaution against danger must come from others. He cannot help his abnormal situation. This is roughly how we ourselves regard marginal people in a secular, not a ritual context. Social workers in our society, concerned with the after-care of ex-prisoners, report a difficulty of resettling them in steady jobs, a difficulty which comes from the attitude of society at large. A man who has spent any time 'inside' is put permanently 'outside' the ordinary social system. With no rite of aggregation which can definitively assign him to a new position he remains in the margins, with other people who are similarly credited with unreliability, unteachability, and all the wrong social attitudes.

. . .

To plot a map of the powers and dangers in a primitive universe, we need to underline the interplay of ideas of form and formlessness.

So many ideas about power are based on an idea of society as a series of forms contrasted with surrounding non-form. There is power in the forms and other power in the inarticulate area, margins, confused lines, and beyond the external boundaries. If pollution is a particular class of danger, to see where it belongs in the universe of dangers we need an inventory of all the possible sources of power. In a primitive culture the physical agency of misfortune is not so significant as the personal intervention to which it can be traced. The effects are the same the world over: drought is drought, hunger is hunger; epidemic, child labour, infirmity – most of the experiences are held in common. But each culture knows a distinctive set of laws governing the way these disasters fall. The main links between persons and misfortunes are personal links. So our inventory of powers must proceed by classifying all kinds of personal intervention in the fortunes of others.

The spiritual powers which human action can unleash can roughly be divided into two classes – internal and external. The first reside within the psyche of the agent – such as evil eye, witchcraft, gifts of vision or prophecy. The second are external symbols on which the agent must consciously work: spells, blessings, curses, charms and formulas and invocations. These powers require actions by which spiritual power is discharged.

This distinction between internal and external sources of power is often correlated with another distinction, between uncontrolled and controlled power. According to widespread beliefs, the internal psychic powers are not necessarily triggered off by the intention of the agent. He may be quite unaware that he possesses them or that they are active. These beliefs vary from place to place. For example, Joan of Arc did not know when her voices would speak to her, could not summon them at will, was often startled by what they said and by the train of events which her obedience to them started. The Azande believe that a witch does not necessarily know that his witchcraft is at work, yet if he is warned, he can exert some control to check its action.

By contrast, the magician cannot utter a spell by mistake; specific intention is a condition of the result. A father's curse usually needs to be pronounced to have effect.

Where does pollution come in the contrast between uncontrolled and controlled power, between psyche and symbol? As I see it, pollution is a source of danger altogether in a different class: the distinctions of voluntary, involuntary, internal, external, are not relevant. It must be identified in a different way.

First to continue with the inventory of spiritual powers, there is another classification according to the social position of those endangering and endangered. Some powers are exerted on behalf of the social structure; they protect society from malefactors against whom their danger is directed. Their use must be approved by all good men. Other powers are supposed to be a danger to society and their use is disapproved; those who use them are malefactors, their victims are innocent and all good men would try to hound them down – these are witches and sorcerers. This is the old distinction between white and black magic.

Are these two classifications completely unconnected? Here I tentatively suggest a correlation: where the social system explicitly recognises positions of authority, those holding such positions are endowed with explicit spiritual power, controlled, conscious, external and approved – powers to bless or curse. Where the social system requires people to hold dangerously ambiguous roles, these persons are credited with uncontrolled, unconscious, dangerous, disapproved powers – such as witchcraft and evil eye.

In other words, where the social system is well-articulated, I look for articulate powers vested in the points of authority; where the social system is ill-articulated, I look for inarticulate powers vested in those who are a source of disorder. I am suggesting that the contrast between form and surrounding non-form accounts for the distribution of symbolic and psychic powers: external symbolism upholds the explicit social structure and internal, unformed psychic powers threaten it from the non-structure.

. . .

To sum up, beliefs which attribute spiritual power to individuals are never neutral or free of the dominant patterns of social structure. If some beliefs seem to attribute free-floating spiritual powers in a haphazard manner, closer inspection shows consistency. The only circumstances in which spiritual powers seem to flourish independently of the formal social system are when the system itself is exceptionally devoid of formal structure, when legitimate authority is always under challenge or when the rival segments of an acephalous political system resort to mediation. Then the main contenders for political power have to court for their side the holders of free-floating spiritual power. Thus it is beyond doubt that the social system is thought of as quick with creative and sustaining powers.

Now is the time to identify pollution. Granted that all spiritual powers are part of the social system. They express it and provide institutions for manipulating it. This means that the power in the universe is ultimately hitched to society, since so many changes of fortune are set off by persons in one kind of social position or another. But there are other dangers to be reckoned with, which persons may set off knowingly or unknowingly, which are not part of the psyche and which are not to be bought or learned by initiation and training. These are pollution powers which inhere in the structure of ideas itself and which punish a symbolic breaking of that which should be joined or joining of that which should be separate. It follows from this that pollution is a type of danger which is not likely to occur except where the lines of structure, cosmic or social, are clearly defined.

A polluting person is always in the wrong. He has developed some wrong condition or simply crossed some line which should not have been crossed and this displacement unleashes danger for someone. Bringing pollution, unlike sorcery and witchcraft, is a capacity which men share with animals, for pollution is not always set off by humans. Pollution can be committed intentionally, but intention is irrelevant to its effect – it is more likely to happen inadvertently.

This is as near as I can get to defining a particular class of dangers which are not powers vested in humans, but which can be released by human action. The power which presents a danger for careless humans is very evidently a power inhering in the structure of ideas, a power by which the structure is expected to protect itself.

References

F. C. Bartlett, *Remembering* (Cambridge: Cambridge University Press 1932).

Anton Ehrenzweig, *The Psychoanalysis of Artistic Vision and Hearing* (London: Routledge & Kegan Paul 1953).

E. E. Evans-Pritchard, *Nuer Religion* (Oxford: Clarendon Press 1956).

Leon Festinger, *A Theory of Cognitive Dissonance* (Evanston, IL: Row, Peterson 1957).

E. B. Harper, 'Ritual Pollution as an Integrator of Caste and Religion', *Journal of Asian Studies* 23 (1964), 151–97.

William James, *The Varieties of Religious Experience* (London: Longmans, Green 1902).

Lucien Lévy-Bruhl, *Primitives and the Supernatural* (London: G. Allen 1936).

A. R. Radcliffe-Brown, *The Andaman Islanders* (Cambridge: Cambridge University Press 1933).

Jean-Paul Sartre, *L'Être et le Néant* (3rd edn, Paris: Gallimard 1943).

Arnold Van Gennep, *The Rites of Passage* (London: Routledge & Kegan Paul 1960).

Hutton Webster, *Primitive Secret Societies* (New York: Macmillan 1908).

Hutton Webster, *Magic. A Sociological Study* (Stanford: Stanford University Press 1948).

★★★

Natural Symbols

Chapter 4: A rule of method

It is illuminating to consider ritual as a restricted code. But more problems arise in applying this insight than I am ready to handle. Bernstein argues that the restricted code has many forms; any structured group that is a group to the extent that its members know one another very well, for example in cricket, science or local government, will develop its special form of restricted code which shortens the process of communication by condensing units into pre-arranged coded forms. The code enables a given pattern of values to be enforced and allows members to internalise the structure of the group and its norms in the very process of interaction. Much of the writings and conference proceedings of anthropologists, or of every other body of scholars, would have to be classed as ritualistic or restricted code in so far as the citing of fieldwork, the reference to (often impossible) procedures, the footnotes etc., are given as pre-coded items of social interaction. Allegiances, patronage, clientship, challenge of hierarchy, assertion of hierarchy and so on, these are being obliquely and silently expressed along the explicit verbal channels. If this is so, then Bernstein, by working within the broad framework of a dichotomy of restricted and elaborated codes, is at the stage of Durkheim when he distinguished mechanical and organic solidarity, or of Maine, distinguishing societies governed by contract or by status. As he himself says, the distinction between restricted and elaborated codes must be relative within a given culture or within the speech forms of a given group. Thus the question of whether there are primitive cultures in which all speech is in the restricted code is meaningless, since it ascribes absolute value to the definition. Bernstein would suppose that in any social group there are some areas of social life more responsible for policy decisions and more exposed to the need to communicate with outsiders. Therefore in any tribal system he would expect to find some people who had been forced to develop a more elaborated code in which universal principles can be made explicit and meanings detached from a purely local context. I am not convinced of this myself. If the situations requiring policy decisions were only part of a repetitive cycle it would be possible to discuss them fully in terms of pre-organised units of speech. Only the need for innovation in policy would call forth the effort to use an elaborated speech code. This question poses intriguing problems of method for the ethno-linguists. But it is not central to my theme. More pertinent is how to use the idea of the restricted code to interpret different degrees of ritualisation.

If ritual is taken to be a form of restricted code, and if the condition for a restricted code to emerge is that the members of a group should know one another so well that they share a common backcloth of assumptions which never need to be made explicit, then tribes may well vary on this basis. One can well suppose that the pygmies might never get to know each other very well. Their social intercourse might be likened in intensity and structure to that of the provisioners of a French seaside resort who move down from Paris in June to open their shops and hotels for the tourist season. They know each other quite well, there is a field of common assumptions to be sure, but it by no means exhausts their interests. They could be expected to develop a restricted code with reference to their local concerns. So we can also suppose that the pygmies and the Persian nomads who join their respective hunting or pastoral camps for a season and may not necessarily be together for next year, use one restricted code for those of their common concerns to which an enduring social structure corresponds, and variant forms of restricted code for communication within their own families. This analogy from speech codes suggests good reason for the poverty of ritual forms in the two cases. It fits the Durkheimian premise that society and God can be equated: to the extent that society is impoverished and confused in its structure of relations, to that extent is the idea of God poor and unstable in content.

The restricted code is used economically to convey information and to sustain a particular social form. It is a system of control as well as a system of communication. Similarly ritual creates solidarity and religious ideas have their punitive implications. We would expect this function to be less and less important the less is effective social coherence valued. We cannot therefore be surprised that the pygmies have not developed the punitive aspects of religion. They are content with a minimal level of organisation. Here again a range of comparison is suggested which would predict something about the presence and absence of ritualism in human societies. We need some way of comparing the value set on organisation and social control. It is all very well to illustrate my theme by references to exotic tribes. At some point the problem of comparison must be brought under control. Not only is it dubious practice to compare preachers with pygmies. It is just as dubious to compare hunters with pastoralists, or hunters in Africa with hunters in Australia. I will try to control this problem of cultural variation by proposing a methodological restraint. But first, the task is to adapt Bernstein's diagram of systems of family control. It was designed to reflect the increasing influence of the division of labour in industrial society on two variables, speech and techniques of control. Our first step, then, is to eliminate the effect of the division of labour by choosing slightly different variables. Since Bernstein's work relates to the structure of London families it is concerned with personal face-to-face relations. Consequently it needs very little adaptation for tribal society. His two lines measure different aspects of what he calls positional behaviour in families. Where the division of labour has least effect, the speech code and the control system support a differentiated structure of relations in the family. If we want to follow his work closely we must first do violence to the subtlety of his thought. We have to ignore the speech code and divide our personal relations into different kinds of positionings. In Bernstein's diagram, speech codes respond to the pressure exerted from the decision-making areas at the centre-top of industrial society for more and more verbal articulateness. Family control systems respond to the same set of pressures demanding children capable of mastering intellectual abstractions concerning human behaviour. His quadrant was designed to show how the two responses are not produced in the same combination in all sectors of industrial society. The area of maximum structuring of social relations in the family is on the left: the area of maximal openness and freedom from structuring is on the right. In the bottom right the individual emerges as free as possible from a system of socially structured controls. His diagram illustrates some effects of a single pressure to move from the positional to the personal control system. The vertical line expresses changes in the use of speech. It shows the possibility of speech being used as an intensifier of positional control, with this possibility diminishing as the central pressure to be intellectually, verbally and symbolically free of the local positional structure develops. The people who have been freed most completely from structured personal relations are among those most involved in the complexity of modern industrial structure. Inevitably this model has to be dismantled to be adapted to tribal society. In what follows we are working with only a very crude and limping parody of his idea. The concept of the positional control system has to be divided into two independent variables affecting the structuring of personal relations. The one I call group, the other, grid (see Figure 4.1, p. 61). To the extent that the family is a bounded unit, contained in a set of rooms, known by a common name, sharing a common interest in some property, it is a group, however ephemeral. To the extent that roles within it are allocated on principles of sex, age and seniority, there is a grid controlling the flow of behaviour. So we can adapt Bernstein's diagram to small-scale primitive societies by considering their subjection to these two variables. I start with a line expressing horizontally the minimum experience of group boundaries, towards the maximum. This is to concentrate entirely on group allegiances and on experiences of inclusion and exclusion.

It expresses the possible range from the lowest possible of associations to tightly knit, closed groups. A group essentially has a temporal dimension. It must endure through time to be recognisable. So this line also measures the permanence or temporary nature of people's associations with one another. A group must essentially have some corporate identity, some recognisable signs of inclusion and exclusion. The further we travel along the line from left to right, the more permanent, inescapable and clearly bounded the social groups.

There are other internal forms of structuring which are dependent on group organisation, such as hierarchy of command and delegation of responsibility from the centre. These I will suppose to be increasing concomitantly with the increase in the importance of bounded groups in the organisation of society.

For the vertical line, consider the way a man's life can be organised in a grid of ego-centred social categories. For us the classification according to sex controls a great deal of our behaviour. It did still more our grandparents. Even so, this strict control did not produce groups defined or recruited by sex. Incest categories invariably affect a man in an ego-focussed radius, but his sexual life is none the less made to flow into a prescribed grid. Among some primitive peoples there is a women's group and a men's group; but more usually groups recruited by sex are rare. Similarly for categories of age: for most people the relevance of age to behaviour is ego-focussed. Each individual needs to know who is older and younger than himself, and to know in which part of the age-categorisation he at present belongs. In some tribes, groups are recruited on a basis of age; in some of our schools also. But age does not necessarily produce grouping. As a social category it can vary independently . . . I have chosen ego-centred categories of behaviour, because they are capable of varying independently of group.

This frame of analysis is first intended to express the character of social relations, the degree to which they are structured or unstructured.

But it also expresses a higher degree of organisation of relationships in square C where both effects are maximised, and a lesser degree in B. In this square B a man is bound neither by grid nor group. He is free of constraints of a social kind. Conventions do not irk him. All his human relations are in the interpersonal, optional mode. In square A he belongs to no bounded group. But he is constrained in his relations with other people by a set of categories defined with reference to himself. In square D all statuses are

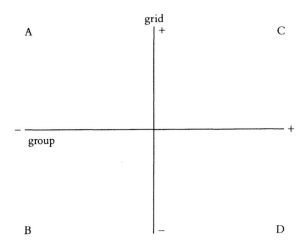

Figure 4.1 Grid and group (a)

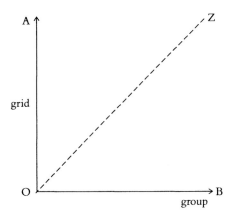

Figure 4.2 Grid and group (b)

insignificant compared with one kind, the status involved in not belonging or belonging to a defined group. In square C society is cut across by both grids and groups of various kinds. An individual is involved with other people and separated from them by numerous lines and boundaries. Role definition is at a minimum in square B and maximum in C. We can redraw the diagram as shown in Figure 4.2.

Z is the direction of maximal involvement of the individual in formalised social interaction. OB is in the direction of maximum group organisation. Moving along the line to B, group becomes a more and more effective principle of organisation and so it imposes group-focussed roles upon its members: stratification, leadership and sub-groupings will develop. OA goes towards the maximum for ego-centred categories of behaviour and the minimum for restraints of group. Somewhere near zero is the minimum for either kinds of social variable. Here are the people who are free to move away if they quarrel. In tribal society this freedom may be produced by mobility, lack of fixed assets, a general low level of organisation.

Where populations are sparse and social relations infrequent, interrupted and irregular, a person does not have the impression of inhabiting a man-dominated world. What preoccupations about his fate he may entertain concern drought, pasture, livestock, movements of game, pests or growth of crops. He is controlled by objects not persons. Objects do not respond to personal modes of approach. The essential difference between cultures placed near zero on this diagram, and those in any other position on it, is that the principal determinants of social life are not seen in the form of fellow humans. Fellow humans do not put their imprint on the universe as models of controlling influence. It is not an anthropomorphic cosmos. Therefore there is no call for articulate forms of social intercourse with non-human beings and no need for a set of symbols with which to send and receive special communications. Hence one cause of the low regard for ritual in this social sector.

Fellow humans are fellow sufferers, fellow victims. Hence the benign view of human nature which is typical of cultures located in this sector among tribal societies. As for industrial society, anyone who wants that freedom from social constraints can drop out of the higher levels of organisation and go as near to zero point as they find worth the material sacrifices it entails. The choice of becoming an academic, writer or painter, compared with the choice to try entrepreneurship, is a preference for expressive rather than organising roles. And within any profession or discipline comparable options of withdrawal from top responsibility are available. There is a possible total drop-out by way of alcoholism or drug addiction, or by retreating to the anchorite cell. No doubt, the seductiveness of dropping out towards zero lies in the benign cosmology of peace and tolerance of fellow men which seems to accompany experience in this social dimension.

We can now start to explain some of the similarity between the world view of pygmies in the Ituri forest and that of certain Londoners deeply implicated in industrial society. Not only in London, but everywhere is heard the complaint that industrial society is impersonal. Some more than others feel their lives controlled, not by persons, but by things. They wander through a forest of regulations, imponderable forces are represented by forms to complete in triplicate, parking meters, inexorable laws. Their cosmos is dominated by objects of which they and fellow humans are victims. The essential difference between a cosmos dominated by persons and one dominated by objects is the impossibility of bringing moral pressures to bear upon the controllers: there is no person-to-person communication with them. Hence the paradox that some of the people whose metaphysics are most fuzzy and who respond only to very diffuse symbols – in short, who in their cosmology are most like pygmies and Arizona peyotists – are those who are much involved in certain sectors of industrial society. To this paradox I shall return.

By considering only one aspect of social relations in modern industrial society we may overcome the main difficulty of drawing comparisons between industrial and pre-industrial societies. The division of labour has been abstracted out of our diagram, but its effects are there in so far as it influences the hounding or positioning of social relationships. The other effects are a distraction to the task in hand. We can ignore them, for it will soon be clear that religious behaviour is strongly influenced by social experiences which can be studied under the head of grid and group. What it is that strengthens or weakens one or the other seems to make very little difference to the regularities we shall be observing. How many social relationships can anyone have at any one time? Fifty? A hundred? Probably no more within the meaning of the word. The milkman who delivers milk and is paid, the lawyer who is consulted by post, the office colleagues who are rarely seen outside the office, the old friends and cousins whose relationship has dwindled to an annual exchange of cards, the personal element is extremely attenuated in those relationships. Suppose we take fifty friends and relations arbitrarily as representing the capacity of the average individual to enter and sustain personal relations – then we can ask concerning those fifty how close-knit and regular is the web of reciprocity. How clear the hierarchy? How strong the sense of mutual obligation? To how many people can a widower with small children, or orphans bereft of parents, turn in various sectors of modern London for help or fostering? How long-term are loyalties? How disruptive are quarrels? How clearly aligned the pattern of relationships? If we confine our comparisons to experiences in this dimension we can solve the problem of how to derive insights about ourselves from primitive society, and solve the problem of extending Bernstein's insights about Londoners to tribal studies.

Another problem of method still remains: how to control cultural variation. There is only one solution to this and it is the old question of *ceteris paribus* – how to isolate the things we mean to compare from irrelevant variables. If we are trying to compare forms of expression, symbolic orders, we are involved in assessing behaviour in the physical dimension. The range of physical variables is so astonishingly great that it obviously contains a large cultural element. As Lévi-Strauss has said:

> The thresholds of excitement, the limits of resistance are different in each culture. The 'impossible' effort, the 'unbearable' pain, the 'unbounded' pleasure are less individual functions than criteria sanctioned by collective approval, and disapproval. Each technique, each item of behaviour, traditionally learnt and transmitted, is based on certain nervous and muscular syndromes which constitute true systems, related within a total sociological context (1950: xii).

It follows that no objective physiological limits to the range from most complete bodily control to most utter abandonment are relevant. Similarly for all the possible range of symbolic expressions: each social environment sets its own limits to the modes of expression. From London to the north standard stimulants shift from beer to whisky, within some social circles they shift from weak tea to coffee, to shandy. And with these shifts go special ranges of noise and quiet, and of bodily gesture. There is no way of controlling the cultural differences. And yet, without some method, the cross-cultural comparison falls to the ground and with it the whole interest of this exercise. If we cannot bring the argument back from pygmy to ourselves, there is little point in starting it at all. The same goes for the experience of social control. What it feels like to have other people controlling one's behaviour varies with the quality of restraints and freedoms they can use. Each social environment sets limits to the possibilities of remoteness or nearness of other humans, and limits the costs and rewards of group allegiance and conformity to social categories. To compare across cultures is like trying to compare the worth of primitive currencies where no common standard of value applies. And yet the problem is basically the same as that faced by linguists in comparing tonal languages in which the variations in tone occur within a range of relative pitch and not in relation to absolute pitch. One way to solve the comparative problem is to limit the predictions of a hypothesis to any given social environment. Even here the difficulty of defining a social environment is great. The methodological rule is merely a rough kind of safeguard against the wildest kinds of cultural selections.

It serves to counter the effects of Bongo-Bongoism, the trap of all anthropological discussion. Hitherto when a generalisation is tentatively advanced, it is rejected out of court by any field-workers who can say: 'This is all very well, but it doesn't apply to the Bongo-Bongo'. To enter this present discussion the Bongoist must precisely specify the cultural field within which his comparisons are drawn.

The hypothesis which I will propose about concordance between symbolic and social experience will always have to be tested within a given social environment. One of the arguments will be that the more value people set on social constraints, the more the value they set on symbols of bodily control. The rule of comparison will not allow me to compare Lloyd George's unruly hair with Disraeli's flowing locks, for they belonged to different cultural periods in English history. Strictly it should not allow me to compare Lloyd George with a younger generation of more close-cropped contemporaries. The latitude allowed by the term 'given social environment' is a matter of discretion. It does not allow me to claim that the comparison of Congo net hunters with Arizona sheep herders validates my thesis. Only if various pygmy bands, net hunters and archers and their neighbouring Bantu farmers were compared would the conclusions be interesting. The more limited the cultural ranges within which the comparison is made, the more significant the results. I now will leave the general subject of ritual and anti-ritual. It is too vast. I will try to reduce it to more manageable proportions by focussing on the symbolic uses of the body and how these may be expected to vary.

Chapter 5: The two bodies

The social body constrains the way the physical body is perceived. The physical experience of the body, always modified by the social categories through which it is known, sustains a particular view of society. There is a continual exchange of meanings between the two kinds of bodily experience so that each reinforces the categories of the other. As a result of this interaction the body itself is a highly restricted medium of expression. The forms it adopts in movement and repose express social pressures in manifold ways. The care that is given to it, in grooming, feeding and therapy, the theories about what it needs in the way of sleep and exercise, about the stages it should go through, the pains it can stand, its span of life, all the cultural categories in which it is perceived, must correlate closely with the categories in which society is seen in so far as these also draw upon the same culturally processed idea of the body.

Marcel Mauss, in his essay on the techniques of the body (1936), boldly asserted that there can be no such thing as natural behaviour. Every kind of action carries the imprint of learning, from feeding to washing, from repose to movement and, above all, sex. Nothing is more essentially transmitted by a social process of learning than sexual behaviour, and this of course is closely related to morality (ibid.: 383). Mauss saw that the study of bodily techniques would have to take place within a study of symbolic systems. He hoped that the sociologists would co-ordinate their approaches with those of perception theory as it was being developed then by Cambridge psychologists (ibid.: 372). But this is as far as he got, in this gem of an essay, to suggesting a programme for organising the study of 'l'homme total'.

Whereas Mauss was concerned to emphasise the culturally learnt control of the body, other scholars, before and after, have noticed unconscious correspondences between bodily and emotional states. Psychoanalysis takes considerable account of what Freud called 'conversion' of the emotional into the physical condition. This insight has had immense therapeutic and theoretical importance. But the corresponding lessons have not yet been drawn for sociology.

. . .

Lévi-Strauss has given us a technique. It is for us to refine it for our own problems. To be useful, the structural analysis of symbols has somehow to be related to a hypothesis about role structure. From here the argument will go in two stages. First, the drive to achieve consonance in all levels of experience produces concordance among the means of expression, so that the use of the body is co-ordinated with other media. Second, controls exerted from the social system place limits on the use of the body as medium.

The first point is a familiar principle of aesthetics. The style appropriate to any message will co-ordinate all the channels along which it is given. The verbal form, syntactically and lexically, will correspond to the kind of situation to be expressed; tautness, slackness, slowness, speed, will give further information of a non-verbal kind; the metaphors selected will add to the meaning, not diminish it.

> Then let us give praise to the Lord, brethren, by our lives and by our speech, by our hearts and by our voices, by our words and by our ways. For the Lord wants us to sing Alleluia to Him in such a way that there may be no discord in him who gives praise. First, therefore, let our speech agree with our lives, our voice with our conscience. Let our words, I say, agree with our ways, lest fair words bear witness against false ways.

So preached Augustine in Carthage in the year 418. The sermon is quoted more fully by Auerbach and analysed as an example of a peculiar kind of rhetoric (Auerbach, 1965: 27–36). Augustine's problem was how to present the enormously difficult paradox of Christianity as if it were something obvious and acceptable. He tried to solve it by combining the grand sweep of Ciceronian rhetoric with robust simplicity: Cicero had taught that there are three distinct levels of style, the sublime, the intermediate and the lowly; each level was supposed to belong to its own class of subject matter, so that some situations and things were noble in themselves and should be spoken of in the sublime manner and others too humble for anything but the lowly style. The unquestioned assumptions on which such values could be assigned imply a restricted code. But Augustine argued that Christianity turned all previous values around: the most humble objects became sublime. He therefore proceeded to detach the styles of rhetoric from classes of things and acts and related them firmly to the social relations holding between speaker and listener. The sublime style was for rousing emotions, the intermediate for administering praise or blame and the lowly for teaching. It is wholesome for anthropologists struggling to interpret ritual to recall this long tradition of enquiry into the relation of style to subject matter and social relations.

. . .

Mauss's denial that there is any such thing as natural behaviour is confusing. It falsely poses the relation between nature and culture. Here I seek to identify a natural tendency to express situations of a certain kind in an appropriate bodily style. In so far as it is unconscious, in so far as it is obeyed universally in all cultures, the tendency is natural. It is generated in response to a perceived social situation, but the latter must always come clothed in its local history and culture. Therefore the natural expression is culturally determined. I am merely relating what has long been well-known of literary style to the total bodily style.

. . .

Now for the second stage of the argument. The scope of the body as a medium of expression is limited by controls exerted from the social system. Just as the experience of cognitive dissonance is disturbing, so the experience of consonance in layer after layer of experience and context after context is satisfying. I have argued before that there are pressures to create consonance between the perception of social and physiological levels of experience (Douglas, 1966: 114–128). Some of my friends still find it unconvincing. I hope to bring them round by going much further, following Mauss in maintaining that the human body is always treated as an image of society and that there can be no natural way of considering the body that does not involve at the same time a social dimension. Interest in its apertures depends on the preoccupation with social exits and entrances, escape routes and invasions. If there is no concern to preserve social boundaries, I would not expect to find concern with bodily boundaries. The relation of head to feet, of brain and sexual organs, of mouth and anus are commonly treated so that they express the relevant patterns of hierarchy. Consequently I now advance the hypothesis that bodily control is an expression of social control – abandonment of bodily control in ritual responds to the requirements of a social experience which is being expressed. Furthermore, there is little prospect of successfully imposing bodily control without the corresponding social forms. And lastly, the same drive that seeks harmoniously to relate the experience of physical and social, must affect ideology. Consequently, when once the correspondence between bodily and social controls is traced, the basis will be laid for considering co-varying attitudes in political thought and in theology.

This approach takes the vertical dimension of experience more seriously than the current trend in the structural analysis of symbolism. It is what Rodney Needham, following the phenomenologists and Bachelard, has called analysis in depth (1967: 612). In linguistics it may well have been a blind alley to seek to interpret the selection of sounds by reference to their physical associations. Structural analysis of language has foregone considering whether sibilants have onomatopoeic associations with running water, snakes and the like. Structural analysis should, perhaps, not be interested in the psychological significance, or social, of a particular symbol. Meanings are found horizontally, as it were, by the relation of elements in a given pattern. But when anthropologists apply this technique to the analysis of ritual and myth, the vertical references to physical and social experience are generally slipped in, without apology, as extensions of the total structure. Surely the account we take of the vertical dimensions of analysis must be made explicit, in order to understand the basis of natural symbols. A study of anti-ritualism must focus on the expression of formality and informality. It seems not too bold to suggest that where role structure is strongly defined, formal behaviour will be valued. If we were to proceed to analyse a range of symbolism under the general opposition of formal/informal we would expect the formal side of every contrasted pair to be valued where role structure is more dense and more clearly articulated. Formality signifies social distance, well-defined, public, insulated roles. Informality is appropriate to role confusion, familiarity, intimacy. Bodily control will be appropriate where formality is valued, and most appropriate where the valuing of culture above nature is most emphasised. All this is very obvious. It goes without saying that any individual moves between areas of social life where formality is required and others where it is inappropriate. Great discrepancies can be tolerated in differently defined sectors of behaviour. And definition may be in terms of time, place or dramatis personae, as Goffman showed when he considered what criteria women use to decide when it is and is not permissible to walk in the street in slippers and hair nets (1959: 127). Some individuals groom their whole appearance to the same pitch of formality, while others are careful here and relaxed there. James Thurber once remarked that if some writers dressed as carelessly as they wrote they would be prosecuted for indecency. This range of personal experience can build up a demand for more and more formal symbols of distance and power where a crescendo is held appropriate – and vice versa a diminuendo in symbols of formality on other occasions. The need and ability to switch from the one set of symbols to its contrary is often discussed in terms of reversals. But here I am concerned not with reversal, but with the possibility of a fading out of control, a general détente, and its symbolic expression.

. . .

It seems that the freedom to be completely relaxed must be culturally controlled. What do we make, therefore, of the fact that most revivalist movements go, in an early phase, through what Durkheim called 'effervescence'? Emotions run high, formalism of all kinds is denounced, the favoured patterns of religious worship include trance or glossolalia, trembling, shaking or other expressions of incoherence and dissociation. Doctrinal differentiation is deplored. The movement is seen to be universal in potential membership. Generally the stage of effervescence gives way to various forms of sectarianism or to the growth of a religious denomination. But it is not true that effervescence must either be routinised or fizzle out. It is possible for it to be sustained indefinitely as the normal form of worship. The only requirement is that the level of social organisation be sufficiently low and the pattern of roles sufficiently unstructured. We do not have to look for strain, change, deprivation or tension to account for effervescent religious forms. They can be found in steady state religions. Talcott Parsons's definition of the contrast of structured and unstructured helps to identify those tribes which celebrate social solidarity by the greatest abandonment of conscious control.

> In a highly structured situation there are a minimum of possible responses other than the ones required by the norms of the situation; adaptation is carefully defined; and usually the situation is not very confusing psychologically (1956: 236).

The less highly structured, the more the value on informality, the more the tendency to abandon reason and to follow panics or crazes, and the more the permitted scope for bodily expressions of abandonment. We can summarise the general social requirements for religious formality and informality, that is for ritualism and effervescence, as follows:

Symbolic dimension	Symbolic order
A *Conditions for ritualism* (i) articulated for social structure; control by social grid and group	condensed symbolic system; ritual differentiation of roles and situations
	magical efficacy attributed to symbolic acts (e.g. sin and sacraments
(ii) assumption that interpersonal relations must be subordinate to public patterns of roles	symbolic distinctions between inside and outside
(iii) society differentiated and exalted above self	symbols express high value set on control of consciousness
B *Conditions for effervescence* (i) lack of articulation in social structure; weak control on individuals by social grid and group	diffuse symbols; preference for spontaneous expression, no interest in ritual differentiation; no magicality
(ii) little distinction recognised between interpersonal and public patterns of relations	no interest in symbolic expressions of inside/outside
(iii) society not differentiated from self	control of consciousness not exalted

The second case provides the social conditions for a religion of ecstasy as distinct from a religion of control. Ethnographic reading suggests that the attitude to consciousness is not merely neutral, as I have written it here, but that there is a positive affirmation of the high value of consciousness whenever the corresponding social structure demands control of individual behaviour. So we tend to find trance-like states feared as dangerous where the social dimension is highly structured, but welcomed and even deliberately induced where this is not the case. According to my general hypothesis, the inarticulateness of the social organisation in itself gains symbolic expression in bodily dissociation. The religious cult of trance is material especially suitable to the present thesis.

. . .

It would be inconsistent with the whole argument about the culturally conditioned experience of the body if we seemed to be asserting something absolute about the place of trance in religion. What I am saying is that the full possibilities of abandoning conscious control are only available to the extent that the social system relaxes its control on the individual. This has many implications for the deprivation approach to religious behaviour. For religious movements which take this form are expressing social solidarity without differentiation: the question of whether this state occurs as a result of deprivation must be considered separately in each instance.

We can add this case to other ranges of symbolic behaviour in which a tendency to replicate the social situation is observed. Van Gennep first discerned the common form in all ceremonies of transition (1960). Where the transfer from one social status to another is to be expressed he noted how material symbols of transition were inevitably used and also how the rite itself takes the form of preliminary separation from and re-integration into the community. As this applies across cultural boundaries it is a natural symbolic form. At a more profound level, the social experience of disorder is expressed by powerfully efficacious symbols of impurity and danger.

References

Erich Auerbach, *Literary Language and Its Public* (London: Routledge & Kegan Paul 1965).

Basil Bernstein, 'Some Sociological Determinants of Perception', *British Journal of Sociology* 9 (1958), 159–74.

Basil Bernstein, 'A Public Language – some sociological implications of a linguistic form', *British Journal of Sociology* 10 (1959), 311–26.

Basil Bernstein, 'Linguistic Codes, Hesitation Phenomena and Intelligence', *Language and Speech* 5 (1962), 31–46.

Basil Bernstein, 'Social Class and Psycho-therapy', *British Journal of Sociology* 15 (1964), 54–64.

Basil Bernstein, 'A Socio-Linguistic Approach to Social Learning', in Julius Gould, ed., *Penguin Survey of the Social Sciences* (London: Penguin 1965).

Basil Bernstein, 'A Socio-Linguistic Approach to Socialisation', in J. Gumperz and D. Hymes, eds, *Directions in Socio-Linguistics* (New York: Holt, Rinehart & Winston 1970).

Mary Douglas, *Natural Symbols: Explorations in Cosmology* (London: Barrie & Rockliff 1970).

Emile Durkheim, *The Elementary Forms of the Religious Life* (London: George Allen & Unwin 1915).

Erving Goffman, *The Presentation of Self in Everyday Life* (Edinburgh: Edinburgh University 1959).

Claude Lévi-Strauss, Introduction to Marcel Mauss, *Sociologie et anthropologie* (Paris: Presses Universitaires de France 1950).

Marcel Mauss, 'Les techniques du corps', *Journal de la Psychologie* 32 (1936).

Rodney Needham, 'Percussion and Transition', *Man* (N.S.) 2 (1967), 606–14.

Talcott Parsons and Neil Smelser, *Society and Economy* (London: Routledge & Kegan Paul 1956).

Arnold Van Gennep, *The Rites of Passage* (London: Routledge & Kegan Paul 1960).

5

Victor Turner

Introduction

> Liminality and communitas have become two of the most widely used
> concepts in ritual studies. Arnold van Gennep was the first to use the
> image of threshold (limen) as a metaphor for being 'betwixt and between'
> social states. Liminality refers to the transition, or middle, phase of a rite
> of passage. (Ronald L. Grimes, *Readings in Ritual Studies* [Upper Saddle
> River, NJ: Prentice Hall 1996], 511)

Born in Scotland and educated in England, Victor Turner wrote his
dissertation, *Schism and Continuity*, treating ritual in a single chapter
and from a purely functional perspective. His later publications, however, showed a radical shift toward ritual as his major concern. One
of his major contributions, perhaps the most important, is his expan-
sion of the notion of liminality, derived initially from Arnold Van
Gennep. His applications of the notion to modern, as distinct from
traditional, societies is insightful, and can be seen in the first of the
two samples of his writing here, consisting of extracts from Chapter
3, 'Liminality and Communitas', of his book, *The Ritual Process:
Structure and Anti-Structure* (Chicago, Aldine 1969), 94–97, 106–09,
110–12, 125–30.

Turner's discussion of symbols is particularly useful for liturgists.
The distinction between dominant and instrumental symbols and their
properties is important, if not crucial. Likewise, his fields of meaning offers helpful insights. This is illustrated in the second sample,
extracts from his book, *The Forest of Symbols: Aspects of Ndembu Ritual*
(Ithaca, NY: Cornell University Press 1967), 27–32, 35–39, 45–47,
50–55, 58.

Victor Turner was professor at Colgate University, the University
of Chicago, and the University of Virginia, where he died in 1983.

For further reading

Bobby Alexander, *Victor Turner Revisited: Ritual as Social Change* (AAR Academy
Series No. 74; Atlanta, GA: Scholars Press 1991).
Caroline Walker Bynum, 'Women's Stories, Women's Symbols: A Critique of
Victor Turner's Theory of Liminality', in Robert L. Moore and Frank E.
Reynolds, eds, *Anthropology and the Study of Religion* (Chicago: Center for
the Scientific Study of Religion 1984).

Matthieu Deflem, 'Ritual, Anti-Structure and Religion: A Discussion of Victor Turner's Processual Symbolic Analysis', *Journal for the Scientific Study of Religion* 30 (1991), 1–25.

Dan Sperber, *Rethinking Symbolism* (Cambridge: Cambridge University Press 1974).

★★★

Liminality and communitas

Form and attributes of rites of passage

In this Chapter I take up a theme I have discussed briefly elsewhere (Turner, 1967, pp. 93–111), note some of its variations, and consider some of its further implications for the study of culture and society. This theme is in the first place represented by the nature and characteristics of what Arnold van Gennep (1960) has called the 'liminal phase' of *rites de passage*. Van Gennep himself defined *rites de passage* as 'rites which accompany every change of place, state, social position and age'. To point up the contrast between 'state' and 'transition', I employ 'state' to include all his other terms. It is a more inclusive concept than 'status' or 'office', and refers to any type of stable or recurrent condition that is culturally recognized. Van Gennep has shown that all rites of passage or 'transition' are marked by three phases: separation, margin (or *limen*, signifying 'threshold' in Latin), and aggregation. The first phase (of separation) comprises symbolic behaviour signifying the detachment of the individual or group either from an earlier fixed point in the social structure, from a set of cultural conditions (a 'state'), or from both. During the intervening 'liminal' period, the characteristics of the ritual subject (the 'passenger') are ambiguous; he passes through a cultural realm that has few or none of the attributes of the past or coming state. In the third phase (reaggregation or reincorporation), the passage is consummated. The ritual subject, individual or corporate, is in a relatively stable state once more and, by virtue of this, has rights and obligations vis-à-vis others of a clearly defined and 'structural' type; he is expected to behave in accordance with certain customary norms and ethical standards binding on incumbents of social position in a system of such positions.

Liminality

The attributes of liminality or of liminal *personae* ('threshold people') are necessarily ambiguous, since this condition and these persons elude or slip through the network of classifications that normally locate states and positions in cultural space. Liminal entities are neither here nor there; they are betwixt and between the positions assigned and arrayed by law, custom, convention, and ceremonial. As such, their ambiguous and indeterminate attributes are expressed by a rich variety of symbols in the many societies that ritualize social and cultural transitions. Thus, liminality is frequently likened to death, to being in the womb, to invisibility, to darkness, to bisexuality, to the wilderness, and to an eclipse of the sun or moon.

Liminal entities, such as neophytes in initiation or puberty rites, may be represented as possessing nothing. They may be disguised as monsters, wear only a strip of clothing, or even go naked, to demonstrate that as liminal beings they have no status, property, insignia, secular clothing indicating rank or role, position in a kinship system – in short, nothing that may distinguish them from their fellow neophytes or initiands. Their behaviour is normally passive or humble; they must obey their instructors implicitly, and accept arbitrary punishment without complaint. It is as though they are being reduced or ground down to a uniform condition to be fashioned anew and endowed with additional powers to enable them to cope with their new station in life. Among themselves, neophytes tend to develop an intense comradeship and egalitarianism. Secular distinctions of rank and status disappear or are homogenized. The condition of the patient and her husband in *Isoma* had some of these attributes – passivity, humility, near-nakedness – in a symbolic milieu that represented both a grave and a womb. In initiations with a long period of seclusion, such as the circumcision rites of many tribal societies or induction into secret societies, there is often a rich proliferation of liminal symbols.

Communitas

What is interesting about liminal phenomena for our present purposes is the blend they offer of lowliness and sacredness, of homogeneity and comradeship. We are presented, in such rites, with a 'moment in and out of time', and in and out of secular social structure, which reveals, however fleetingly, some recognition (in symbol if not always in language) of a generalized social bond that has ceased to be and has simultaneously yet to be fragmented into a multiplicity of structural ties. These are the ties organized in terms either of caste, class, or rank hierarchies or of segmentary oppositions in the stateless societies beloved of political anthropologists. It is as though there are here two major 'models' for human interrelatedness, juxtaposed and alternating. The first is of society as a structured, differentiated, and often hierarchical system of politico-legal-economic positions with many types of evaluation, separating men in terms of 'more' or 'less'. The second, which emerges recognizably in the liminal period, is of society as an unstructured or rudimentarily structured and relatively undifferentiated *comitatus*, community, or even communion of equal individuals who submit together to the general authority of the ritual elders.

I prefer the Latin term 'communitas' to 'community', to distinguish this modality of social relationship from an 'area of common living'. The distinction between structure and communitas is not simply the familiar one between 'secular' and 'sacred', or that, for example, between politics and religion. Certain fixed offices in tribal societies have *many* sacred attributes; indeed, every social position has *some* sacred characteristics. But this 'sacred' component is acquired by the incumbents of positions during the *rites de passage*, through which they changed positions. Something of the sacredness of that transient humility and modelessness goes over, and tempers the pride of the incumbent of a higher position or office. This is not simply, as Fortes (1962, p. 86) has cogently argued, a matter of giving a general stamp of legitimacy to a society's structural positions. It is rather a matter of giving recognition to an essential and generic human bond, without which there could be *no* society. Liminality implies that the high could not be high unless the low existed, and he who is high must experience what it is like to be low. No doubt something of this thinking, a few years ago, lay behind Prince Philip's decision to send his son, the heir apparent to the British throne, to a bush school in Australia for a time, where he could learn how 'to rough it'.

Dialectic of the developmental cycle

From all this I infer that, for individuals and groups, social life is a type of dialectical process that involves successive experience of high and low, communitas and structure, homogeneity and differentiation, equality and inequality. The passage from lower to higher status is through a limbo of statuslessness. In such a process, the opposites, as it were, constitute one another and are mutually indispensable. Furthermore, since any concrete tribal society is made up of multiple personae, groups, and categories, each of which has its own developmental cycle, at a given moment many incumbencies of fixed positions coexist with many passages between positions. In other words, each individual's life experience contains alternating exposure to structure and communitas, and to states and transitions.

. . .

Liminality contrasted with status system

Let us now, rather in the fashion of Lévi-Strauss, express the difference between the properties of liminality and those of the status system in terms of a series of binary oppositions or discriminations. They can be ordered as follows:

Transition/state
Totality/partiality
Homogeneity/heterogeneity
Communitas/structure
Equality/inequality
Anonymity/systems of nomenclature
Absence of property/property
Absence of status/status
Nakedness or uniform clothing/distinctions of clothing
Sexual continence/sexuality
Minimization of sex distinctions/maximization of sex distinctions
Absence of rank/distinctions of rank
Humility/just pride of position
Disregard for personal appearance/care for personal appearance
No distinctions of wealth/distinctions of wealth
Unselfishness/selfishness
Total obedience/obedience only to superior rank
Sacredness/secularity
Sacred instruction/technical knowledge
Silence/speech
Suspension of kinship rights and obligations/kinship rights and obligations
Continuous reference to mystical powers/intermittent reference to
   mystical powers
Foolishness/sagacity
Simplicity/complexity
Acceptance of pain and suffering/avoidance of pain and suffering
Heteronomy/degrees of autonomy

This list could be considerably lengthened if we were to widen the span of liminal situations considered. Moreover, the symbols in which these properties are manifested and embodied are manifold and various, and often relate to the physiological processes of death and birth, anabolism and katabolism. The reader will have noticed immediately that many of these properties constitute what we think of as characteristics of the religious life in the Christian tradition. Undoubtedly, Muslims, Buddhists, Hindus, and Jews would number many of them among their religious characteristics, too. What appears to have happened is that with the increasing specialization of society and culture, with progressive complexity in the social division of labour, what was in tribal society principally a set of transitional qualities 'betwixt and between' defined states of culture, and society has become itself an institutionalized state. But traces of the *passage* quality of the religious life remain in such formulations as: 'The Christian is a stranger to the world, a pilgrim, a traveller, with no place to rest his head.' Transition has here become a permanent condition. Nowhere has this institutionalization of liminality been more clearly marked and defined than in the monastic and mendicant states in the great world religions.

For example, the Western Christian Rule of St Benedict 'provides for the life of men who wish to live in *community* and devote themselves entirely to God's service by *self-discipline*, prayer, and *work*. They are to be essentially families, in the care and under the *absolute control* of a father (the abbot); individually they are bound to personal *poverty*, *abstention from marriage*, and *obedience to their superiors*, and by the vows of stability and conversion of manners [originally a synonym for '*common life*', 'monasticity' as distinguished from secular life]; a moderate degree of austerity is imposed by the night office, fasting, abstinence from fleshmeat, and *restraint in conversation*' (Attwater, 1961, p. 51 – my emphases). I have stressed features that bear a remarkable similarity to the condition of the chief-elect during his transition to the public installation rites, when he enters his kingdom. The Ndembu circumcision rites (*Mukanda*) present further parallels between the neophytes and the monks of St Benedict. Erving Goffman (*Asylums*, 1962) discusses what he calls the 'characteristics of total institutions'. Among these he includes monasteries, and devotes a good deal of attention to 'the stripping and levelling processes which . . . directly cut across the various social distinctions with which the recruits enter'. He then quotes from St Benedict's advice to the abbot: 'Let him make no distinction of persons in the monastery. Let not one be loved more than another, unless he be found to excel in good works or in obedience. Let not one of noble birth be raised above him who was formerly a slave, unless some other reasonable cause intervene' (p. 119).

Here parallels with *Mukanda* are striking. The novices are 'stripped' of their secular clothing when they are passed beneath a symbolic gateway; they are 'levelled' in that their former names are discarded and all are assigned the common designation *mwadyi*, or 'novice', and treated alike. One of the songs sung by circumcisers to the mothers of the novices on the night before circumcision contains the following line: 'Even if your child is a chief's son, tomorrow he will be like a slave' – just as a chief-elect is treated like a slave before *his* installation. Moreover, the senior instructor in the seclusion lodge is chosen partly because he is father of several boys undergoing the rites and becomes a father for the whole group, a sort of 'abbot', though his title *Mfumwa tubwiku*, means literally 'husband of the novices', to emphasize their passive role.

Mystical danger and the powers of the weak

One may well ask why it is that liminal situations and roles are almost everywhere attributed with magico-religious properties, or why these should so often be regarded as dangerous, inauspicious, or polluting to persons, objects, events, and relationships that have not been ritually incorporated into the liminal context. My view is briefly that from the perspectival viewpoint of those concerned with the maintenance of 'structure', all sustained manifestations of communitas must appear as dangerous and anarchical, and have to be hedged around with prescriptions, prohibitions, and conditions. And, as Mary Douglas (1966) has recently argued, that which cannot be clearly classified in terms of traditional criteria of classification, or falls between classificatory boundaries, is almost everywhere regarded as 'polluting' and 'dangerous' (passim).

To repeat what I said earlier, liminality is not the only cultural manifestation of communitas. In most societies, there are other areas of manifestation to be readily recognized by the symbols that cluster around them and the beliefs that attach to them, such as 'the powers of the weak', or, in other words, the permanently or transiently sacred attributes of low status or position. Within stable structural systems, there are many dimensions of organization. We have already noted that mystical and moral powers are wielded by subjugated autochthones over the total welfare of societies whose political frame is constituted by the lineage or territorial organization of incoming conquerors. In other societies – the Ndembu and Lamba of Zambia, for example – we can point to the cult associations whose members have gained entry through common misfortune and debilitating circumstances to therapeutic powers with regard to such common goods of mankind as health, fertility, and climate. These associations transect such important components of the secular political system as lineages, villages, subchiefdoms, and chiefdoms. We could also mention the role of structurally small and politically insignificant nations within systems of nations as upholders of religious and moral values, such as the Hebrews in the ancient Near East, the Irish in early medieval Christendom, and the Swiss in modern Europe.

. . .

Folk literature abounds in symbolic figures, such as 'holy beggars', 'third sons', 'little tailors', and 'simpletons', who strip off the pretensions of holders of high rank and office and reduce them to the level of common humanity and mortality. Again, in the traditional 'Western', we have all read of the homeless and mysterious 'stranger' without wealth or name who restores ethical and legal equilibrium to a local set of political power relations by eliminating the unjust secular 'bosses' who are oppressing the smallholders. Members of despised or outlawed ethnic and cultural groups play major roles in myths and popular tales as representatives or expressions of universal-human values. Famous among these are the good Samaritan, the Jewish fiddler Rothschild in Chekhov's tale 'Rothschild's Fiddle', Mark Twain's fugitive Negro slave Jim in *Huckleberry Finn*, and Dostoevsky's Sonya, the prostitute who redeems the would-be Nietzschean 'super-man' Raskolnikov, in *Crime and Punishment*.

All these mythic types are structurally inferior or 'marginal', yet represent what Henri Bergson would have called 'open' as against 'closed morality', the latter being essentially the normative system of bounded, structured, particularistic groups. Bergson speaks of how an in-group preserves its identity against members of out-groups, protects itself against threats to its way of life, and renews the will to maintain the norms on which the routine behaviour necessary for its social life depends. In closed or structured societies, it is the marginal or 'inferior' person or the 'outsider' who often comes to symbolize what David Hume has called 'the sentiment for humanity', which in its turn relates to the model we have termed 'communitas'.

Millenarian movements

Among the more striking manifestations of communitas are to be found the so-called millenarian religious movements, which arise among what Norman Cohn (1961) has called 'uprooted and desperate masses in town and countryside . . . living on the margin of society' (pp. 31–32) (i.e., structured society), or where formerly tribal societies are brought under the alien overlordship of complex, industrial societies. The attributes of such movements will be well known to most of my readers. Here I would merely recall some of the properties of liminality in tribal rituals that I mentioned earlier. Many of these correspond pretty closely with those of millenarian movements: homogeneity, equality, anonymity, absence of property (many movements actually enjoin on their members the destruction of what property they possess to bring nearer the coming of the perfect state of unison and communion they desire, for property rights are linked with structural distinctions both vertical and horizontal), reduction of all to the same status level, the wearing of uniform apparel (sometimes for both sexes), sexual continence (or its antithesis, sexual community, both continence and sexual community liquidate marriage and the family, which legitimate structural status), minimization of sex distinctions (all are 'equal in the sight of God' or the ancestors), abolition of rank, humility, disregard for personal appearance, unselfishness, total obedience to the prophet or leader, sacred instruction, the maximization of religious, as opposed to secular, attitudes and behaviour, suspension of kinship rights and obligations (all are siblings or comrades of one another regardless of previous secular ties), simplicity of speech and manners, sacred folly, acceptance of pain and suffering (even to the point of undergoing martyrdom), and so forth.

It is noteworthy that many of these movements cut right across tribal and national divisions dosing their initial momentum. Communitas, or the 'open society', differs in this from structure, or the 'closed society', in that it is potentially or ideally extensible to the limits of humanity. In practice, of course, the impetus soon becomes exhausted, and the 'movement' becomes itself an institution among other institutions – often one more fanatical and militant than the rest, for the reason that it feels itself to be the unique bearer of universal-human truths. Mostly, such movements occur during phases of history that are in many respects 'homologous' to the liminal periods of important rituals in stable and repetitive societies, when major groups or social categories in those societies are passing from one cultural state to another. They are essentially phenomena of transition. This is perhaps why in so many of these movements much of their mythology and symbolism is borrowed from those of traditional *rites de passage*, either in the cultures in which they originate or in the cultures with which they are in dramatic contact.

. . .

Liminality, low status, and communitas

The time has now come to make a careful review of a hypothesis that seeks to account for the attributes of such seemingly diverse phenomena as neophytes in the liminal phase of ritual, subjugated autochthones, small nations, court jesters, holy mendicants, good Samaritans, millenarian movements, 'dharma bums', matrilaterality in patrilineal systems, patrilaterality in matrilineal systems, and monastic orders. Surely an ill-assorted bunch of social phenomena! Yet all have this common characteristic: they are persons or principles that (1) fall in the interstices of social structure, (2) are on its margins, or (3) occupy its lowest rungs. This leads us back to the problem of the definition of social structure.

. . .

Most definitions contain the notion of an arrangement of positions or statuses. Most involve the institutionalization and perdurance of groups and relationships. Classical mechanics, the morphology and physiology of animals and plants, and, more recently, with Lévi-Strauss, structural linguistics have been ransacked for concepts, models, and homologous forms by social scientists. All share in common the notion of a superorganic arrangement of parts or positions that

81

continues, with modifications more or less gradual, through time. The concept of 'conflict' has come to be connected with the concept of 'social structure', since the differentiation of parts becomes opposition between parts, and scarce status becomes the object of struggles between persons and groups who lay claim to it.

The other dimension of 'society' with which I have been concerned is less easy to define. G. A. Hillery (1955) reviewed 94 definitions of the term 'community' and reached the conclusion that 'beyond the concept that people are involved in community, there is no complete agreement as to the nature of community' (p. 119). The field would, therefore, seem to be still open for new attempts! I have tried to eschew the notion that communitas has a specific territorial locus, often limited in character, which pervades many definitions. For me, communitas emerges where social structure is not. Perhaps the best way of putting this difficult concept into words is Martin Buber's – though I feel that perhaps he should be regarded as a gifted native informant rather than as a social scientist! Buber (1961) uses the term 'community' for 'communitas': 'Community is the being no longer side by side (and, one might add, above and below) but *with* one another of a multitude of persons. And this multitude, though it moves towards one goal, yet experiences everywhere a turning to, a dynamic facing of, the others, a flowing from *I* to *Thou*. Community is where community happens' (p. 51).

Buber lays his finger on the spontaneous, immediate, concrete nature of communitas, as opposed to the norm-governed, institutionalized, abstract nature of social structure. Yet, communitas is made evident or accessible, so to speak, only through its juxtaposition to, or hybridization with, aspects of social structure. Just as in *Gestalt* psychology, figure and ground are mutually determinative, or, as some rare elements are never found in nature in their purity but only as components of chemical compounds, so communitas can be grasped only in some relation to structure. Just because the communitas component is elusive, hard to pin down, it is not unimportant. Here the story of Lao-tse's chariot wheel may be apposite. The spokes of the wheel and the nave (i.e., the central block of the wheel holding the axle and spokes) to which they are attached would be useless, he said, but for the hole, the gap, the emptiness at the centre. Communitas, with its unstructured character, representing the 'quick' of human interrelatedness, what Buber has called *das Zwischenmenschliche*, might well be represented by the 'emptiness at the centre', which is nevertheless indispensable to the functioning of the structure of the wheel.

It is neither by chance nor by lack of scientific precision that, along with others who have considered the conception of communitas, I find myself forced to have recourse to metaphor and analogy. For communitas has an existential quality; it involves the whole man in his relation to other whole men. Structure, on the other hand, has cognitive quality; as Lévi-Strauss has perceived, it is essentially a set of classifications, a model for thinking about culture and nature and ordering one's public life. Communitas has also an aspect of potentiality: it is often in the subjunctive mood. Relations between total beings are generative of symbols and metaphors and comparisons; art and religion are their products rather than legal and political structures. Bergson saw in the words and writings of prophets and great artists the creation of an 'open morality' which was itself an expression of what he called the *élan vital*, or evolutionary 'life-force'. Prophets and artists tend to be liminal and marginal people, 'edgemen', who strive with a passionate sincerity to rid themselves of the clichés associated with status incumbency and role-playing and to enter into vital relations with other men in fact or imagination. In their productions we may catch glimpses of that unused evolutionary potential in mankind which has not yet been externalized and fixed in structure.

Communitas breaks in through the interstices of structure, in liminality; at the edges of structure, in marginality; and from beneath structure, in inferiority. It is almost everywhere held to be sacred or 'holy', possibly because it transgresses or dissolves the norms that govern structured and institutionalized relationships and is accompanied by experiences of unprecedented potency. The processes of 'levelling' and 'stripping', to which Goffman has drawn our attention, often appear to flood their subjects with affect. Instinctual energies are surely liberated by these processes, but I am now inclined to think that communitas is not solely the product of biologically inherited drives released from cultural constraints. Rather it is the product of peculiarly human faculties, which include rationality, volition, and memory, and which develop with experience of life in society – just as among the Tallensi it is only mature men who undergo the experiences that induce them to receive *bakologo* shrines.

The notion that there is a generic bond between men, and its related sentiment of 'humankindness', are not epiphenomena of some kind of herd instinct but are products of 'men in their wholeness wholly attending'. Liminality, marginality, and structural inferiority are conditions in which are frequently generated myths, symbols, rituals, philosophical systems, and works of art. These cultural forms provide men with a set of templates or models which are, at one level, periodical reclassifications of reality and man's relationship to society, nature, and culture. But they are more than classifications, since they incite men to action as well as to thought. Each of these productions has a multivocal character, having many meanings, and each is capable of moving people at many psychobiological levels simultaneously.

There is a dialectic here, for the immediacy of communitas gives way to the mediacy of structure, while, in *rites de passage*, men are released from structure into communitas only to return to structure revitalized by their experience of communitas. What is certain is that no society can function adequately without this dialectic. Exaggeration of structure may well lead to pathological manifestations of communitas outside or against 'the law'. Exaggerations of communitas, in certain religious or political movements of the levelling type, may be speedily followed by despotism, overbureaucratization, or other modes of structural rigidification. For, like the neophytes in the African circumcision lodge, or the Benedictine monks, or the members of a millenarian movement, those living in community seem to require, sooner or later, an absolute authority, whether this be a religious commandment, a divinely inspired leader, or a dictator. Communitas cannot stand alone if the material and organizational needs of human beings are to be adequately met. Maximization of communitas provokes maximization of structure, which in its turn produces revolutionary strivings for renewed communitas. The history of any great society provides evidence at the political level for this oscillation.

. . .

[A]s most anthropologists would now confirm, customary norms and differences of status and prestige in preliterate societies allow of little scope for individual liberty and choice – the individualist is often regarded as a witch; for true equality between, for example, men and women, elders and juniors, chiefs and commoners; while fraternity itself frequently succumbs to the sharp distinction of status between older and junior sibling. Membership of rivalrous segments in such societies as the Tallensi, Nuer, and Tiv does not allow even of tribal brotherhood: such membership commits the individual to structure and to the conflicts that are inseparable from structural differentiation. However, even in the simplest societies, the distinction between structure and communitas exists and obtains symbolic expression in the cultural attributes of liminality, marginality, and inferiority. In different societies and at different periods in each society, one or the other of these 'immortal antagonists' (to borrow terms that Freud used in a different sense) comes uppermost. But together they constitute the 'human condition', as regards man's relations with his fellow man.

References

Donald Attwater, ed., *A Catholic Encyclopedia* (New York: Macmillan 1961).

Henri Bergson, *L'evolution créatrice* (Paris 1907).

Martin Buber, *I and Thou* (Edinburgh: T & T Clark 1961).

Norman Cohn, *The Pursuit of the Millennium* (New York: Harper Torch Books 1961).

Mary Douglas, *Purity and Danger* (London: Routledge & Kegan Paul 1966).

Meyer Fortes, 'Ritual and Office', in Max Gluckman, ed., *Essays on the Ritual of Social Relations* (Manchester: Manchester University Press 1962).

Erving Goffman, *Asylums: Essays on the Social Situation of Mental Patients and Other Inmates* (Chicago: Aldine 1962).

G. A. Hillery, 'Definitions of community: areas of agreement', *Rural Sociology* 20 (1955).

David Hume, *Enquiry concerning the Principles of Morals* (Oxford: Clarendon 1975).

Claude Lévi-Strauss, *Le cru et le cuit* (Paris: Plon 1964).

Victor Turner, *The Forest of Symbols: Aspects of Ndembu Ritual* (Ithaca, NY: Cornell University Press 1967).

Arnold Van Gennep, *The Rites of Passage* (London: Routledge & Kegan Paul 1960).

★★★

The Forest of Symbols

Chapter 1: Symbols in Ndembu ritual

Three properties of ritual symbols

The simplest property is that of *condensation*. Many things and actions are represented in a single formation. Secondly, a dominant symbol is a *unification of disparate significata*. The disparate *significata* are interconnected by virtue of their common possession of analogous qualities or by association in fact or thought. Such qualities or links of association may in themselves be quite trivial or random or widely distributed over a range of phenomena. Their very generality enables them to bracket together the most diverse ideas and phenomena. Thus, as we have seen, the milk tree stands for, *inter alia*, women's breasts, motherhood, a novice at *Nkang'a*, the principle of matriliny, a specific matrilineage, learning, and the unity and persistence of Ndembu society. The themes of nourishment and dependence run through all these diverse *significata*.

The third important property of dominant ritual symbols is *polarization of meaning*. Not only the milk tree but all other dominant Ndembu symbols possess two clearly distinguishable poles of meaning. At one pole is found a cluster of *significata* that refer to components of the moral and social orders of Ndembu society, to principles of social organization, to kinds of corporate grouping, and to the norms and values inherent in structural relationships. At the other pole, the *significata* are usually natural and physiological phenomena and processes. Let us call the first of these the 'ideological pole', and the second the 'sensory pole'. At the sensory pole, the meaning content is closely related to the outward form of the symbol. Thus one meaning of the milk tree – breast milk – is closely related to the exudation of milky latex from the tree. One sensory meaning of another dominant symbol, the *mukula* tree, is blood; this tree secretes a dusky red gum.

At the sensory pole are concentrated those *significata* that may be expected to arouse desires and feelings; at the ideological pole one finds an arrangement of norms and values that guide and control persons as members of social groups and categories. The sensory, emotional *significata* tend to be 'gross' in a double sense. In the first place, they are gross in a general way, taking no account of detail or the precise qualities of emotion. It cannot be sufficiently stressed that such symbols are social facts, 'collective representations', even though their appeal is to the lowest common denominator of human feeling. The second sense of 'gross' is 'frankly, even flagrantly, physiological'. Thus, the milk tree has the gross meanings of breast milk, breasts, and the process of breast feeding. These are also gross in the sense that they represent items of universal Ndembu experience. Other Ndembu symbols, at their sensory poles of meaning, represent such themes as blood, male and female genitalia, semen, urine, and feces. The same symbols, at their ideological poles of meaning, represent the unity and continuity of social groups, primary and associational, domestic, and political.

Reference and condensation

It has long been recognized in anthropological literature that ritual symbols are stimuli of emotion. Perhaps the most striking statement of this position is that made by Edward Sapir in the *Encyclopaedia of the Social Sciences* (xiv, 492–93). Sapir distinguishes, in a way which recalls Jung's distinction, between two principal classes of symbols. The first he calls 'referential' symbols. These include such forms as oral speech, writing, national flags, flag signalling, and other organizations of symbols which are agreed upon as economical devices for purposes of reference. Like Jung's 'sign', the referential symbol is predominantly cognitive and refers to known facts. The second class, which includes most ritual symbols, consists of 'condensation' symbols, which Sapir defines as 'highly condensed forms of substitutive behaviour for direct expression, allowing for the ready release of emotional tension in conscious or unconscious form'. The condensation symbol is 'saturated with emotional quality'. The chief difference in development between these types of symbolism, in Sapir's view, is that 'while referential symbolism grows with formal elaboration in the conscious, condensation symbolism strikes deeper and deeper roots in the unconscious, and diffuses its emotional quality to types of behaviour and situations apparently far removed from the original meaning of the symbol.'

Sapir's formulation is most illuminating. He lays explicit stress on four main attributes of ritual symbols: (1) the condensation of many meanings in a single form; (2) economy of reference; (3) predominance of emotional or orectic quality; (4) associational linkages with regions of the unconscious. Nevertheless, he tends to underestimate the importance of what I have called the ideological (or, I would add, normative) pole of meaning. Ritual symbols are at one and the same time referential and condensation symbols, though each symbol is multireferential rather than unireferential. Their essential quality consists in their juxtaposition of the grossly physical and the structurally normative, of the organic and the social. Such symbols are coincidences of opposite qualities, unions of 'high' and 'low'. We do not need a detailed acquaintance with any of the current depth psychologies to suspect that this juxtaposition, and even interpenetration, of opposites in the symbol is connected with its social function. Durkheim was fascinated by the problem of why many social norms and imperatives were felt to be at the same time 'obligatory' and 'desirable'. Ritual, scholars are coming to see, is precisely a mechanism that periodically converts the obligatory into the desirable. The basic unit of ritual, the dominant symbol, encapsulates the major properties of the total ritual process which brings about this transmutation. Within its framework of meanings, the dominant symbol brings the ethical and jural norms of society into close contact with strong emotional stimuli. In the action situation of ritual, with its social excitement and directly physiological stimuli, such as music, singing, dancing, alcohol, incense, and bizarre modes of dress, the ritual symbol, we may perhaps say, effects an interchange of qualities between its poles of meaning. Norms and values, on the one hand, become saturated with emotion, while the gross and basic emotions become ennobled through contact with social values. The irksomeness of moral constraint is transformed into the 'love of virtue'.

Before proceeding any further with our analysis, it might be as well to restate the major empirical properties of dominant symbols derived from our classification of the relevant descriptive data: (1) condensation; (2) unification of disparate meanings in a single symbolic formation; (3) polarization of meaning.

Dominant and instrumental symbols

Certain ritual symbols, as I have said, are regarded by Ndembu as dominant. In rituals performed to propitiate ancestor spirits who are believed to have afflicted their living kin with reproductive disorders, illness, or bad luck at hunting, there are two main classes of dominant symbols. The first class is represented by the first tree or plant in a series of trees or plants from which portions of leaves, bark, or roots are collected by practitioners or adepts in the curative cult. The subjects of ritual are marked with these portions mixed with water, or given them, mixed in a potion, to drink. The first tree so treated is called the 'place of greeting' (*ishikenu*), or the 'elder' (*mukulumpi*). The adepts encircle it several times to sacralize it. Then the senior practitioner prays at its base, which he sprinkles with powdered white clay. Prayer is made either to the named spirit, believed to be afflicting the principal subject of ritual, or to the tree itself, which is in some way identified with the afflicting spirit. Each *ishikenu* can be allotted several meanings by adepts. The second class of dominant symbols in curative rituals consists of shrines where the subjects of such rituals sit while the practitioners wash them with vegetable substances mixed with water and perform actions on their behalf of a symbolic or ritualistic nature. Such shrines are often composite, consisting of several objects in configuration. Both classes of dominant symbols are closely associated with nonempirical beings. Some are regarded as their repositories; others, as being identified with them; others again, as representing them. In life-crisis rituals, on the other hand, dominant symbols seem to represent not beings but nonempirical powers or kinds of efficacy. For example, in the boys' circumcision ritual, the dominant symbol for the whole ritual is a 'medicine' (*yitumbu*), called '*nfunda*', which is compounded from many ingredients, e.g., the ash of the burnt lodge which means 'death', and the urine of an apprentice circumciser which means 'virility'. Each of these and other ingredients have many other meanings. The dominant symbol at the camp where the novices' parents assemble and prepare food for the boys is the *chikoli* tree, which represents, among other things, an erect phallus, adult masculinity, strength, hunting prowess, and health continuing into old age. The dominant symbol during the process of circumcision is the milk tree, beneath which novices are circumcised. The dominant symbol in the immediate post-circumcision phase is the red *mukula* tree, on which the novices sit until their wounds stop bleeding. Other symbols are dominant at various phases of seclusion. Each of these symbols is described as '*mukulumpi*' (elder, senior). Dominant symbols appear in many different ritual contexts, sometimes presiding over the whole procedure, sometimes over particular phases. The meaning-content of certain dominant symbols possesses a high degree of constancy and consistency throughout the total symbolic system, exemplifying Radcliffe-Brown's proposition that a symbol recurring in a cycle of rituals is likely to have the same significance in each. Such symbols also possess considerable autonomy with regard to the aims of the rituals in which they appear. Precisely because of these properties, dominant symbols are readily analyzable in a cultural framework of reference. They may be regarded for this purpose as what Whitehead would have called 'eternal objects'.[1] They are the relatively fixed points in both the social and cultural structures, and indeed constitute points of junction between these two kinds of structure. They may be regarded irrespective of their order of appearance in a given ritual as ends in themselves, as representative of the axiomatic values of the widest Ndembu society. This does not mean that they cannot also be studied, as we have indeed studied them, as factors of social action, in an action frame of reference, but their social properties make them more appropriate objects of morphological study than the class of symbols we will now consider.

These symbols may be termed 'instrumental symbols'. An instrumental symbol must be seen in terms of its wider context, i.e., in terms of the total system of symbols which makes up a given kind of ritual. Each kind of ritual has its specific mode of interrelating symbols. This mode is often dependent upon the ostensible purposes of that kind of ritual. In other words, each ritual has its own teleology. It has its explicitly expressed goals, and instrumental symbols may be regarded as means of attaining those goals. For example, in rituals performed for the overt purpose of making women fruitful, among the instrumental symbols used are portions of fruit-bearing trees or of trees that possess innumerable rootlets. These fruits and rootlets are said by Ndembu to represent children. They are also thought of as having efficacy to make the woman fruitful. They are means to the main end of the ritual. Perhaps such symbols could be regarded as mere signs or referential symbols, were it not for the fact that the meanings of each are associated with powerful conscious and unconscious emotions and wishes. At the psychological level of analysis, I suspect that these symbols too would approximate to the condition of condensation symbols, but here we touch upon the present limits of competence of anthropological explanation.

. . .

---

[1] I.e., objects not of indefinite duration but to which the category of time is not applicable.

Provinces of explanation

I consider that if we conceptualize a dominant symbol as having two poles of meaning, we can more exactly demarcate the limits within which anthropological analysis may be fruitfully applied. Psychoanalysts, in treating most indigenous interpretations of symbols as irrelevant, are guilty of a naïve and one-sided approach. For those interpretations that show how a dominant symbol expresses important components of the social and moral orders are by no means equivalent to the 'rationalizations', and the 'secondary elaborations' of material deriving from endopsychic conflicts. They refer to social facts that have an empirical reality exterior to the psyches of individuals. On the other hand, those anthropologists who regard only indigenous interpretations as relevant, are being equally one-sided. This is because they tend to examine symbols within two analytical frameworks only, the cultural and the structural. This approach is essentially a static one, and it does not deal with processes involving temporal changes in social relations.

Nevertheless, the crucial properties of a ritual symbol involve these dynamic developments. Symbols instigate social action. In a field context they may even be described as 'forces', in that they are determinable influences inclining persons and groups to action. It is in a field context, moreover, that the properties we have described, namely, polarization of meanings, transference of affectual quality, discrepancy between meanings, and condensations of meanings, become most significant. The symbol as a unit of action, possessing these properties, becomes an object of study both for anthropology and for psychology. Both disciplines, in so far as they are concerned with human actions must conceptualize the ritual symbol in the same way.

The techniques and concepts of the anthropologist enable him to analyze competently the interrelations between the data associated with the ideological pole of meaning. They also enable him to analyze the social behaviour directed upon the total dominant symbol. He cannot, however, with his present skills, discriminate between the precise sources of unconscious feeling and wishing, which shape much of the outward form of the symbol; select some natural objects rather than others to serve as symbols; and account for certain aspects of the behaviour associated with symbols. For him, it is enough that the symbol should evoke motion. He is interested in the fact that emotion is evoked and not in the specific qualities of its constituents. He may indeed find it situationally relevant for his analysis to distinguish whether the emotion evoked by a specific symbol possesses the gross character, say, of aggression, fear, friendliness, anxiety, or sexual pleasure, but he need go no further than this. For him the ritual symbol is primarily a factor in group dynamics, and, as such, its references to the groups, relationships, values, norms, and beliefs of a society are his principal items of study. In other words, the anthropologist treats the sensory pole of meaning as a constant, and the social and ideological aspects as variables whose interdependencies he seeks to explain.

The psychoanalyst, on the other hand, must, I think, attach greater significance than he now does to social factors in the analysis of ritual symbolism. He must cease to regard interpretations, beliefs, and dogmas as mere rationalizations when, often enough, these refer to social and natural realities. For, as Durkheim wrote (1915, 2–3), 'primitive religions hold to reality and express it. One must learn to go underneath the symbol to the reality which it represents and which gives it its meaning. No religions are false, all answer, though in different ways, to the given conditions of human existence.' Among those given conditions, the arrangement of society into structured groupings, discrepancies between the principles that organize these groupings, economic collaboration and competition, schism within groups and opposition between groups – in short, all those things with which the social aspect of ritual symbolism is concerned – are surely of at least equal importance with biopsychical drives and early conditioning in the elementary family. After all, the ritual symbol has, in common with the dream symbol, the characteristic, discovered by Freud, of being a compromise formation between two main opposing tendencies. It is a compromise between the need for social control, and certain innate and universal human drives whose complete gratification would result in a breakdown of that control. Ritual symbols refer to what is normative, general, and characteristic of unique individuals. Thus, Ndembu symbols refer among other things, to the basic needs of social existence (hunting, agriculture, female fertility, favourable climatic conditions, and so forth), and to shared values on which communal life depends (generosity, comradeship, respect for elders, the importance of kinship, hospitality, and the like). In distinguishing between ritual symbols and individual psychic symbols, we may perhaps say that while ritual symbols are gross means of handling social and natural reality, psychic symbols are dominantly fashioned under the influence of inner drives. In analyzing the former, attention must mainly be paid to relations between data external to the psyche; in analyzing the latter, to endopsychic data.

For this reason, the study of ritual symbolism falls more within the province of the social anthropologist than that of the psychologist or psychoanalyst, although the latter can assist the anthropologist by examining the nature and interconnections of the data clustered at the sensory pole of ritual symbolism. He can also, I believe, illuminate certain aspects of the stereotyped behaviour associated with symbols in field contexts, which the actors themselves are unable to explain. For, as we have seen, much of this behaviour is suggestive of attitudes that differ radically from those deemed appropriate in terms of traditional exegesis. Indeed, certain conflicts would appear to be so basic that they totally block exegesis.

The interpretation of observed emotions

Can we really say that behaviour portraying conflict between persons and groups, who are represented by the symbols themselves as being in harmony, is in the full Freudian sense unconscious behaviour? The Ndembu themselves in many situations outside *Nkang'a*, both secular and ritual, are perfectly aware of and ready to speak about hostility in the relationships between particular mothers and daughters, between particular sublineages, and between particular young girls and the adult women in their villages. It is rather as though there existed in certain precisely defined public situations, usually of a ritual or ceremonial type, a norm obstructing the verbal statement of conflicts in any way connected with the principle and rules celebrated or dramatized in those situations. Evidences of human passion and frailty are just not spoken about when the occasion is given up to the public commemoration and reanimation of norms and values in their abstract purity.

Yet, as we have seen, recurrent kinds of conflict may be acted out in the ritual or ceremonial form. On great ritual occasions, common practice, as well as highest principle, receives its symbolic or stereotyped expression, but practice, which is dominantly under the sway of what all societies consider man's 'lower nature', is rife with expressions of conflict. Selfish and factional interests, oath breaking, disloyalty, sins of omission as well as sins of commission, pollute and disfigure those ideal prototypes of behaviour which in precept, prayer, formula, and symbol are held up before the ritual assembly for its exclusive attention. In the orthodox interpretation of ritual it is pretended that common practice has no efficacy and that men and women really are as they ideally should be. Yet, as I have argued above, the 'energy' required to reanimate the values and norms enshrined in dominant symbols and expressed in various kinds of verbal behaviour is 'borrowed', to speak metaphorically in lieu at the moment of a more rigorous language, from the miming of well-known and normally mentionable conflicts. The raw energies of conflict are domesticated into the service of social order.

I should say here that I believe it possible, and indeed necessary, to analyze symbols in a context of observed emotions. If the investigator is well acquainted with the common idiom in which a society expresses such emotions as friendship, love, hate, joy, sorrow, contentment, and fear, he cannot fail to observe that these are experienced in ritual situations. Thus, in *Nkang'a* when the women laugh and jeer at the men, tease the novice and her mother, fight one another for the 'porridge of *chipwampwilu*', and so on, the observer can hardly doubt that emotions are really aroused in the actors as well as formally represented by ritual custom. ('What's Hecuba to him or he to Hecuba, that he should weep for her?')

These emotions are portrayed and evoked in close relation to the dominant symbols of tribal cohesion and continuity, often by the performance of instrumentally symbolic behaviour. However, since they are often associated with the mimesis of interpersonal and intergroup conflict, such emotions and acts of behaviour obtain no place among the official, verbal meanings attributed to such dominant symbols.

. . .

Conclusion: the analysis of symbols in social processes

Let me outline briefly the way in which I think ritual symbols may fruitfully be analyzed. Performances of ritual are phases in broad social processes, the span and complexity of which are roughly proportional to the size and degree of differentiation of the groups in which they occur. One class of ritual is situated near the apex of a whole hierarchy of redressive and regulative institutions that correct deflections and deviations from customarily prescribed behaviour. Another class anticipates deviations and conflicts. This class includes periodic rituals and life-crisis rituals. Each kind of ritual is a patterned process in time, the units of which are symbolic objects and serialized items of symbolic behaviour.

The symbolic constituents may themselves be classed into structural elements, or 'dominant symbols', which tend to be ends in themselves, and variable elements, or 'instrumental symbols', which serve as means to the explicit or implicit goals of the given ritual. In order to give an adequate explanation of the meaning of a particular symbol, it is necessary first to examine the widest action-field context, that, namely, in which the ritual itself is simply a phase. Here one must consider what kinds of circumstances give rise to a performance of ritual, whether these are concerned with natural phenomena, economic and technological processes, human life-crises, or with the breach of crucial social relationships. The circumstances will probably determine what sort of ritual is performed. The goals of the ritual will have overt and implicit reference to the antecedent circumstances and will in turn help to determine the meaning of the symbols. Symbols must now be examined within the context of the specific ritual. It is here that we enlist the aid of indigenous informants. It is here also that we may be able to speak legitimately of 'levels' of interpretation, for laymen will give the investigator simple and exoteric meanings, while specialists will give him esoteric explanations and more elaborate texts. Next, behaviour directed towards each symbol should be noted, for such behaviour is an important component of its total meaning.

We are now in a position to exhibit the ritual as a system of meanings, but this system acquires additional richness and depth if it is regarded as itself constituting a sector of the Ndembu ritual system, as interpreted by informants and as observed in action. It is in comparison with other sectors of the total system, and by reference to the dominant articulating principles of the total system, that we often become aware that the overt and ostensible aims and purposes of a given ritual conceal unavowed, and even 'unconscious', wishes and goals. We also become aware that a complex relationship exists between the overt and the submerged, and the manifest and latent patterns of meaning. As social anthropologists we are potentially capable of analyzing the social aspect of this relationship. We can examine, for example, the relations of dependence and independence between the total society and its parts, and the relations between different kinds of parts, and between different parts of the same kind. We can see how the same dominant symbol, which in one kind of ritual stands for one kind of social group or for one principle of organization, in another kind of ritual stands for another kind of group or principle, and in its aggregate of meanings stands for unity and continuity of the widest Ndembu society, embracing its contradictions.

The limits of contemporary anthropological competence

Our analysis must needs be incomplete when we consider the relationship between the normative elements in social life and the individual. For this relationship, too, finds its way into the meaning of ritual symbols. Here we come to the confines of our present anthropological competence, for we are now dealing with the structure and properties of psyches, a scientific field traditionally studied by other disciplines than ours. At one end of the symbol's spectrum of meanings we encounter the individual psychologist and the social psychologist, and even beyond them (if one may make a friendly tilt at an envied friend), brandishing his Medusa's head, the psychoanalyst, ready to turn to stone the foolhardy interloper into his caverns of terminology.

We shudder back thankfully into the light of social day. Here the significant elements of a symbol's meaning are related to what it does and what is done to it by and for whom. These aspects can only be understood if one takes into account from the beginning, and represents by appropriate theoretical constructs, the total field situation in which the symbol occurs. This situation would include the structure of the group that performs the ritual we observe, its basic organizing principles and perdurable relationships, and, in addition, its extant division into transient alliances and factions on the basis of immediate interest and ambitions, for both abiding structure and recurrent forms of conflict and selfish interest are stereotyped in ritual symbolism. Once we have collected informants' interpretations of a given symbol, our work of analysis has indeed just begun. We must gradually approximate to the action-meaning of our symbol by way of what Lewin calls (1949, 149) 'a stepwise increasing specificity' from widest to narrowest significant action context. Informants' 'meanings' only become meaningful as objects of scientific study in the course of this analytical process.

Chapter 2: Ritual symbolism, morality, and social structure among the Ndembu

When we talk about the 'meaning' of a symbol, we must be careful to distinguish between at least three levels or fields of meaning. These I propose to call: (1) the level of indigenous interpretation (or, briefly, the exegetical meaning); (2) the operational meaning; and (3) the positional meaning. The exegetical meaning is obtained from questioning indigenous informants about observed ritual behaviour. Here again one must distinguish between information given by ritual specialists and information given by laymen, that is, between esoteric and exoteric interpretations. One must also be careful to ascertain whether a given explanation is truly representative of either of these categories or whether it is a uniquely personal view.

On the other hand, much light may be shed on the role of the ritual symbol by equating its meaning with its use, by observing what the Ndembu do with it, and not only what they say about it. This is what I call the operational meaning, and this level has the most bearing on problems of social dynamics. For the observer must consider not only the symbol but the structure and composition of the group that handles it or performs mimetic acts with direct reference to it. He must further note the affective qualities of these acts, whether they are aggressive, sad, penitent, joyful, derisive, and so on. He must also inquire why certain persons and groups are absent on given occasions, and if absent, whether and why they have been ritually excluded from the presence of the symbol.

The positional meaning of a symbol derives from its relationship to other symbols in a totality, a *Gestalt*, whose elements acquire their significance from the system as a whole. This level of meaning is directly related to the important property of ritual symbols mentioned earlier, their polysemy. Such symbols possess many senses, but contextually it may be necessary to stress one or a few of them only. Thus the *mukula* tree viewed in abstraction for 'matriliny', 'huntsmanship', 'menstrual blood', 'the meat of wild animals', and many other concepts and things. The associational link between its various senses is provided by the red gum it secretes, which Ndembu liken to blood. Now in the boys' circumcision ritual (*Mukanda*) the meaning of *mukula* is determined by its symbolic context. A log of this wood is placed near the site where the boys are circumcised. They are circumcised under a *mudyi* tree, which, as we shall see, stands *inter alia* for motherhood and the mother–child relationship. Then they are lifted over a cutting of the *muyombu* tree, which is customarily planted quickset as a shrine to the village ancestor spirits, and placed still bleeding on the *mukula* log. Here the *mukula* log stands mainly for two things. It represents the wish of the elders that the circumcision wounds will heal quickly (from the fact that *mukula* gum quickly coagulates like a scab). It also represents, I was told, masculinity (*wuyala*) and the life of an adult male, who as hunter and warrior has to shed blood. The rite represents (1) the removal of the boy from dependence on his mother (the passage from the *mudyi* tree); (2) his ritual death and subsequent association with the ancestors (the passage over the *muyombu* tree); and (3) his incorporation into the male moral community of tribesmen (the collective setting on the *mukula* tree where the boys are ceremonially fed as though they were infants by the circumcisers and by their fathers. Each boy is given a ball of cassava mush to be eaten directly from the circumciser's knife). In this rite the position of the *mukula* symbol with reference to other symbolic objects and acts is the crucial semantic factor.

The same symbol may be reckoned to have different senses at different phases in a ritual performance, or rather, different senses become paramount at different times. Which sense shall become paramount is determined by the ostensible purpose of the phase of the ritual in which it appears. For a ritual, like a space rocket, is phased, and each phase is directed towards a limited end which itself becomes a means to the ultimate end of the total performance. Thus the act of circumcision is the aim and culmination of a symbol-loaded phase of the *Mukanda* ritual, but itself becomes a means to the final end of turning a boy into a tribesman. There is a consistent relationship between the end or aim of each phase in a ritual, the kind of symbolic configuration employed in that phase, and the senses that become paramount in multivocal symbols in that configuration.

I should now like to consider the exegetical meaning of one of the principal Ndembu ritual symbols, the *mudyi* tree. This symbol is found in more than half a dozen different kinds of ritual, but its *locus classicus* is in the girls' puberty ritual (*Nkang'a*). The novice is laid, wrapped in a blanket, at the foot of a slender young *mudyi* sapling. Ndembu say that its pliancy stands for the youth of the girl. The sapling has been previously consecrated by the novice's ritual instructress (*nkong'u*) and her mother. They have trampled down the grass in a circle around the tree, thus making it sacred — 'set apart' (*chakumbadyi*) or 'forbidden' (*chakujila*). The site, like that of circumcision for the boys, is called *ifwilu* or 'the place of dying'. Both sites are also known as *ihung'u*, 'the place of suffering' or 'ordeal'. *Ihung'u* is also applied to a hut where a woman is in labour. It is a 'place of suffering' because the novice must not move her limbs until nearly nightfall on penalty of being pinched all over by the older women; nor may she eat or speak all day. The association of the *mudyi* tree with suffering and dying should be borne in mind as an aspect of its positional meaning.

Ndembu begin the exposition of *mudyi*'s meaning by pointing out that if its bark is scratched, beads of milky latex are promptly secreted. For this reason they say that *mudyi* or 'milk tree' is a symbol (*chinjikijilu*) for 'breasts' and 'breast milk' — both called in Chindembu *mayeli*. They go on from there to say that *mudyi* means 'a mother and her child', a social relationship. They further extend this sense to signify a matrilineage (*ivumu*, literally 'a womb or stomach'). A text which I collected well expresses this view:

Mudyi diku kwakaminiyi nkakulula hakumutembwisha ni ankukulula
The milk tree is the place where slept the (founding) ancestress, where they initiated her and another ancestress

mukwawu nimukwawu ni kudi nkaka ni kudi mama ninetu anyana;
and (then) another down to the grandmother and the mother and ourselves the children;

diku kumuchidi wetu kutwatachikili ni amayala nawa chochu hamu.
It is the place where our tribe (or tribal custom — literally 'kind') began, also the men in just the same way.

My informant then added the following comments: 'The milk tree is the place of all mothers; it is the ancestress of men and women. *Kutembwisha*, "to initiate a girl", means to dance round and round the milk tree where the novice lies. The milk tree is the place where our ancestors slept, to be initiated there means to become ritually pure or white. An uninitiated girl, a menstruating woman, or an uncircumcised boy is called "one who lacks whiteness (*wunabulakutooka*)".'

Contextually, a particular novice's milk tree may be termed 'her matrilineage'. At one phase of the ritual, the leaves of this tree are said to represent 'the novice's children' – a sense that is concerned with a future wished-for state of affairs rather than with the past or present.

In other phases of the *Nkang'a* ritual the milk tree is said to stand for 'the women' and for 'womanhood'. It also has the situational sense of 'married womanhood'.

Finally, the milk tree stands for the process of learning (*kudiza*), especially for learning 'women's sense' or 'wisdom' (*mana yawambanda*). An informant said that '*mudyi*' is like going to school; 'the girl drinks sense as a baby drinks milk'.

The semantic structure of *mudyi* may itself be likened to a tree. At the root is the primary sense of 'breast milk' and from this proceeds by logical steps series of further senses. The general direction is from the concrete to the increasingly abstract, but there are several different branches along which abstraction proceeds. One line develops as follows: breast, mother–child relationship, matriliny, the Ndembu tribe or tribal custom of which matriliny is the most representative principle. Another line runs: development of the breasts, womanhood, married womanhood, childbearing. Yet another goes from suckling to learning the tasks, rights, and duties of womanhood. As with many other Ndembu symbols, derivative senses themselves become symbols pointing to ideas and phenomena beyond themselves. Thus 'matriliny', a derivative sense from 'the mother–child' relationship, and 'breast-milk', by the principle of *pars pro toto*, itself becomes a symbol for Ndembu culture in its totality.

However, despite this multiplicity of senses, Ndembu speak and think about the milk tree as a unity, almost as a unitary power. They can break down the concept 'milk tree' cognitively into many attributes, but in ritual practice they view it as a single entity. For them it is something like Goethe's 'eternal womanly', a female or maternal principle pervading society and nature. It must not be forgotten that ritual symbols are not merely signs representing known things; they are felt to possess ritual efficacy, to be charged with power from unknown sources, and to be capable of acting on persons and groups coming in contact with them in such a way as to change them for the better or in a desired direction. Symbols, in short, have an orectic as well as a cognitive function. They elicit emotion and express and mobilize desire.

Indeed, it is possible further to conceptualize the exegetic meaning of dominant symbols in polar terms. At one pole cluster a set of referents of a grossly physiological character, relating to general human experience of an emotional kind. At the other pole cluster a set of referents to moral norms and principles governing the social structure. If we call these semantic poles respectively the 'orectic' and the 'normative' pole, and consider Ndembu ritual symbols in terms of this model, we find that the milk tree stands at one and the same time for the physiological aspect of breast feeding with its associated affectual patterns, and for the normative order governed by matriliny. In brief, a single symbol represents both the obligatory and the desirable. Here we have an intimate union of the moral and the material. An exchange of qualities may take place in the psyches of the participants under the stimulating circumstances of the ritual performance, between orectic and normative poles; the former, through its association with the latter, becomes purged of its infantile and regressive character, while the normative pole becomes charged with the pleasurable effect associated with the breast-feeding situation. In one aspect, the tie of milk, under matriliny, develops into the primary structural tie, but in another aspect, and here the polar model is apposite, the former stands opposed to and resists the formation of the latter.

References

Emile Durkheim, *The Elementary Forms of the Religious Life* (London: Allen & Unwin 1915).

Carl Jung, *Psychological Types* (London: Routledge & Kegan Paul 1949).

Kurt Lewin, *Field Theory in Social Science* (London: Tavistock Publications 1949).

Edward Sapir, 'Symbols', in *Encyclopaedia of the Social Sciences*, edited by Edwin R. A. Seligman (New York: Macmillan 1930–1935).

Part 3

THE FIELD OF RITUAL

6

Nathan D. Mitchell

Introduction

Why is it that the term religion does not exhaust all the components – the practices, the ways of being – that comprise it? How did this understanding of the term come about and why is it that you place such emphasis on an alternative conception of the term?

I'm not really concerned to give another definition of religion. I am not concerned to say that we can get a more comprehensive, a more dynamic conception, and so on. I wish only to point to the fact that religion as a category is constantly being defined within social and historical contexts, and that people have specific reasons for defining it one way or another.

Religion is associated with various kinds of experience, various institutions, with various movements, arguments and so on. That is what I am pointing to. In other words, it is not an abstract definition that interests me. People who use abstract definitions of religion are missing a very important point: that religion is a social and historical *fact*, which has legal dimensions, domestic and political dimensions, economic dimensions, and so on. So what one has to look for, in other words, is the ways in which, as circumstances change, people constantly try, as it were, to gather together elements that they think belong, or *should* belong, to the notion of religion. People *use* particular conceptions of religion in social life. This has really been my concern. (*AsiaSource* interview with Talal Asad, 16 December, 2002: http://www.asiasource.org/news/special_reports/asad.cfm)

Drawing predominantly on the thought of Talal Asad and Michel Foucault, Nathan Mitchell offers a provocative essay that sketches some directional paths for future studies of ritual within the orbit of liturgical studies. By exploring the rich metaphor of 'technology of the self', the author teases out implications for understanding varied dimensions of ritual engagement and embodiment. In the final section, he deftly examines the shifting sands of current anthropological theory as it relates to religion and rite.

Nathan Mitchell teaches liturgical studies in the Department of Theology, University of Notre Dame, Indiana, and this is Chapter 3, 'New Directions in Ritual Research', of his book, *Liturgy and the Social Sciences* (Collegeville: The Liturgical Press 1999), 63–93.

For further reading

Talal Asad, 'Remarks on the Anthropology of the Body', in Sarah Coakley, ed., *Religion and the Body* (Cambridge: Cambridge University Press 1997), 42–52.

Talal Asad, 'Towards a Genealogy of the Concept of Ritual', in Wendy James and Douglas H. Johnson, *Vernacular Christianity* (New York: Lilian Barber Press 1988), 73–87.

Alex McHoul and Wendy Grace, *A Foucault Primer: Discourse, Power, and the Subject* (Melbourne: Melbourne University Press 1993).

★★★

New directions in ritual research

At the conclusion of Chapter 2, I noted that, among many Christian scholars, the reigning academic consensus about the 'anthropological' roots and roles of ritual has been linked to the conviction that traditional liturgies constitute a symbol system providing references that point to encoded meanings. This ritual encoding, as anthropologist Roy Rappaport argues, is derived from a 'more or less invariant sequence of formal acts and utterances' that are 'given', i.e., not determined or prescribed by the participants in the ritual:[1]

> Liturgical orders are public, and participation in them constitutes a public acceptance of a public order, regardless of the private state of belief. Acceptance is, thus, a fundamental social act, and it forms a basis for public orders, which unknowable and volatile belief or conviction cannot.[2]

For Rappaport, a liturgical order is by definition a public one that provides the correct categories (about nature and cosmos, social structure, moral rules) which participants are expected to impose upon their private processes. The very performance of the liturgical order establishes a publicly accepted obligation to conform to the rite's rules, norms and values. These obligations, accepted in the liturgical performance, are not nullified by subsequent disbelief or violation. Thus, liturgical orders establish and preserve the conventions they encode, in spite of the vagaries of usage and the real possibility of insincerity or failure on the part of the participants.[3]

Such has been the 'classic consensus' about the nature of those rituals we commonly call 'liturgical orders'. As we have seen, it is a consensus challenged widely today by a substantial number of critics. David Kertzer's work with families subverts the myth of a ritually deprived America; Ronald Grimes demonstrates the importance of

[1] See 'The Obvious Aspects of Ritual', in Roy A. Rappaport, *Ecology, Meaning, and Religion* (Richmond, CA: North Atlantic Books 1979), 173–221.
[2] Ibid., 194.
[3] See ibid., 197.

emerging ritual, especially among marginalized groups and individuals; Catherine Bell questions the adequacy of the theoretical basis for this anthropological consensus and suggests that ritual is not intrinsically about either preserving tradition or promoting change. In the present chapter, my task is to sketch for readers some of the new directions ritual studies is taking among anthropologists and sociologists, and to show how these might reshape our understanding of the rituals of Christian liturgy.

Ritual and the technology of the self

The first of the new approaches that I want to examine flows from the research of Talal Asad, a British scholar who, for two decades or more, has been studying the distinctive contribution of Western monasticism to our understanding of religious ritual.[4] In medieval Benedictine monachism, Asad argues, ritual was not primarily a symbol system aimed at the production of meaning but a *technology* – an acquired aptitude or embodied skill – aimed at the production of a 'virtuous self', i.e., of a person who is obedient, humble, chaste, charitable, compassionate, hospitable, and wise.

Asad's discourse about ritual technology is connected to the work of Michel Foucault. Foucault's project had been, in his own words, 'to sketch out a history of the different ways in our culture that humans develop knowledge about themselves: economics, biology, psychiatry, medicine, penology'.[5] He wished not simply to accept this knowledge at face value, but to look at the sciences just mentioned as ' "truth games" related to specific techniques that human beings use to understand themselves'.[6]

These techniques (technologies) fall into four fundamental categories: (1) technologies of production, 'which permit us to produce, transform, or manipulate things'; (2) technologies of sign systems, 'which permit us to use signs, meanings, symbols, or signification'; (3) technologies of power, 'which determine the conduct of individuals and submit them to certain ends or domination, an objectivizing of the subject'; and finally, (4) technologies of the self, 'which permit individuals to effect by their own means or with the help of others a certain number of operations on their own bodies and souls, thoughts, conduct, and way of being, so as to transform themselves

---

[4] I am indebted to Dr Fred Roberts, professor of anthropology at Michigan State University, for alerting me to Talal Asad's work and for showing me its relevance to the field of ritual studies.

[5] Luther H. Martin, Huck Gutman, and Patrick H. Hutton, eds, *Technologies of the Self: A Seminar with Michel Foucault* (Amherst: The University of Massachusetts Press 1988).

[6] Ibid., 18.

in order to attain a certain state of happiness, purity, wisdom, perfection, or immortality'.[7]

To speak about a technology of the self is thus to discuss 'the history of how an individual acts upon himself', along with the interactions between self and others as these are driven by strategies of domination or power.[8] Note that this technology of the self is not an autistic, idiosyncratic or isolated process. Indeed, the phrase is closely connected to what early Christian writers called *cura animae*, 'care of the soul (self)'.[9] This *cura* is deployed and exercised chiefly through the practices of asceticism (e.g., discipline, control, penance, prayer, and purification). But if self-care is personal, it is also, for Christians, inherently and decisively social. It comes as no surprise, therefore, that the ascetic practices of *cura animae* inevitably involve ritual. Thus, technologies of the self include both the 'rites' practised by individuals and the 'ritual construction' of the whole social order.[10] The reason is that Foucault sees the human body not simply as a private possession but as 'a political field'.[11] As Catherine Bell describes it,

> For Foucault, the body is 'the place where the most minute and local social practices are linked up with the large scale organization of power'. The body is a political field: 'Power relations have an immediate hold upon it; they invest it, mark it, train it, torture it, force it to carry out tasks, to perform ceremonies, to emit signs.' The body is the most basic and fundamental level of power relations, the 'microphysics' of the micropolitics of power. Ritualization, Foucault appears to imply, is a central way that power operates; it constitutes a political technology of the body.[12]

Ritual is thus a way of inscribing the body personal, the body politic and their complex, inevitable interactions. Foucault's work (and that of feminist thinkers like Julia Kristeva) has helped us form a new image of the body. No longer is the body a stepchild, 'the mere physical instrument of the mind; it now denotes a more complex and

---

[7] Ibid. Foucault notes that these technologies rarely function separately. Each of them, moreover, 'implies certain modes of training and modification of individuals, not only in the obvious sense of acquiring certain skills but also in the sense of acquiring certain attitudes'.

[8] Ibid., 19.

[9] See the examples Foucault cites from writers like Gregory of Nyssa; ibid., 20–22.

[10] See Catherine Bell, *Ritual Theory, Ritual Practice* (New York: Oxford University Press 1992) 97–98. Note her critique of Foucault: Even though Foucault 'consistently chooses the nomenclature of "ritual" to evoke the mechanisms and dynamics of power', he is not 'concerned to analyze ritual per se or even to generate a description of ritual as an autonomous phenomenon', 98, 201.

[11] Ibid., 201.

[12] Ibid., 202. It might be noted here that Foucault's project – to produce a history of the 'political technology of the body' – is not so vastly different from what (as I suggested in Chapter 1) Aidan Kavanagh was aiming at with his call for a kind of 'political science' of ritual.

irreducible phenomenon, namely, *the social person*'.[13] This new image
is inescapably linked to ritual:

> For Foucault, the 'body' emerged in the late seventeenth century as the
> arena in which more local social practices were linked to the larger scale
> organization of power. With examples that range from marking the body
> with torture to confessional routines and the control of space, Foucault
> has suggested how 'rituals of power' work to forge a specific political 'tech-
> nology' of the body. As the medium of the play of power, he argued, the
> body came to be linked to a new political rationality specifically rooted
> in the technologies of 'biopower'. This historical emergence of the body
> as a focus, moreover, would constitute a new level of analysis located
> between biology and the institutional vehicles of force, and giving rise to
> the human sciences themselves.[14]

In a real sense, this modern reappropriation of the body – its new
image as an arena for the ritual negotiation of power and politics –
is what made the modern human sciences such as anthropology and
sociology possible.

Technologies of the self thus have roots (and consequences) that
are both ancient and modern. Two familiar axioms of the ancient
world were 'know yourself' and 'take care of yourself'. But as Foucault
notes, 'there has been [in modern life] an inversion between the hierarchy of the[se] two principles . . . In Greco-Roman culture knowledge of oneself appeared as the consequence of taking care of
yourself. In the modern world, knowledge of oneself constitutes the
fundamental principle.'[15]

In many Western cultures today, therefore, self-knowledge is
supreme, while 'taking care of yourself' is regarded with suspicion.
Foucault summarizes the situation this way:

> [T]here has been a profound transformation in the moral principles of
> Western society. We find it difficult to base rigorous morality and austere
> principles on the precept that we should give ourselves more care than
> anything else in the world. We are more inclined to see taking care of our-
> selves as an immorality, as a means of escape from all possible rules. We
> inherit the tradition of Christian morality which makes self-renunciation
> the condition for salvation. To know oneself was paradoxically the way
> to self-renunciation.
>
> We are [also] the inheritors of a social morality which seeks the rules for
> acceptable behaviour in relations with others . . . Therefore, it is difficult
> to see concern with oneself as compatible with morality. 'Know thyself'

---

[13] Ibid., 96.
[14] Ibid., 97.
[15] Martin et al., eds, *Technologies of the Self*, 22.

has obscured 'Take care of yourself' because our morality, a morality of asceticism, insists that the self is that which one can reject.[16]

But it is not only the hierarchical relation between self-knowledge and self-care that has been altered in modern life. As Foucault observes, the course of Christian history shows a close correlation 'between *disclosure* of the self, dramatic or verbalized, and the *renunciation* of self'.[17] Self-disclosure – i.e., showing the truth about oneself – has taken two main forms, each of them a 'technology' rooted in the church's emerging penitential discipline. The first form is what both Greek and Latin Christian literature called *exomologesis* (ἐξομολογησις, usually translated 'confession'), 'a dramatic expression of the situation of the penitent as sinner which makes manifest his status as sinner'.[18] Christianity, Foucault noted, is not only a 'salvational' religion but a 'confessional' one as well.[19] It imposes 'very strict obligations of truth', not only about doctrine but about the *self*.

Each person has the duty to know who he or she is, that is, to try to know what is happening inside oneself, to acknowledge faults, to recognize temptations, to locate desires, and everyone is obliged to disclose these things either to God or to others in the community and hence to bear public or private witness against oneself. The truth obligations of faith and the self are linked together.[20]

Exomologesis was thus a means of discovering and deciphering the terrible truth about oneself. It was an exercise in the 'recognition of fact', a 'ritual of recognizing oneself as a sinner and penitent'.[21] Note that *exomologesis was not* primarily verbal behaviour; rather, it was 'the dramatic recognition of one's status as a penitent'.[22] Thus, for example, the Christian Latin writer Tertullian paraphrased the Greek term with the Latin phrase, *publicatio sui*. By it, he meant not a verbal or mental analysis of thoughts and deeds (as practised by the Stoics, for example), but a *somatic and symbolic* activity.[23] *Publicatio sui* was not a way to explain one's sin but to show and present oneself as a sinner. 'Exposé', therefore, 'is the heart of *exomologesis*'.[24] Christian penance

---

[16] Ibid.
[17] Ibid., 48.
[18] Ibid., 40.
[19] Ibid.
[20] Ibid.
[21] Ibid., 41.
[22] Ibid. On the historical roots of penance as a Christian ritual, see J. A. Favazza, *The Order of Penitents: Historical Roots and Pastoral Future* (Collegeville: The Liturgical Press 1988).
[23] See Martin et al., eds, *Technologies of the Self*, 42. As Foucault notes, 'What was private for the Stoics was public for the Christians.'
[24] Ibid.

constituted a kind of voluntary 'ritual martyrdom', a complete 'rupture with self, past, and world', a means of showing 'that you are able to renounce life and self, to show that you can face and accept death'.[25]

Thus, the ritual technology embedded in the early Christian penitential system was *not* aimed at establishing or maintaining a personal, or corporate identity (the typical goals of ritual as interpreted in the 'classic consensus'). Its purpose, rather, was 'the refusal of self, the breaking away from self'.[26] It represented 'a break with one's past identity . . . Self-revelation is at the same time self-destruction.'[27] Foucault thus summarized the differences between the Christian ritual of *exomologesis* and the (Stoic) tradition of self-examination in this way:

> [I]n the Stoic tradition examination of self, judgment, and discipline show the way to self-knowledge by superimposing truth about self through memory, that is, by memorizing the rules. In *exomologesis*, the penitent superimposes truth about self by violent rupture and dissociation. It is important to emphasize that this *exomologesis is* not verbal. *It is symbolic, ritual, and theatrical.*[28]

Within the context of Christian monasticism, however, the penitential ritual of *exomologesis* changed. As noted above, the older notion of penance as *publicatio sui* aimed at the *ritual* 'showing forth of oneself as a sinner'. But in monasticism, a different ideology took hold, an ideology of obedience and contemplation. Personal autonomy – symbolized, in the *Rule of Benedict*,[29] by 'the vice of private ownership' (*RB* 33) – was disallowed. Anything done without permission was tantamount to stealing: stealing back the freedom, the control which monks renounce and surrender when they enter the monastery.[30] Moreover, the goal of monastic life was understood to be contemplation. 'It is the obligation of the monk', wrote Foucault, 'to turn his thoughts continuously to that point which is God and to make sure that his heart is pure enough to see God.'[31]

Both these factors meant that the technology of the self, as it developed in monasteries, took on distinctive characteristics. Dominated by the ideals of obedience and contemplation, monastic ideology focused more upon thought than upon action. As Foucault comments,

---

[25] Ibid., 43.
[26] Ibid.
[27] Ibid.
[28] Ibid., emphasis added.
[29] Hereafter *RB*.
[30] Martin et al., eds, *Technologies of the Self*, 45.
[31] Ibid.

Since the monk must continuously turn his thoughts toward God, he must scrutinize the actual course of this thought. This scrutiny thus has as its object the permanent discrimination between thoughts which lead toward God and those which don't. This continual concern with the present is different from . . . memorization of deeds and their correspondence with rules. It is what the Greeks referred to with a pejorative word: *logismoi* ('cogitations, reasoning, calculating thought').[32]

The monk's life is a continual scrutiny of conscience, a supreme effort 'to immobilize consciousness, to eliminate movements of the spirit that divert one from God'.[33] Here, we are brought to the beginnings of the 'Christian hermeneutics of the self' that emphasizes 'the deciphering of inner thoughts' and implies 'that there is something hidden in ourselves . . . that we are always in a self-delusion which hides the secret'.[34]

Precisely because of the danger of self-delusion, there is only one way for monks to be certain that their thoughts are spiritual and pure – and that is by telling absolutely *everything* to one's director or superior. Note that this process of self-examination and 'confession' is verbal and analytic. If early Christian penance relied on a strategy that was symbolic and dramatic (ἐξομολόγησις = *publicatio sui*, which was the ritual revelation of oneself as sinner), monastic self-examination stressed the constant need to verbalize one's inner thoughts in obedience to a spiritual 'superior' (ἐξαγόρευσις = verbal 'exegesis' of the self through statements made to another). Foucault notes that these two strategies have one important element in common: *You cannot disclose without renouncing. Exomologesis* had as its model martyrdom. In *exomologesis*, the sinner had to 'kill' himself through ascetic macerations . . . In *exagoresis*, on the other hand, you show that, in permanently verbalizing your thoughts and permanently obeying the master, you are renouncing your will and yourself.[35]

This theme of self-renunciation (through either the ritual martyrdom of penance or the verbal/analytical martyrdom of monastic self-examination and confession) has had vast influence on Christian life.[36] Of the two techniques that promote it, the second (verbalization)

---

[32] Ibid.

[33] Ibid., 46. To illustrate, Foucault appeals to three of the analogies used by John Cassian, who describes how monks must 'care for themselves' through the exercise of constant scrutiny. Commenting on Cassian's analogy of the 'money changer', Foucault notes, 'Conscience is the money changer of the self. It must examine coins, their effigy, their metal, where they came from. . . . As there is the image of the emperor on money, so must the image of God be on our thoughts. We must verify the quality of the thought: This effigy of God, is it real? What is its degree of purity? Is it mixed with desire or concupiscence?' (47).

[34] Ibid., 46.

[35] Ibid., 48.

[36] Ibid.

eventually became the most important, not only within Christianity but within the emerging 'human sciences'. 'From the eighteenth century to the present', Foucault notes, 'the techniques of verbalization have been reinserted in a different context by the so-called human sciences in order to use them without renunciation of the self but to constitute, positively, a new self. To use these techniques without renouncing oneself constitutes a decisive break.'[37] Thus the older Christian 'technology of the self' – and its monastic corollary, the 'hermeneutics of the self' – have been reappropriated and reinterpreted by modern sociology and anthropology. The focus is no longer the renunciation of self (as it was in classical Christian asceticism), but the creation of a new self, the formation of a new identity.

As the research of Talal Asad shows, however, the Western monastic tradition, especially *RB*, combined the older Christian emphasis (self-disclosure as self-renunciation) with a view akin to the 'modern' focus (self-disclosure as creation of a new identity). Asad notes that in *RB*, ritual is not yet recognized as a separate mode or specialized category of human behaviour (the way modern liturgists and anthropologists might like to think of it).[38] Monastic liturgy and ritual are not yet seen as formal activities that are inherently 'symbolic, structured, canonical, invariable, non-technical, traditional, and repetitive' in nature. Indeed, *RB* seems to think of the monks' three principal daily occupations – chanting the Divine Office (*opus Dei*), manual labour, and 'holy reading' (*lectio divina*) – as the same kinds of activity requiring roughly the same amount of time.[39] Nor is *opus Dei* spoken of as though it were some kind of *symbolic* action that was opposed to manual labour and *lectio*. Writing about the idea of monastic 'liturgy' in *RB*, Asad observes:

> The liturgy is not a species of enacted symbolism to be classified separately from activities defined as technical but is *a practice among others essential to the acquisition of Christian virtues*. In other words, the liturgy can be isolated only conceptually, for pedagogic reasons, not in practice, from the [rest of the] monastic program . . . In the *Rule* all prescribed practices, whether they

---

[37] Ibid., 49.

[38] Asad would not quite agree with the opinion of scholars like Catherine Bell who see ritual fundamentally as 'a way of acting that distinguishes itself from other ways of acting'. He writes, 'it does not seem to me to make good sense to say that ritual behavior stands universally in opposition to behavior that is ordinary or pragmatic, any more than religion stands in contrast to reason or to (social) science'. See his essay 'On Discipline and Humility in Medieval Christian Monasticism', in Talal Asad, *Genealogies of Religion* (Baltimore: Johns Hopkins University Press 1993), 167. Asad is also critical of Clifford Geertz's view of religion and ritual. See 'Anthropological Conceptions of Religion: Reflections on Geertz', *Man* (NS) 18:2 (1983), 237–59.

[39] See *RB* 47 and 48.

had to do with the proper ways of eating, sleeping, working, and praying or with proper moral disposition and spiritual aptitudes, are aimed at developing virtues that are put 'to the service of God'.[40]

The virtues of a monastic man or woman were thus formed by cultivating the ability to behave, bodily, in certain ways (humbly, obediently, compassionately) – no matter what the particular activity might be. This is clear from *RB*'s description of the 'twelfth step of humility':

> The twelfth step of humility is that a monk always manifests humility in his bearing no less than in his heart, so that it is evident at the Work of God [the Divine Office], in the oratory, the monastery; or the garden, on a journey or in the field, or anywhere else. Whether he sits, walks or stands, his head must be bowed and his eyes cast down.[41]

In *RB*, ritual is thus perceived as bodily inscription, as embodied practice, rehearsal, routine. It is a way of acting equally applicable to work in the garden, to a business trip outside the monastic enclosure, or to chanting psalms in the oratory. Obviously, such an understanding of ritual has nothing to do with ceremonial grandeur, solemnity or 'canonicity' (in Rappaport's sense of the term as applied to 'liturgical orders'). It aims, rather, 'at the apt performance of what is prescribed, something that depends on intellectual and practical disciplines *but does not itself require decoding*. In other words, apt performance involves not symbols to be interpreted but *abilities to be acquired* according to rules that are sanctioned by those in authority: it presupposes no obscure meanings, but rather the formation of physical and linguistic skills.'[42] In *RB*, ritual means 'thinking' with the skin, 'speaking' with the whole human sensorium. Ritual's role is to teach the body how to develop spiritual virtues by material means. Ritual competence is thus bodily competence, for the body is 'an assemblage of embodied aptitudes, not . . . a medium of symbolic meanings'.[43] Strictly speaking, monastic rituals are cognitively 'empty' and 'meaningless'.[44] Their

---

[40] Talal Asad, 'Toward a Genealogy of the Concept of Ritual', in *Genealogies of Religion*, 63; emphasis added.

[41] *RB* 7.62–63. Translation in *RB 1980: The Rule of St. Benedict in Latin and English with Notes*, Timothy Fry et al., eds (Collegeville: The Liturgical Press 1981), 201.

[42] Asad, 'Toward a Genealogy of the Concept of Ritual', 62; emphasis added.

[43] Ibid., 75.

[44] See Frits Staal, 'The Meaninglessness of Ritual', *Numen* 26:1 (1979), 2–22. 'A widespread but erroneous assumption about ritual is that it consists in symbolic activities which refer to something else. It is characteristic of a ritual performance, however, that it is self-contained and self-absorbed. The performers are totally immersed in the proper execution of their complex tasks. Isolated in their sacred enclosure, they concentrate on correctness of act, recitation and chant. Their primary concern, if not obsession, is with rules. There are no symbolic meanings going through their minds when they are engaged in performing ritual' (4).

significance is acquired and interpreted by the body. Their 'meaning' is inscribed on the skin, borne by the blood, carved in the bone.

According to *RB*, then, the ability to enter into communion with God and others is a function of bodies that have learned how to behave ritually, of bodies that 'practise' virtue in much the same way that a pianist's hands practise music and bring it to life in perform-ance.[45] Early Benedictinism saw ritual as a 'technology of the self' with roots in early Christian *exomologesis* (ritual presentation of self as sinner), in monastic *exagoresis* (self-examination and its verbal expression), and in what modernity calls 'the creation of a new identity'. In *RB*, self-renunciation leads not to martyrdom or self-destruction, but to the creation of a new being. This new monastic identity is not bestowed through a single sacramental stroke; instead, it is gradually gathered through the patient learning of skills inscribed on the body. If ritual rules seem to govern virtually every aspect of life in *RB* (eating, working, walking, sleeping, praying), they are aimed at neither regimentation nor ostentatious display.[46] Rather, the ritual structures provide the social means – the 'institutional resources of organized community life' – that make the 'production of a virtuous self' possible.[47] This virtuous self *is* the new identity disclosed – slowly, perhaps painfully – through the technologies of confession and self-examination, as well as through the myriad rules and rites that accompany work (manual labour), prayer (*opus Dei*) and reading (*lectio divina*).

In sum, 'ritual' in *RB* is a *quality* that characterizes communal behaviour,[48] rather than a separate species or category of human action. It is closer, perhaps, to Herbert Fingarette's description:[49]

> Rite brings out forcefully . . . the inherent and ultimate dignity of human intercourse; it brings out also the moral perfection implicit in dealing with others as beings of equal dignity, as free coparticipants in *li* . . . [T]o act with ceremony [i.e., with *li*] is to be completely open to the other; for ceremony is public, shared, transparent; to act otherwise is to be secret, obscure and devious, or merely tyrannically coercive. It is in this beautiful

---

[45] Asad, 'Toward a Genealogy of the Concept of Ritual', 76.

[46] See Staal, 'The Meaninglessness of Ritual': 'Ritual, then, is primarily activity. It is an activity governed by explicit rules. The important thing is what you do, not what you think, believe or say' (4).

[47] See Talal Asad, 'Notes on Body Pain and Truth in Medieval Christian Ritual', in *Genealogies of Religion*, 83–124.

[48] One might even say that in *RB*, ritual is what renders human behaviour (even if practised individually) communal.

[49] Herbert Fingarette, *Confucius – The Secular as Sacred* (New York: Harper Torchbooks 1972), 16. Fingarette is commenting on the Chinese notion of *li* (usually translated 'holy rite' or 'sacred ceremony'). He argues that ultimately this notion refers not to any 'ritualism' but to the idea that we engage in the art of becoming human by learning the ritual repertoire of the human community, i.e., by dealing with all others as 'beings of equal dignity'.

and dignified, shared and open participation with others who are ultimately like oneself that man realizes himself. This perfect community of men . . . becomes an inextricable part, the chief aspect, of Divine worship.

Instead of being a diversion of attention from the human realm to another transcendent realm, the overtly holy ceremony is to be seen as the central symbol, both expressive of and participating in the holy as a dimension of all truly human existence.[50]

This is also the basic attitude toward ritual in *RB*. Rite is not the formalized presentation of condensed corporate symbols that encode canonical meanings, and guarantee social cohesion. Rather, rite is a technological means of acquiring a new self – one defined by solidarity with all others as 'beings of equal dignity' and by participation in a life that 'in its entirety finally appears as one, vast, spontaneous and holy Rite'.[51]

This is not to say that the Western monastic understanding of ritual lacks roots in the traditions of renunciation and self-surrender (what Foucault called the element of martyrdom). The rituals that *RB* attaches to actions like prayer, work and reading are ascetic ones, and cannot be learned without pain – mental pain, spiritual pain, even bodily pain – not because the body is evil and should be punished; not because Christians should 'suffer like Jesus'; but because the human self is always (if sometimes involuntarily) in bondage to competing feelings, demands and desires. That is why, in the literature of Christian asceticism, physical pain (e.g., the distress of fasting, the weariness of vigils, or the discomfort of denying the body's urge for sex and satisfaction) is viewed as an ordinary, inevitable aspect of the ritualized 'technology of the self'. That is also why this link between ritual and pain is extremely unfashionable today. For many North Americans, pain is pathological. Our analgesic cultures encourage us to greet even the mildest discomfort with horrified denial; with medication or sedation. We feel there is nothing to be learned from pain's presence.

But Christian history reveals a different attitude. The distress and discomfort that inevitably result when one is learning how to inscribe the body with rituals of compassion, hospitality and graciousness (washing the feet of the poor, welcoming the stranger, caring for the sick, lifting the leper, listening to the garrulous) are also *the* way of embodying 'holy rite as a metaphor of human existence'. Perhaps that is why, near the end of Matthew's gospel, these uncomfortable rituals of service and self-surrender are the actions that will form the

---

[50] Ibid., 16–17.
[51] Ibid., 17.

basis for God's judgment. Ritual is not only a way Christians negotiate their access to the Sacred; it is also their way of editing experience, 'rewriting' personal history, and appropriating a new identity.[52] Inescapably, such activity will pose a substantial degree of danger and discomfort. For ultimately, the performance of ritual is the way we discover how and what we *think*. Thus, as Foucault notes, the Christian rituals connected with chastity aim not at inhibition but at openness:

> the opening up of an area . . . which is that of [embodied] thought . . . with its images, memories and perceptions, with movements and impressions transmitted from the body to the mind and the mind to the body. This has nothing to do with a code of permitted or forbidden actions, but is a whole technique for analyzing and diagnosing thought, its origins, its qualities, its dangers, its potential for temptation and all the dark forces that can lurk behind the mask it may assume.[53]

In other words, the goal of all ascetic ritual is purity of heart. The author of *RB* knew that human beings (including monastic recruits) are not just mildly misinformed – they are tragically and radically *self-deceived*. From birth, we humans are addicts, and our deepest addiction is to a mistaken identity, to a false self. We insist on living someone else's life, not our own. In Genesis, the great temptation was not about sex; it was about living someone else's life. 'Eat of this tree', the serpent said, 'and your eyes will be opened! You will be like gods who know good from evil!' The temptation was and 'is to forget that "even in heaven there are ants"',[54] to forget the painful facts of our human vulnerability and failure, of our lies and liabilities. That is why the chapter on humility in *RB* proposes a series of rituals designed to counter our human habit of 'forgetting', of running away, of pretending to be someone else. Forgetting feeds addiction. So *RB* 7.10 warns that we must 'resolutely shun oblivion' if we hope to reach the life with God that creates a new self. To become pure of heart, to discover the terrible truth about oneself, is thus to *remember*, to 'keep the fear of God always before one's eyes, and never

---

[52] Asad explains in one of his essays how the ritual character of medieval chapter sermons (such as those given by Bernard to the monks of Clairvaux) helped new monastic recruits (adults) to 'rewrite' their experience, to reinterpret it in light of a self undergoing the profound change of monastic conversion. See Talal Asad, 'On Discipline and Humility in Medieval Christian Monasticism', in *Genealogies of Religion*, 125–67.

[53] Michel Foucault, 'The Battle for Chastity', in *Politics, Philosophy, Culture: Interviews and Other Writings, 1977–1984*, trans. Alan Sheridan et al., ed. Lawrence D. Kritzman (New York: Routledge 1988), 239.

[54] See Staal, 'The Meaninglessness of Ritual', 2.

to forget it'.[55] It also means what Tertullian called *publicatio sui* – ritually revealing the exact nature of one's life and thoughts to oneself, to God, to another human being.[56]

Thus the goal of the whole battery of ascetic rules and disciplines that comprise *RB*'s 'technology of the self' is to replace rituals of denial with rituals of remembrance. Remembering permits recovery of our real human identity, our original face and form, our true name and nature. Memory gives us our own lives back. Moreover, memory is not merely the mind's habitat; it also belongs to the *body*. *RB* knows that our deepest memories are buried in the skin, borne on the blood and breath, bred in the bone. That is why *RB* 7.9 insists that the 'ladder' of humility (by which we 'return' to paradise) is 'our whole life on earth', built by the *body* as well as the soul.[57]

Thus, as Asad's research suggests, the goal of Western monastic ritual is an *embodied* 'spiritual awakening'. The ritually inscribed body becomes the place where God's presence and power are known. It becomes the place where the cosmos comes to consciousness. As the great Estonian-American architect Louis Kahn wrote: 'All material in nature, the mountains and the streams and the air and we, are made of Light which has been spent, and this crumpled mass called material casts a shadow, and the shadow belongs to Light.'[58] The ritually inscribed body is the place where truth is brought to light and the self's true identity is restored, in a ritual 'process in which [bodily] pain and discomfort [are] inescapable means'.[59]

To summarize, the ritual technology associated with the Western ascetic tradition (of which *RB* is a prime witness) emphasizes these six points:

- *The body's passions play an indispensable role in acquiring virtue*, in 'diagnosing *thought*, its origins, its qualities, its dangers, its power of seduction'.[60] Ritual action gives rise to thought – not the other way around. The body is the essential clue for recovering the self's identity. As *RB*'s Chapter 4 on 'the tools for good works' suggests, one acquires humility not by thinking about it, but by ritually embodied acts (washing another's feet, drying another's tears).

---

[55] *RB* 7.10.
[56] See *RB* 7.44–48.
[57] See *RB* 7.9: 'We may call our body and souls the sides of this ladder, into which our divine vocation has fitted the various steps of humility and discipline as we ascend.'
[58] Quoted in John Lobell, *Between Silence and Light: Spirit in the Architecture of Louis Kahn* (Boulder, CO: Shambhala 1979), 5.
[59] See Asad, 'Notes on Body Pain', 311.
[60] Foucault, *Politics, Philosophy, Culture*, 239.

- *The ritualized body is the privileged place where God's presence and power continue to be visible in human history.* That may well be why Tertullian, an early Christian exponent of asceticism, placed such strong emphasis on the visible, dramatic presentation of oneself as a penitent in *exomologesis.* God's power to forgive and reconcile is revealed in the ritually inscribed body of the penitent.

- *The ritual process is the ritual content.* In the ascetic tradition, ritual is not a 'score' to be performed, but the performance itself. Thus, for example, the ritual technology that teaches the body how to behave humbly is the meaning of humility.[61] As performance, ritual redefines the self by embodying thoughts and emotions never before known, risked or felt. These coincide with (rather than are shaped or evoked by) the ritual performance. This point is paramount. As the British art historian R. G. Collingwood once put it: 'The expression of emotion is not, as it were, a dress made to fit an emotion already existing, but is *an activity without which the experience of that emotion cannot exist. Take away the language, and you take away what is expressed.*'[62] To put the matter another way, a ritual's 'spiritual content' cannot be separated from bodily performance. 'The meanings of conventional [everyday] performances and the feelings and intentions of performers are not sharply separated', writes Asad. 'On the contrary . . . it is precisely their interrelation that is central.'[63]

- *The Rites found in Western ascetic sources like* RB *do not claim to be representative of broad cross-cultural patterns found in virtually all human societies, as an earlier generation of anthropologists claimed to be true of many rituals* (e.g., rites of passage). Rather, they ritualize 'historically specific emotions that are structured internally and related to each other in historically determined ways'.[64]

- *The ritual repertoire represented by the Western ascetic tradition does not belong to the 'rites of passage' category.* For instance, the rites and rules of *RB* do not, in fact, ritualize passages that every (Christian) human

---

[61] Note the ritual provision in *RB*: If one wishes to 'know' the content of humility, one must 'embrace suffering' (*RB* 7.35); one must bow the head and lower the eyes (*RB* 7.63); at times one must lay the body down at the entrance of the oratory, begging forgiveness from all who pass by (cf. *RB* 44.1–31). If one wants to know the content of 'being hospitable', one must wash a guest's hands and feet (*RB* 53.12, 14) and welcome a stranger 'with all the courtesy of love' (*RB* 53.3). If one wants to know the content of 'compassion', one must console the grieving and never lose hope in God's mercy (cf. *RB* 4.19, 74). In *RB*, the 'content' and 'meaning' of virtue emerge not from the grammar of thought or theology, but from the grammar of ritual performance.

[62] Talal Asad, 'On Discipline and Humility in Medieval Christian Monasticism', in *Genealogies of Religion*, 130–31, n. 6; emphasis added.

[63] Ibid., 130.

[64] Ibid., 134.

being experiences (e.g., the transition from puberty to adulthood, or youth to old age, or life to death). Novitiate is not catechumenate; monastic profession is not a 'life-crisis rite' in the way initiation or marriage may be; the election of an abbot or abbess is not ordination. Rites of passage use encoded symbols to produce meanings that will support specific definitions of reality, reinforce social identity and cohesion, and guarantee the 'success' of critical human transitions. But the rituals of asceticism do not try to produce meanings. They are, as Frits Staal suggests, 'primarily activity . . . The important thing is what you do, not what you think, believe or say.'[65] Moreover, life-crisis rites are, by definition, terminal. They have an obvious beginning, middle and end. What the ritual doesn't finish, nature will. By contrast, ascetic rites are open-ended. They lack both the social drama of a life-crisis event (like marriage) and the high symbolic stakes of a sacrament (like initiation or eucharist). Furthermore, life-crisis rites attend to involuntary transitions (like the onset of menstruation or the coming of death), while ascetic rites are chosen and voluntary. The ritual technologies of a monastery are thus voluntary routines whose goal is embodied virtue. These virtues are not values ritually reviewed and renewed, as the classic anthropological consensus might have it, but acts aimed at unselfconscious goodness. They are similar to the deeds praised by the Chinese sage Chuang-Tzu in his chapters on the *Tao Te Ching*:

> [I]n the world of perfect peace, no value [is] placed upon exalting the wise, or putting the capable . . . in positions of power. The ruler [is] like the top of a tree (unconsciously there), and the people live like the deer of the forest. Doing right, they do not know it is called justice. Kind to one another, they do not know it is called humanity. They are upright and do not know it is called faithfulness. They are proper and do not know it is called honesty. They move about and call to one another for help, and do not call it favor. Therefore their actions leave no trace and their deeds leave no record.[66]

• Finally, *the models typically used by anthropologists to interpret ritual negotiations of power* (ritual as catharsis, rhetoric, persuasion or metaphysical theatre) are *not especially helpful for interpreting the kind of power being negotiated in ascetic rituals*. The ritual strategies of *RB* do not claim to represent, symbolically, the ultimate nature of reality or to justify power among a hierarchical elite. Rather, they are

[65] Staal, 'The Meaninglessness of Ritual', 4.
[66] *The Wisdom of Laotse*, trans. Lin Yutang (New York: Modern Library 1948), 57; text slightly altered.

'essential *to* the disciplined development of the self'.[67] In this sense, the gradual formalization of rites in monasteries (especially in the medieval epoch) did *not* signify the increasing domination of inferior subjects by repressive, superior leaders. In fact, as Asad's research shows, it was precisely those persons *excluded* from full participation in monastic rites such as 'lay brothers' and peasants attached to the monastery's lands or businesses who were most likely to suffer repression and exploitation. Even when formalized, ritual was not viewed as an activity inherently symbolic or canonical. In the monasticism envisioned by *RB*,

> The liturgy is not a species of enacted symbolism to be classified separately from activities defined as technical but is a practice among others essential to the acquisition of Christian virtues . . . It presupposes no obscure meanings, but rather the formation of physical and linguistic skills.[68]

Ritual competence is bodily competence, for the body is an ensemble of *'embodied aptitudes, not* . . . a medium of symbolic meanings'.[69]

Ritual, religion and 'critical' anthropology

The innovative studies of scholars like Talal Asad are but one example of the revolution that has been taking place in the fields of social and cultural anthropology over the past quarter-century. This revolution has important repercussions for the way Christian liturgists make use of anthropological data, as I hope to show in this final section.

Of course, anthropology has been changing throughout the twentieth century. The introduction of field method, early in this century, marked a major shift in the way anthropologists go about collecting data.[70] Gone was the anecdotal, 'armchair' approach to the study of other cultures, ancient or modern; in its place came direct inquiry and participant observation. The anthropologist's task was to describe in detail a culture or society, 'to record as accurately as possible the modes of life of other people'.[71] This approach to ethnography – with its emphasis on actual experience and accurate recording – was a welcome improvement, but it also suffered limitations. 'The chief experience of ethnographers was that of "culture shock" ', writes John

---

[67] See Asad, 'On Discipline and Humility in Medieval Christian Monasticism', 134–35.
[68] Asad, 'Toward a Genealogy of the Concept of Ritual', 63, 62.
[69] Ibid., 75.
[70] John Saliba, 'The New Ethnography and the Study of Religion', *Journal for the Scientific Study of Religion* 13 (1974), 145.
[71] Ibid., 146.

Saliba, 'which was obviously not shared by the indigenous people.'[72] Moreover, anthropologists often seemed more eager to discover 'what anthropology is' than, for example, 'what this ritual means to the life of an Eskimo village'. 'In a sense anthropologists were studying only one culture – the culture of anthropology.'[73]

In reaction, therefore, a new ethnography (a 'cognitive anthropology') emerged, one whose aim was not to formulate a grand unified theory of culture (as advanced by the older ethnographers), but to concentrate on competent descriptions of *particular* cultures and their cognitive systems.[74] The ethnographer's task is 'to discover how different peoples organize and use their own cultures' by seeking answers to two basic questions: (1) What phenomena are most important to the people who share a common culture? and (2) How do the people organize these phenomena? This newer approach sought, above all, 'to avoid imposing on an alien culture a preconceived order [and] to elicit that culture's own semantic categories'.[75] In short, the goal was to describe cultures from the inside out rather than from the outside in. Both questions and answers must come from the culture of the people under investigation – and not from some preexisting order (usually Western) imposed by the ethnographer.[76]

While these changes were happening within the field of anthropology itself, new developments in the ethnoscientific study of religion were also underway. First, researchers began to see that Western categories for what constitutes 'religion' or 'religious experience' are not universally applicable, and hence cannot be applied indiscriminately.[77] Secondly, they began to question their use of the familiar, contrasting categories commonly applied to religious phenomena (sacred/profane, natural/supernatural). These, again, may be of some relevance to the study of Western Christian practices, but they are not very useful for understanding the native religious experience of indigenous peoples in Asia or Africa. Thirdly, researchers began to

---

[72] Ibid.

[73] Ibid. The quotation is from Stephen Tyler's edited collection, *Cognitive Anthropology* (New York: Holt, Rinehart and Winston 1969), 203.

[74] Saliba, 'The New Ethnography and the Study of Religion', 146–47.

[75] Ibid., 147.

[76] The 'new ethnography' did not abandon the field method, but it did propose a newer way of getting at the native point of view through 'controlled eliciting'. The ethnographer is thus trained 'to elicit from [native persons in the culture] the relevant questions they ask about themselves and the world around them. . . . [T]he ethnographer must be prepared to listen to his informants and to let them do most of the talking; to allow them to choose, as often as possible, the topics of conversation and to discuss the issues they have in mind' (ibid., 148).

[77] Ibid., 151.

realize that religious experience cannot be fully or accurately described simply on the basis of official texts or surveys. As John Saliba notes,

> The primary lesson of ethnoscience for the study of religion is the emphasis on field work. If religious experience has to be stressed, then one cannot really base one's conclusions on sacred books or statistical surveys ... Up to now fieldwork, as understood by anthropologists, has not as a rule been diligently pursued by those historians of religions whose main area of study is contemporary religious beliefs and rituals.[78]

Recently, moreover, anthropology's landscape has begun to change again – partly as a result of critique from feminist scholars, and partly because of new challenges posed by the anthropology of science, technology and economics.[79] Some would argue that the discipline is suffering an identity crisis from which it may never recover. Others argue that the changes are needed in order to restore balance to a discipline long dominated by patriarchal, Eurocentric and colonialist assumptions. While it is not possible to chronicle all of the changes in anthropology over the past quarter-century, four of the major ones are noted here:

- First, *the 'starting point' for anthropology is changing*. It was noted above that the new ethnography of the 1970s emphasized the importance of eliciting questions and answers from the native peoples under investigation. Today, as David Hess observes,

> The idea of the 'native's point of view' should not be taken too literally or too narrowly. As in the term 'native New Yorker', the natives ...
> are often quite cosmopolitan and well-educated; these 'natives' include artificial intelligence researchers, space scientists, or the inventors of new bio- and reproductive technologies ... The term 'natives', then, is a less formal way of referring to the Other, the members of a society or social group who have a culture or perspective different from one's own, even if the Other is merely a different segment of one's own society (because anthropologists are studying with greater frequency groups within their home societies). Furthermore, it may be better to speak now of the starting point of the anthropologist's task as interpreting the natives' *points* of view.[80]

Anthropology today 'retains a thoroughgoing scepticism of most universalistic statements about human beings and their social world'.[81] But this does not mean that the modern ethnographer

---

[78] Ibid., 154.
[79] See David J. Hess, 'The New Ethnography and the Anthropology of Science and Technology', *Knowledge and Society* 9 (1992), 1–26.
[80] Ibid., 2–3.
[81] Ibid., 3.

is paralyzed by what conservative critics derisively describe as 'political correctness'. Ethnography continues to practise participant observation. This does not suggest merely 'watching people's behaviour'; rather, it means 'talking to and interacting with people, and ultimately attempting to understand their symbolic worlds and social action'.[82]

• Second, *anthropologists are finding it increasingly necessary to critique the assumptions and conventions of their craft.* This necessity has led Clifford Geertz to complain that exaggerated scrupulosity may soon render the anthropologist aphasiac. He speaks of a 'pervasive nervousness' that hovers about his field today:

> What is at hand is a pervasive nervousness about the whole business of claiming to explain enigmatical others on the grounds that you have gone about with them in their native habitat or combed the writings of those who have. This nervousness brings on, in turn, various responses, variously excited: deconstructive attacks on canonical works, and on the very idea of canonicity as such; *Ideologiekritik* unmaskings of anthropological writings as the continuation of imperialism by other means; clarion calls to reflexivity, dialogue, heteroglossia, linguistic play, rhetorical self-consciousness, performative translation, verbatim recording, and first-person narrative as forms of cure . . .

> Both the world that anthropologists . . . study, which once was called primitive, tribal, traditional, or folk and now is called emergent, modernizing, peripheral, or submerged, and the one that they . . . study it from, academia, have vastly changed . . . The end of colonialism altered radically the nature of the social relationship between those who ask and look and those who are asked and looked at. The decline of faith in brute fact, set procedures, and unsituated knowledge in the human sciences . . . altered no less radically the askers' and lookers' conception of what it was they were trying to do.[83]

Because his field keeps changing, Geertz wonders whether the very 'right to write' ethnography is not now at risk.[84] In less combative moments, however, he admits (as many of his colleagues surely would) that ethnographic texts are '*made*, and made to *persuade*'.[85] In other words, one must recognize that in anthropology there is (and has ever been) as much art as science. Anthropology is a work of the *imagination*, 'like quantum mechanics or the Italian opera'.[86] To say this is not to deny that ethnography deals also with

---

[82] Ibid., 4.
[83] Clifford Geertz, *Works and Lives: The Anthropologist as Author* (Stanford, CA: Stanford University Press 1988), 130–32.
[84] Ibid., 133.
[85] Ibid., 138; emphasis added.
[86] Ibid., 140.

the actual, the factual, with what Geertz calls 'vitality phrased'.[87] The art of persuasion should not, therefore, be dismissed as mere drama or deception:

> This capacity to persuade readers . . . that what they are reading is an authentic account by someone personally acquainted with how life proceeds in some place, at some time, among some group, is the basis upon which anything else ethnography seeks to do – analyze, explain, amuse, disconcert, celebrate, edify, excuse, astonish, subvert – finally rests. The textual connection of the Being Here and Being There sides of anthropology, the imaginative reconstruction of a common ground between the Written At and the Written About . . . is the *fons et origo* of whatever power anthropology has to convince anyone of anything.[88]

In other words, the call to critique assumptions should not be construed as a call to abandon the anthropologist's art. What is needed is greater honesty about what anthropology is (craft, persuasion, rhetoric, art, science) and how it is practised and written. Unquestionably, imperialist and colonialist assumptions *have* sometimes compromised the integrity and results of field work. Nor can anyone doubt that 'dispassionate science' is sometimes only political ideology. In an effort to be more self-critical about their work, modern anthropologists have proposed new methods and metaphors. With Claude Lévi-Strauss, for instance, 'the metaphors of society shifted from biological ones, the analysis of society in terms of the functional integration of organs/institutions, to musical and informational ones: the analysis of society as the decoding of ciphers'.[89] With Clifford Geertz, a different metaphor appears: the ethnographer is 'a *reader*' who examines native rituals as 'cultural *texts*' that can be read through a variety of lenses: 'political, economic, psychological, status/local, and aesthetic'.[90] The point is that, while no science is utterly free of assumptions, honesty about their nature and presence is a first step toward overcoming the limits they impose.

- Third, *anthropology today seeks what some call a 'dialogical' or 'polyphonic' ethnography*. This means, to some degree, 'surrendering authorship of the ethnography to one's informants or . . . surrendering large spaces of the ethnographic text to direct . . . transcriptions of the informants' voices'.[91] There is, of course, a

---

[87] Ibid., 143.
[88] Ibid., 143–44.
[89] Hess, 'The New Ethnography', 7.
[90] Ibid., 7–8. As Hess notes, some critics have accused Geertz of simply 'reinscribing in the ethnographic text the colonial relationship between anthropologist and informant', 8.
[91] Ibid., 9.

potentially serious shortcoming in such efforts to respect native informants. Informants bring assumptions and prejudices of their own to descriptions of their culture and social world. They may be as blind as the alien anthropologist to 'oppressive systems of imperialism, race, class, and gender'.[92] As feminist scholars note, culture is never neutral; it 'is composed of seriously contested codes of meaning . . . language and politics are inseparable, constructing the "other" entails relations of domination'.[93]

- Finally, *there is widespread recognition among anthropologists that their art must be both reflexive and critical – though not everyone agrees how this should be accomplished.* Many insist that 'because values and politics will be inscribed in texts', anthropologists should 'self-consciously decide what their politics are and contribute to the critique of knowledge-power-technology systems that are bound up with (and legitimate) structures of oppression'.[94] Virtually everyone agrees that anthropology needs to provide room for *second voices* or *other* voices that might never get heard. This will necessitate a regular review – a 'political and theoretical critique' – of every anthropologist's 'discipline and discourse'.[95]

These changes in the way anthropologists understand and practise their craft also have a bearing on their views of religion and ritual. Until recently the majority of anthropologists tended to place religion generally – and ritual specifically – in the category of symbolic or expressive action (as opposed to natural/biological or technical actions).[96] As Talal Asad comments,

> Studies of the social functions of religion tend to be either reductionist ways of arriving at its meanings, or (more usefully) ways of describing social consequences which, although brought about by religious institutions, may also be secured by 'secular' ones. Religion itself is rarely approached in terms of 'technical action' – that is to say, the disciplining of the body, of speech, which is used to produce religion in its variety.[97]

To put it another way, religious reality (including ritual) must be allowed to be itself, and not simply a system of symbols that points to something else. Moreover, one cannot assume that the meaning

---

[92] Ibid., 10.
[93] Ibid., 10–11.
[94] Ibid., 11.
[95] Ibid., 18.
[96] Talal Asad, 'Anthropological Conceptions of Religion: Reflections on Geertz', in *Genealogies of Religion*, 251.
[97] Ibid.

of religion (and hence, of ritual) is absolutely univocal, and thus constant from one historical epoch to another. Religion, argues Asad, is usually linked to *power*, not merely power in the political sense, but 'in the sense in which power constructs religious ideology, establishes the preconditions for distinctive kinds of religious personality, authorizes specifiable religious practices and utterances, produces religiously defined knowledge'.[98] But over the course of history, such power is deployed and distributed differently, to achieve quite different goals and purposes.[99]

This is the case even if discussion is confined to a single religious tradition, e.g., Christianity. It is widely assumed that, for Christians, ritual provides a symbolic means of negotiating power (just as it does in other social groups). Obviously, this does not mean that ritual is mere artifice designed 'to disguise the crude instruments of power' or coercion.[100] The power linked to ritual cannot simply be defined, then, as political manipulation or as the violent oppression of the weak by the powerful. Indeed, there are two distinct sets of questions that need to be raised about the relation between ritual and power: (1) What *kind* of power does ritual create, possess, or transmit? and (2) How does religious power, ritually expressed, create religious *truth*?

The first of these questions has been cogently formulated by Catherine Bell. 'If ritual is not merely a *mask* for power,' she asks, then '[H]ow does ritual do what we keep saying it does: How does it actually inculcate cultural or political values, converting beliefs about another world into facts about this one and vice versa, and "inventing" traditions even as it purports to be transmitting them?'[101] Traditionally – as is evident from the 'classic consensus' arrived at by Christian liturgists using anthropological categories – ritual is seen as an *instrumental* agent, as a way to impose social control by celebrating canons of correct belief and behaviour (*lex orandi, lex credendi*) and by transmitting tradition (meanings and values). But today, many anthropologists will argue that ritual is neither an instrument of power 'nor does it refer, express, or symbolize anything outside itself'.[102] Political rituals, for instance, 'do not *refer* to politics . . . they *are* politics. Ritual is the thing itself. It *is* power; it acts and it actuates.'[103] In a word, ritual is not a 'referential instrument', not a 'functional

---

[98] Ibid., 237.
[99] Ibid., 238.
[100] Bell, *Ritual Theory, Ritual Practice*, 194.
[101] Ibid.
[102] Ibid., 195.
[103] Ibid. Bell is alluding, here, to the position developed by Clifford Geertz in his *Negara: The Theatre State in Nineteenth Century Bali* (Princeton, NJ: Princeton University Press 1980).

mechanism or expressive medium in the service of social solidarity and control'.[104] Rather, ritualization is 'a strategic mode of practice' that 'produces nuanced relationships of power, relationships characterized by acceptance and resistance, negotiated appropriation, and redemptive reinterpretation of the hegemonic order'.[105]

But if ritual power is not instrumental or political or coercive or authoritative, *what is it?* Bell suggests that we try to answer this question by returning to the work of Michel Foucault. 'For Foucault,' she notes, 'power is contingent, local, imprecise, relational, and organizational'.[106] In other words, Foucault broke with the long-standing Western tradition that sees power as substantive, centralized, sovereign or hypostasized (e.g., in the person of a monarch). Instead, power is distributed all over the social body; it is 'a matter of techniques and discursive practices that comprise the micropolitics of everyday life'.[107] *Power is thus the way ordinary people define and negotiate the reality of their daily lives* – whether they're haggling over the price of a croissant at the corner bakery or staking a claim on a parking space in front of the apartment building. Power is, therefore, deeply embedded in the network of ordinary social relations. It is not something external to those relations, but rather, arises from within the local, 'petty calculations of daily life'.[108] Power of this sort always includes the potential for conflict, resistance, confrontation, struggle. It's the kind of power found, for instance, in the rituals of an Italian–American family around the kitchen table in the film *Moonstruck*. Rituals are *practices*: actions that act upon others.

Ritual is thus an imprecise way to organize the world of 'local reality' by the seat of the pants, and so to construct '*particular* relationships of power effective in *particular* social situations'.[109] This way of acting is closely linked to Foucault's notion of the body as a 'political field' (a point noted in the previous section of this chapter). 'Power relations', he writes, 'have an immediate hold on [the body]; they invest it, mark it, train it, torture it, force it to carry out tasks, to perform ceremonies, to emit signs.'[110] Or, as Bell comments, 'The body is the most basic and fundamental level of power relations, the "microphysics" of the micropolitics of power. Ritualization, Foucault

---

[104] Bell, *Ritual Theory, Ritual Practice*, 197.
[105] Ibid., 196.
[106] Ibid., 199.
[107] Ibid.
[108] Ibid., 200.
[109] Ibid., 202.
[110] See Michel Foucault, *Discipline and Punish: The Birth of the Prison*, trans. Alan Sheridan (New York: Vintage Books 1979), 25.

seems to imply, is a central way that power operates; it constitutes a political technology of the body.'[111] Thus,

> It is in ritual – as practices that act upon the actions of others, as the mute interplay of complex strategies within a field structured by engagements of power, as the arena for prescribed sequences of repetitive movements of the body that simultaneously constitute the body, the person, and the macro- and micronetworks of power – that we can see a fundamental strategy of power. In ritualization, power is not external to its workings; it exists only insofar as it is constituted with and through the lived body, which is both the body of society and the social body. Ritualization is a strategic play of power, of domination and resistance, within the arena of the social body.[112]

The power of ritual is thus far more local, strategic, messy, imprecise, ordinary, flexible, ambiguous, and indeterminate than the high church liturgist might wish us to believe.

But if this is the case, how does religious power, ritually expressed, create religious truth (the second of the two questions posed above)? Can ritual make any claims to truth? The question cannot be answered (or dismissed) simply by arguing that the effectiveness of rites are independent of those who use them, or that truth always transcends (flawed) performance. After all, as Asad points out, 'a deeply committed Christian surely cannot be unconcerned at the existence of "truthful" religious symbols that appear to be largely powerless [or irrelevant] in modern society'.[113] One cannot respond adequately to this situation by appealing to a theological defence of ritual effectiveness (to the rite's 'objective efficacy', apart from a minister's worthiness or a participant's intentions). Ritual (as I argued above) is practice – and the discourse of practice (the discourse that *is* practice) is not the same as discourse *about* practice (theology).[114]

Moreover, Christian history shows that the discourse which serves as an authorizing 'model' for truth has varied enormously:

> [T]he ways in which authorizing discourses, based on a cosmology, systematically redefined religious spaces, have been of profound importance in the history of Western society. In the Middle Ages such discourses ranged over an enormous space, defining and creating religion: rejecting 'pagan' practices or accepting them; authenticating particular miracles and relics . . . ; authorizing shrines; compiling saints' lives, both as a model of and as model for the Truth; requiring the regular telling of sinful thoughts,

---

[111] Bell, *Ritual Theory, Ritual Practice*, 202.
[112] Ibid., 204.
[113] Asad, 'Anthropological Conceptions of Religion: Reflections on Geertz', in *Genealogies of Religion*, 242.
[114] On this point, see ibid., 243.

words, and deeds to a priestly confessor, and giving absolution to a penitent, regularizing popular social movements into Rule-following Orders (for example, the Franciscans), or denouncing them for heresy . . . The medieval Church did not attempt to establish absolute uniformity of practice; on the contrary, its authoritative discourse was always concerned to specify differences, gradations, exceptions.[115]

Truth, in other words, was not authorized or guaranteed by a rigid uniformity of ritual practice. Rather, *truth emerged from a locally bro-kered ensemble of diverse practices, diverse discourses* – some of them overtly 'pagan' (and thinly Christianized), some of them sacramental, some of them devotional, some of them juridical, some of them penal. All these competing discourses collectively constituted the religion and the ritual of the Middle Ages.

It cannot be argued on historical grounds, therefore, that the Christian churches have deployed rituals primarily as responses to our deeply human 'dread of disorder'.[116] Ritual is not an antidote to chaos – indeed, it often contributes to it. As medieval Christian history shows, local ritual variations were common and widespread; they were the norm, not the exception – and these variations pro-duced a rich 'polyphonic ritualism' rather than liturgical monody. It never seemed to occur to anyone in that period that ritual's claims to truth required absolute uniformity. Moreover, the authoritative imposition of a single rite upon all of Western Christendom was quite unthinkable prior to the invention of movable type.

Medieval Christianity understood instinctively that rituals do not contain meaning and truth in quite the same way that a vase con-tains water or a book contains 'content'. That is why the 'stimulus–response model of how ritual works will not do'.[117] Religious ritual is indeed, as Geertz suggests, a type of cultural performance, but it is one where claims to truth and meaning are *literally* played out in *practice*:

> [I]f we are to understand how this happens, we must examine not only the ritual itself, but the entire range of available disciplinary activities, of institutional forms of knowledge and practice, within which selves are formed, and the possibilities of 'attaining to faith' are marked out. In other words, for the anthropologist to explain 'faith' must be primarily a matter of describing a dependence on authoritative practices and discourses, and not of intuiting a mental state laying beyond them said to be caused by ritual.[118]

---

[115] Ibid., 244.
[116] See ibid., 246.
[117] Ibid., 249.
[118] Ibid.

Ritual *does* embody religious dispositions, faith and truth – but it does so in a manner that is far more homely, local and imprecise than some anthropologists (and some liturgists) might assume. Religious ritual is a kind of *bricolage*, an act cobbled together from whatever is immediately at hand and available for use. It is not some heroic, Kierkegaardian leap of faith that beckons participants into a 'framework of meaning which religious conceptions define, and the ritual ended, return[s] again to the common-sense world'.[119] The stuff of ritual *is* the stuff of the common-sense world. On this point, the Christian liturgy has stubbornly insisted for almost two millennia. It is the stuff of spittle, salt, water, oil, bread, wine, light, fragrance, touch, taste, smell.

Ritual is not a source of truth independent of all the other practices, disciplines, dispositions, technologies and embodied inscriptions that, together, produce knowledge, faith, and social life (in both religion and the common-sense world). The ritual symbols of Christian liturgy inhabit precisely this common-sense world. Access to their truth does not require a leap into some other world. If it did, the result would be not Christianity, but *gnosticism* – the idea that Truth can be known and measured only by privileged observers whose powers derive from another (alien and superior) culture, another world.

In short, religion and ritual are precisely *products* of human culture. (Note that I did not say they can be 'reduced' to human culture.) It is because of that, ritual can make claims to truth. Thus, instead of approaching religion 'with questions about the social meaning of doctrines and practices, or . . . about the psychological effects of symbols and rituals', we need to study 'the historical conditions (movements, classes, institutions, ideologies) necessary for the existence of particular religious practices and discourses'.[120] In other words, as Michel Foucault and Catherine Bell might ask, 'How does *power* create religion? How does it create ritual?' These questions can be answered only through a careful study of the social disciplines and forces 'which come together at particular historical moments, to make particular religious discourses, practices and spaces possible'. In other words, we must examine how each historical culture and society produces knowledge, including the knowledge and truth embodied in religion and ritual. In short, Christian liturgists and professional anthropologists must continue their dialogue.

---

[119] Clifford Geertz, *The Interpretation of Cultures* (New York: Basic Books 1973), 122. The result of this ritual leap, Geertz goes on to suggest, is that 'a man is . . . changed. And as he is changed, so also is the common-sense world, for it is now seen as but the partial form of a wider reality which corrects and completes it.'

[120] Asad, 'Anthropological Conceptions of Religion: Reflections on Geertz', 252.

For the fact is that in every human life and in every age religion (like ritual) is woven together from an exuberant variety of sources, some official and authorized, some not. This entire ensemble, this riotously imperfect babble is what constitutes the several discourses of religious and ritual truth in any historical period. Medieval believers understood this, as do many modern ones. In his lovely essay 'Sweet Chariot', Mark Doty explains how he grew up in 'two religions'.[121] The first and most enduring of these, a religion of images, he learned from his fundamentalist Christian grandmother:

> She would set me up on her lap and, rocking all the while, read Bible verses to me. I'm not sure if I remember especially her readings from Revelations, but it simply feels to me now, whenever I hear someone mention a phrase like 'last days' or 'apocalypse', that the scent of her – lavender and peppermint and clean old dresses – and the textures of her clothes and the Bible's leatherette cover and onionskin pages are forever commingled with those words; some essence of her imbues them. It was she who presented me with my first religion . . . the religion of images, and they were given to me in Bible verses and in the songs we'd sing on the porch swing, summer nights: the sweet chariot coming to carry us home, the moon turning to blood, the angels sounding the trumpet so that all the dead would clap hands and arise.[122]

This 'ritual of the rocking chair' is a perfect example of how religion creates power and power creates religion. It happens summer evenings, on the front porch, in a beloved grandmother's lap, as much as it does during the solemn grandeur of a papal liturgy. For religion and ritual are always – and inevitably – polyphonic, as are societies, cultures and the human beings who create them.

---

[121] Mark Doty, 'Sweet Chariot', in Brian Bouldrey, ed., *Wrestling with the Angel* (New York: Riverhead Books 1995), 1–10.
[122] Ibid., 2.

7

Ronald L. Grimes

Introduction

[R]itual studies or ritology, is a new field, not because doing ritual or thinking about it is new, but because the effort to consolidate methods from the humanities and social sciences for the study of ritual in a context that is free to be cross-cultural and comparative is new . . . The time for beginning ritual studies is ripe. (Grimes, *Beginnings in Ritual Studies*, xxv)

Founding editor of the *Journal of Ritual Studies*, Ronald Grimes has been a major force in bringing the area of ritual studies to a certain prominence. In the first extract from his writings, Chapter 3, 'Modes of Ritual Sensibility', of his book, *Beginnings in Ritual Studies* (Lanham, MD: University Press of America 1982), Grimes orientates students of ritual studies to basic assumptions and methods. First, in mapping the field of ritual, Grimes sets out categories of investigation which can lead to a full 'evocative description' by a participant observer. Second, rather than provide a taxonomy of rituals, he distinguishes between six modes of ritual sensibility, that is, 'embodied attitudes' which arise in the unfolding of a ritual event. In *Beginnings in Ritual Studies*, Grimes does not intend to provide a systematic theory of ritual, but rather to make forays into the field offering viewpoints for further consideration.

In celebration I do not care to protest that symbols are merely penultimate. I am little interested in distinguishing what is merely fictional, playful, dramatic, and imaginative, on the one hand, from what is metaphysical, real, and eternal, on the other. In festivity I know there is no difference in value (though there may be in form) between what is utterly serious and what is playful. (Grimes, *Beginnings in Ritual Studies*, revised edn [Columbia, SC: University of South Carolina Press 1995], 55)

In our second extract, originally a paper delivered at the Notre Dame Center for Pastoral Liturgy's symposium entitled 'Reclaiming our Rites', held at the University of Notre Dame, Indiana in 1992 and published in *Studia Liturgica* 23 (1993), 51–69, Ronald Grimes explores the notion of 'ritual authority' by contrasting two different 'postures' or attitudes toward what constitutes ritual authority and what ritual itself authorizes. While the article exhibits a playful style, the issues considered are anything but what one would usually consider playful.

Ritual authority can be considered as that which is endorsed, traditional, performed according to rules, functions according to social context or is morally just. The author considers rites which are endorsed, traditional and rule-performed, but then raises important questions concerning rituals which do not fit those exact criteria, yet can be functional and moral. Grimes then avers that ritual ought to have authority only insofar as it is grounded in, forged by, and answerable to its infrastructures, which are bodily, cultural, ecological, and spiritual. While this article gives no definitive answers to the issue of ritual authority, it raises serious questions that need to be given equally serious attention by those involved in matters liturgical.

Ronald L. Grimes is Professor of Religion and Culture at Wilfred Laurier University in Waterloo, Canada.

For further reading

William D. Dinges, 'Ritual Conflict as Social Conflict: Liturgical Reform in the Roman Catholic Church', *Sociological Analysis* 48 (Summer 1987), 138–57.

Ronald L. Grimes, 'Emerging Ritual', *Proceedings of the North American Academy of Liturgy* (1990), 15–31.

Evan Imber-Black and Janine Roberts, *Rituals for our Times: Celebrating, Healing and Changing our Lives and Relationships* (New York: HarperCollins Publishers 1992), esp. Chapters 1 and 2.

Margaret Mary Kelleher, 'Hermeneutics in the Study of Liturgical Performance', *Worship* 67 (1993), 292–318.

Jeffrey VanderWilt, 'Rites of Passage: Ludic Recombination and the Formation of Ecclesial Being', *Worship* 66 (1992), 398–416.

★★★

Modes of ritual sensibility

Ritual studies is differentiated from liturgics insofar as it conceives liturgy, or sacred ritual, as one among several kinds of ritual. If 'ritual' is used as a synonym for 'religious rite', or 'vain repetition' (cf. Mitchell, 1977: ix–xii), we are unlikely to attend to the ritual dimensions of ordinary life. If 'liturgy' is used as a synonym for 'Christian rite', or even more narrowly, 'Christian Eucharist', we probably will look down on the word 'ritual', regarding it as a pejorative term for other people's practices in the same way popular usage treats 'magic' and 'myth'.

I suggest that ritual pervades more of our life than just an isolated realm designated 'religious'. It suffuses our biogenetic, psychosocial, political, economic, and artistic lives as well. I also suggest that liturgy is not just Christian, but characterizes other traditions as well. There is pressing need in ritual studies for a set of distinctions among types of ritual sensibility. The usual distinctions, sacred/profane or rites of passage/seasonal rites, are insufficient. As a beginning, I propose to distinguish six modes of ritual sensibility: ritualization, decorum, ceremony, liturgy, magic, and celebration. I regard these, not so much as types of ritual, as sensibilities, or embodied attitudes, that may arise in the course of a ritual. If one of them dominates, then, of course, I would speak of a 'ritual of decorum', for example.

Ritualization   *embodied actions, enculturated, not utilitarian*

Often we begin to speak of ritual in far too lofty a way by referring to ultimacy, sacredness, awe, sacrifice, or eternality, or in too specific and normative a way by confessing our faith regarding specific personages or religious traditions. As a result, we sometimes unwittingly disincarnate ourselves from our own bodies, our own present, and our own ordinariness. This beginning leads to pretentious ritual studies and gnostic liturgies.

Ritual begins with ritualization. 'Ritualization' is the term used by ethologists (e.g., Huxley, 1966) to designate the stylized, repeated gesturing and posturing of animals. Ritualization is most obvious in the mating and aggressive behaviour of many species, and typically, it consists of a sequence of actions having no obvious adaptive or pragmatic functions such as getting food or fleeing an attacker.

An example of ritualization is the so-called 'inciting ceremony' of ducks. When the common European shellduck threatens, she extends and lowers her neck and then runs straight toward her enemy. Then she returns to her mate with head raised. If she stops in front of her mate and threatens the enemy again, she cranes her neck over her back. Her behaviour is appropriate to the physiology of the duck and to the pragmatics of the situation.

On the other hand, if we watch a mallard duck threaten, something else happens. The mallard always incites with her head craned over her shoulder; the more excited she gets, the sharper the angle of her neck and body. Her movement becomes stylized and ritually fixed. As Konrad Lorenz notes, she seems to be saying gesturally, 'I want to threaten that odious, strange drake but my head is being pulled in another direction' (Lorenz, 1966:50). Her gesture is analogous to symbolic ones that arise in the history of every religion. When meaning, communication, or performance become more important than function and pragmatic end, ritualization has begun to occur.

I see no reason why we should not view ourselves as ritualizing animals. The time is past when, with romantic existentialists and anti-Darwinians, we need to insist that humans are utterly different from 'lower' nature, from animals. We are somewhat different, not wholly different, and if we forget our kinship with beasts and plants, we are likely to become in a perverse way what we deny. We are animals – sometimes rational ones, sometimes divine ones, sometimes social ones – but still animals. And our most sacred rituals still concern our 'animal' functions – eating, drinking, moving about, reproducing, dying, mating, fighting.

The grounds of ritualization as a human necessity are ecological, biogenetic, and psychosomatic. We cannot escape ritualization without escaping our own bodies and psyches, the rhythms and structures of which arise on their own. They flow with or without our conscious assent; they are uttered – exclamations of nature and our bodies. Among the modes of ritual action, ritualization leaves us the least choice. Whether we are involved in ritualization is not ours to decide. We can only choose whether to be attentive or repressive in the face of actions that compel us.

Anthropologists sometimes speak of us as 'programmed' or 'enculturated'. Our heads are filled with 'mazeways' and our bodies with 'bio-rhythms', of which we are only diffusely aware. Psychologists refer to our 'repetition-compulsions' and 'obsessive neuroses'. These terms are ways of calling attention to what is given, preconscious, or determined about the patternings so characteristic of us animals.

Not every pattern constitutes ritualization, but every instance of ritualization presupposes a process, a dancelike quality (see Capra, 1975), of interaction between the ecosystem and persons. The rituals which embody ritualization processes most fully are seasonal, agricultural, fertility, divinatory, funerary, and healing ones, because they make explicit the interdependence of people with their physical environments and bodies. Therefore, ritual studies must pay attention to the systemic connections between unintentional symptoms and mannerisms, since they are latent ritual gestures.

Because of its ecological and psychosomatic roots, ritual has survival implications (see Rappaport, 1971). Ritualization can contain both survival values and disease liabilities; so it is not mere decoration because of its dependence on exteriority and physicality. Ritual can become decadent, in which case it becomes an actional illness, a dis-ease of body and environment.

Ritualization is presupposed in all the other ritual modes: decorum, ceremony, liturgy, magic, and celebration. Yet a process can be presupposed as much by being denied as by being affirmed. Ritualization has been rejected or repressed by some practitioners of Western, so-called 'historical' religions; ritualization is treated as belonging to 'nature', fertility, or pagan religion. But even the most spiritualized monistic and dualistic religions depend on physical and biological *all religions have ritual*

processes in their meditative rituals, even if to deny, chastise, or mutilate the body. And even the most thoroughly historical religions embed their re-presentings and rememberings in repeated liturgical seasons and rhythmic incantations. Moreover, even ritual-denying Protestant groups depend heavily on psychosomatically informed processes like 'being moved', 'feeling the spirit', or 'having a full heart'. As far as I can see, there is no escaping ritualization – the stylized cultivation or suppression of biogenetic and psychosomatic rhythms and repetitions. The history of the renewal of ritual action is the story of the eternal return to what are commonly called 'nature' and 'the body'.

Ritualization is not just a symbolic way of pursuing survival, but is a quest for a specific style of being in our bodies and world (see Booth, 1979). Ritualization is how we stylize our genetic heritage. We have no choice: anatomy is destiny, though what we do with a given anatomy – say, reduce it to gender – is modifiable.

Coming together and pushing apart – intimacy and aggression, symbiosis and isolation – are the most basic rhythms of which ritualization is constructed; hence, they are quite susceptible to habituation (see Kane, 1978). No ritual should fail to deal with the systole and diastole of human action. Habituation is the bane of ritualization. It is imposed in the form of ought-filled, unmindful heteronomy, and then the secret of this imposition is glossed over. So authentic (eco-logical, holistic) ritualization should not be dismissed by our linking it to habituated personalities who impose actions on themselves.

Ritualization includes the patterned and the random (the repeated and the idiosyncratic, the routine and the non-pragmatic, the habitual and useless) elements of action and interaction. Of course, a single action may have both characteristics, for example, cigarette smoking can be at once useless and habitual, but also communicative.

On closer consideration we often find that useless or random activities are not so meaningless as one might initially think. A duck's inciting gesture, which is useless as a means of attack, may in some species communicate an invitation to pair. The gesture is combatively dysfunctional – it is an 'actional remnant' – but still functions as a communication of intention, even though its meaning is indirect and symbolic. Likewise, a smoked pipe is relatively useless for me, but among Sioux it symbolizes the totality of the cosmos, which is brought to witness and ratify the sacred, peaceful intention of the acts which follow the smoking. Noting this, I reconsider my pipe smoking and find that I usually do it when I am drifty and relaxed or else anxiety-ridden. The action encodes at least two different messages.

135

Ritualization among animals sometimes takes the form of scuffling and mock fighting. Even though the combat is theatrical, and therefore in a special frame, it helps socialize the animal, perhaps even prepare it for self-defence by keeping it from confusing genuine aggression with mere testing and display. So a useless element of our behaviour often has unconscious, hidden, or slow-to-surface meanings visible only to the intuitive or trained eye.

Repetitious actions bother us almost as much as useless ones. The latter offend our pragmatic sensibilities, the former, our craving for excitement and things different. We know that repetition is inevitable, but we create diversions so we do not have to be directly aware of the fact of repetition. We turn on the radio to distract ourselves from washing dishes. We learn a good habit so well that we can afford to forget it. 'It' will do itself without my having to waste time thinking about, or deciding upon, it. Practically considered, habits free us to pursue other, more exciting or important things such as holidays, recreation, leisure, religion – that is, 'useless' or ultimate things. So we see that the repeated and the useless exist in symbiotic relation to one another.

The roots of ritual are inescapably biological and natural. Since religious ritual is a rhythmic response to the patternings and events which precede and define us, we only understand the fruits of ritual by considering the change of seasons, the fluctuations of mood, the periodicity of history, and the flowing curvature of rivers and trees. Ritualization is rooted in the rhythms which we are – the combined repetitiousness, indirection, and playfulness characteristic of us as biological animals.

Decorum

A second mode of ritual is decorum, which springs from our civic and social life, just as ritualization springs from our organic and biological nature. Ritualization is the issue of 'genetic culture'; so it has an instinctual, inescapable quality about it. Decorum, on the other hand, occurs at the moment a society or group, reflecting on the ritualizations it cannot help, decides to use gestures and postures for the purpose of regulating face-to-face interaction. When our patterning, indirection, and repetition become part of a system of expectations to which we are supposed to conform, we have passed from ritualization to decorum. The rules of etiquette are only the tip of a social iceberg laden with implicit rules for regularizing everyday behaviour. Erving Goffman (1959; 1967), who has written many provocative works on this subject, calls this 'interaction ritual'. Such ritual is almost invisible to its practitioners until it ceases, or they find themselves in a foreign culture (see Hall, 1976).

We social animals say 'Good morning' when it is not, 'Come again' when we mean only 'Goodbye'. We brush our teeth twice a day, get off at five every afternoon, and, without thinking, kiss our children at every departure and arrival (see La Fontaine, 1972:1–71). Our speech is full of stock phrases, and our gestures repeat themselves endlessly without significant variation. With little conscious intention, we sit and dress in such a manner as to display our national origin, economic status, psychological state, and occupation.

By virtue of my co-operation and shared patterns, I am considered a reliable employee, a trustworthy friend, a consistent thinker, and a psychologically healthy human being. Without decorum I fail to communicate with my fellows and traumatize my children with my inconstancy.

What is distinctive about ritual decorum is its courteous formalization and stylization. No longer elicited primarily by natural rhythms of the biological, genetic, and seasonal kind, decorous action marks the rhythm of social occasions. 'Occasions' are moments in social interaction, which, because they are moments of crossing a social boundary, demand a ritual bridge. Occasions such as greeting, leave-taking, and socializing are marked, facilitated, and complicated by the use of formulaic language and stereotypical gestures. 'Good morning' and 'How are you?' along with handshaking, kissing, and making eye contact are formalities about which we often complain, but which we continue to practise because they are expected of us.

Some decorous gestures, for example, leg-crossing for women, are grafted upon biological factors such as sexuality or age; no absolute distinction between ritualization and decorum is possible. Whether the stereotypical male swagger is rooted in biology or sociology is hard to determine except in a cross-cultural perspective.

Decorum is conventionalized behaviour. Convention is a mutual, socially reinforced agreement about the form, though not necessarily the meaning, of an action. We shake hands or kiss after a quarrel. We have formalized our conclusion of the matter. Yet the convention may serve as much to mask residual ill feeling as to declare our intention to let go of it.

The social conservatism implicit in many rituals derives from the decorous layer of symbolic interaction. Even though decorum, like its etymological cousin, 'decoration', is inessential, because it is a feature added on to the biological substratum of action, it is usually taken to be symbolic of my social identity. One who violates the decorum of an occasion, say, by wearing a sweatsuit instead of a robe when saying Mass, will be heard by a congregation as saying ritually that he or she does not participate in the solemnity of the occasion.

Decorum ordinarily carries a lightweight cultural 'ought' with it. One 'ought to behave', that is, act decorously, and the sanctions for breaking rules of decorum are usually light. The result of a violation is that I am ignored, snubbed, gossiped about, or frowned at. I am not imprisoned or excommunicated, nor do I so quickly get ill, as is the case when I ignore biological rhythms. Decorum is enforced socially, not religiously, legally, or psychobiologically. The voice of decorum is not assertive but interrogative. Its actions have the quality of 'How are you?'

Decorum is rhythmic and responsive, as is ritualization. Walking decorously down a crowded street requires many stylizations of which we are only half aware, such as stepping to the right, not following too closely, averting one's gaze, not touching from behind, and so on. Pedestrian traffic is as predictable as rigorously choreographed dance or heavily rubricated liturgy. Yet we are seldom instructed on how to walk down a sidewalk.

Decorum is a way of displaying our roles, statuses, and interpersonal intentions. It is also a way of affirming sociability itself. Although I may be able, on a given occasion, to ignore or violate some aspect of decorum without heavy censure, repeated or full violation may have psychosomatic or legal implications. I may, for example, become legally stigmatized as 'insane' if I never change my sweatsuit, wearing it not only to Mass, but to bed, to town shopping, in the shower, and finally to the psychiatrist's office. Decorum is adiaphora (ritually optional) only if I continue to observe its rules.

Much of our decorum, such as our patterning of social space, is invisible to us, so the apparent optional character of it can fade almost completely; it becomes a 'social unconsciousness'. At this point it is virtually inescapable for a given member of society and thus resembles the psychosomatic necessity of ritualization.

The Japanese tea ceremony is as rich and complex an example of decorous ritual that I know. E. F. Bleiler calls it a 'social sacrament' (in Okakura, 1964:xvi). In some forms, well over a hundred customary rules inform the participation of host and guests. At times in Japanese history, collecting and admiring tea ware was an elaborate social display of wealth and power. Tea became the setting for great political intrigues, such as the conflict between Hideyoshi and Rikyu, the founder of *cha-no-yu*, the tea ceremony (see Castile, 1971). Yet, the way of tea is also one of simplicity, especially as sometimes practised in Zen monasteries, where one 'just drinks tea, nothing else'; this turns the interaction into a potential vehicle of enlightenment.

So the sanctification of interaction can become as thorough as the reverence for bodily and environmental rhythms is when ritualization processes develop into healing rites.

Ceremony *intentional, body politic, surrender to the "cause"*

Thus far I have identified ritual modes which seem biologically inescapable or socially obligatory. When we turn to the next mode, ceremony, we are considering rituals which seem less ordinary and more intentional. Ceremoniousness is of legal, tribal, or racial import; it includes gestures such as standing for a national anthem, wearing a tribal lip disc, or bearing a clan's coat of arms into battle. The distinction between decorum and ceremony hinges largely on the differences between face-to-face and large-group, political interaction. Labour rallies, political fanfares, coronations, inaugurations, convocations, Olympic games, and courtroom sessions are all laden with the pomp of ceremony. On a decorous occasion the ritual director is a host, but at a ceremonious event he or she is an officiant.

Ceremony invites the participant to surrender idiosyncrasies and independence to some larger cause, for which one is willing to fight, die, or pay homage. This cause is not only considered righteous, it is legally enforced and therefore binding under direct threat. Nevertheless, I am expected to give myself to it not only willingly but even joyously. Whereas decorum is of secondary, or at least of unofficial, importance and is a means of expressing one's character and recognizing other participants in the occasion (Goffman, 1967:54), ceremony has imperative force; it symbolizes respect for the offices, histories, and causes that are condensed into its gestures, objects, and actions.

Implicit in ceremony is what symbolic anthropologists call 'social drama' (Turner, 1974: ch. 2–3). Ceremony is manifestly competitive, sometimes conflict-laden. This is obvious in demonstrations, revolutionary congresses, and military parades. At times such as thanksgivings, independence days, and states of the nation addresses, an implicit we/they distinction is extolled. Whereas decorous actions are typified by their politeness and exaggerated courtesy, ceremonious protagonists are so certain, and yet defensive, of their ideological territory that they dramatize their own victorious heroism. Gracious understatement gives way to solemnly pious, political overstatement. Ceremony is no longer face-to-face. The 'other side' is caricatured, since ceremony both expresses and creates 'our' solidarity as opposed to 'theirs'.

Power is a central consideration in ceremony. Not that it is irrelevant to either ritualization or decorum, but in ceremony the actions often symbolize power itself – either the power to conserve or to make change. Power of whatever kind – political, military, legislative, influential, economic – is always ambiguous; it is both a source of conflict and a means of resolving it. Whenever a ritual symbol masks an ambiguity or covers a social contradiction – and it often does – we have to do with ceremoniousness, even if that symbol appears in an explicitly religious ritual. So it is easy to see how the symbolism of power presented for public veneration and draped in such a way as to expose only its righteous, legitimate qualities, easily becomes the core of a religio-political system. Japanese Shinto, Chinese Confucianism, and Maoism, along with certain rituals of Judaism, Christianity, and Islam are as ceremonious as they are liturgical. They contain elements of 'civil religion' (Bellah, 1974) and spawn 'rites of rebellion' (Gluckman, 1963). By now it should be obvious that the modes of ritual sensibility fade in varying degrees into one another.

Liturgy   *ultimate frame*

I do not restrict 'liturgy' to Christian rites. Rather, I call 'liturgical' any ritual action with an ultimate frame of reference and the doing of which is felt to be of cosmic necessity. Work is not extraneous to liturgy, as its etymology, 'work of the people', suggests. Power is the capacity to do work, but power is more comprehensively understood in liturgy than in ceremony. And work is understood in a less goal-oriented way than it is in magic. Liturgical power is not mere force, but is a mode of tapping the way (*tao*) things flow, connecting with the order and reason (*logos*) things manifest. Liturgy is a way of coming to rest in heart of cosmic change and order.

Liturgy is as far 'beyond' us as ritualization is 'below' us. We are not animals only, but spirits, soul-searchers, Chosen People, Made People (Ortiz, 1969:17), and so on. We participate as surely in the dances of angels on the heads of pins as we do in the aping of chimpanzees. In liturgical rituals we overstep ourselves, and as a result there is always something inherently clumsy about the liturgical stride. For this we ritually apologize by confessions of sin, cleansings, baptisms, and incensations.

What is unique to liturgy is not that it communicates (decorum communicates), proclaims (ceremony proclaims), or exclaims (ritualization exclaims). Liturgically, one approaches the sacred in a reverent, 'interrogative' mood, does necessary ritual work (makes a 'sacrifice of praise', for instance), waits 'in passive voice', and finally is 'declarative' of the way things ultimately are. In liturgy we 'actively act' in order to be acted upon. Liturgy is 'meet, right, and fitting so to do', while at the same time it is an action done through us. This paradoxical pursuit of and by power runs through liturgical acts as diverse as the Christian Eucharist, Sufi dance, Taoist alchemy, Zen meditation, and shamanic trance. Liturgy occurs in moments when power does not need to be seized and held, as is the case in ceremony, or put to immediate use, as in magic. In liturgy we wait upon power.

Liturgy is a symbolic action in which a deep receptivity, sometimes in the form of meditative rites or contemplative exercises, is cultivated. In it we actively await what gives itself and what is beyond our command. This is what separates liturgy from magic and what lends it an implicitly meditative and mystical character. Since liturgy is a structured waiting upon an influx of whole-making (holy) power, it is inescapably a 'spiritual exercise'. There is a sense in which a liturgical rite is but a mere preparatory exercise, a way of biding valued time; this is the origin of inevitable liturgical monotony. But there is another sense in which the exercise *is* the hierophany. Ritual symbols and gestures bear the sacred. Bread does bear the Presence. Dogs do have Buddha nature. If either dogs or bread is incapable of bearing the sacred load, so is everything else, including written and oral Torah, preached words, incarnate lords, warmed hearts, chanted syllables, and visions beheld.

Liturgical action is a vehicle capable of carrying us – but only part way. Then the Christian begins a protest on principle, the Zen Buddhist reminds us that the raft is not the shore, and the Hindu repeatedly utters, '*Neti, neti, neti*' ('No, no, no') – 'the Holy is not that.' In the end, liturgy, even though it is not causal work, must always reverse itself as a form of action. It aspires to more than it has power to produce. It must become reception – what we sometimes call 'passion' or 'deep receptivity'.

Every liturgy attempts to answer every question, to declare, 'This is the way things are.' Of course, it does so in the words of a specific tradition. A liturgy tries to focus all things through a few things. Like speakers who try to say everything, such liturgies must be monotonous, but monotony is appropriate to liturgy. Like any work, a liturgy needs monotony. Only when monotony, a quality we do not know how to appreciate, degenerates into boredom, does the liturgical vehicle break down. Boredom is what occurs when the excitement-obsessed must abide in the monotonous. Instead of having our defences lulled, which is one of the many good uses of monotony, we defend ourselves against repetition and sameness. What many students of ritual consistently fail to recognize is that a ritual does not have to be exciting to exercise power.

Liturgy as a form of work does not surprise, though it may keep us open to the serendipitous moment by its very monotony. When I hear the word 'monotony', I think of 'monochrome' paintings. From the point of view of a Walt Disney cartoon, a Japanese ink painting or a Doré illustration is monotonously monochromatic, but what these lack in colour spectrum they more than make up by what they do to our usual perceptual cravings for splashy colour. They teach us to see the colourfulness of black and white. Liturgy is a full emptiness, a monotony without boredom, a reverent waiting without expectation. If this way of putting it sounds excessively paradoxical, I can only say that I do not know a single religious tradition which does not find itself eventually in a *vacuum plenum* (full/emptiness) paradox when it tries to speak about the relationship between ritual work and sacred referents.

Liturgies do two things. They 're-present' events and 'event-ualize' structures. An event is literally unrepeatable; by definition this is so. So every event, not just the exodus of the Hebrews, the incarnation of Christ, or the enlightenment of Buddha, is unique. Some unique events (to be redundant), however, become definitive ones. We allow those events to define us, much as we define words. Jesus dies on a cross. Buddha sits under the Bo tree. Moses comes down a mountain. In these events some people find themselves defined, that is, judged, enlightened, and put into fundamental touch. But not one of these events is repeatable on the same level at which it occurred. So we must re-present them in enactments. One of these definitive events and consequent performances may save us, but just as surely, we, by our ritual action, save such events from becoming mere artefacts from the past. Without rituals such events have no presence.

Liturgies not only present events, they event-ualize structures. Certain processes, for example, changing seasons, growing up, growing old, and childbirth, appear to be relatively stable structures. They seem always to be there, just as surely as events seem always to be receding into the past. Yet a structure is but a patterning of events, so no absolute difference obtains between events (of history) and structures (of nature), and consequently, between liturgy and ritualization. The commonly accepted dichotomy between the historicity of Christianity, Judaism, and Islam, and the naturalness of other religions has been grossly overstated. Events threaten to evaporate because of their specificity, and structures, to become commonplace because of their generality. Rituals rescue structures by concentrating them punctually, as it were, into events. Death in general is transformed by a funeral into the event of this man's, John Doe's, dying. His 'natural' demise is made for his family and friends an 'historical' occurrence.

Magic intentional, transformative, transcendence

'Magic', as I use it here, does not refer only to other people's rituals but to ours as well. It is not a pejorative term. The word refers to any element of pragmatic, ritual work. If a ritual not only has meaning but also 'works', it is magical. Insofar as it is a deed having transcendent reference and accomplishing some desired empirical result, a rite is magical.

Westerners regularly include curses, divination, and fertility rites in the category of magic. Some also include healing rites, unless they are sanctioned by their own traditions and belief system, in which case they refer to them as miracles and deny that such happenings are rituals at all. For example, a prayer, if one expects it to precipitate specifiable results such as healing or world peace, is magical. If the person praying is simply adjuring us to be peaceful, the prayer is hortatory and ceremonial.

Liturgy speaks in an interrogative voice, then a declarative one: 'Can this be?' then 'This is the case.' Magic depends on the declarative to reach the imperative: 'This is how things work; therefore, let this be the case.' Magic has in common with ceremony a propensity for performative utterances, but the frame of reference of the former is political, while that of the latter is transcendent. Magic uses a transcendent frame of reference to effect change in the ordinary reality of social interaction.

Healing rites, whether of the shamanic sort or the modern therapeutic and medical varieties, provide provocative insights into magic. If a doctor gives me a placebo, treats me with 'fictive medicine', or even performs a mock operation (Kiev, 1964:x), I may be healed. Our consensus is that the frame of reference is chemical and physiological, but the healer 'transcends' it, albeit in a fictive-theatrical direction rather than a supernatural one, as might be the case in a theistic worldview.

The force of magic lies in its use of desire as a major contributing factor in causing hoped-for results. The usual mood of magic is anxiety (Neale, 1969:121). Since the dominant mood of ritualization is ambivalence, it is often found in tandem with magic because of the similarity in dominant moods. Whereas ritualization seems to be uncontrolled, magic restores, or takes, control by employing symbols more for their consequences than for their meaning. Of course, they would have no consequences if they had no meaning.

Magical rituals are not automatically manipulative, any more than ceremonies are. Having control is not manipulation; hiding control is. If a sick person calls a medicine man or requests anointing with oil, and healers use their symbols in accord with this desire, the action is not manipulative, even though it may involve trickery. But as soon as magic is put in the service of ceremony, as happened when Hitler wanted to heal Germany by consolidating Aryans against Jews, magic-as-manipulation can begin. Magic can be employed to hide and horde power or to share and control it. But any ritual sensibility, not just magic, has its pathological forms.

Whereas liturgy is likely to evoke interpretation, magic often provokes a search for explanation, especially in the modern world. Explanation is how we account for causes and consequences; interpretation, for meanings and interconnectedness. If a magical ritual leads to other responses, awe or thankfulness, for instance, it is one step nearer liturgy or celebration.

Magical rituals are often associated with trickery. Since trickery can be manipulative or playful, magic can in some circumstances move toward the playfulness of celebration. This is what we mean by speaking of a 'magical evening'. If magician and audience collude, agreeing to enjoy illusion without expecting empirical results, a festive ethos displaces an anxiety-laden one. Collusion undermines magical 'transcendence', by which I mean not only supernatural reference but any frame not immediately shared by the participants. To agree to be deceived, like suspending disbelief while seeing a performance or reading fiction, is a ludic frame of mind; so speaking of celebrations as 'magical' is not an entirely incorrect usage. It at least recognizes that wonder in the face of mystery, not just causal explanation when confronted by a problem, can be a response to rituals that work.

Magical acts seldom displace pragmatic or scientific ones (see Malinowski, 1954:85–87), and we have no reason to assume that magic is absent from technological societies, although it is probably adumbrated in them. I suspect magic is minimal in modern agriculture, but modern therapy and modern sexuality are as laden with magical thinking as healing and fertility rites ever were. In addition, advertising is full of it. People deny that they believe in magic, but ingest this pill and use that shampoo expecting 'somehow' (the cue for magical transcendence) to become what they desire. A more responsible example of modern magic is Carl Simonton's (1975) use of imagery in therapy for cancer patients. A person treated in his clinic wills and imagines a cancer as soft or dissolvable and surrenders images of it as a rock, army, or steel armour. Considerable success is had in directly using symbols for such concrete ends.

Celebration ~~ravels in misfit w/ cosmic order, playful, unmotivated~~

I have now sketched all but one of what I take to be fundamental impulses of ritual: ritualization, decorum, ceremony, liturgy, and magic. Each arises from a different concatenation of forces; each has its own kind of weight or necessity. Ritualization is compelled; decorum is expected. Ceremony can be enforced. Liturgy is a cosmic necessity, and magic is desired. The final sensibility for consideration is celebration, but, unlike the other modes of ritual, its root, play, is distinctive, because in an important respect it seems unmotivated, spontaneous. For this reason, the ludic element of ritual is at once the most relevant and most irrelevant to liturgical rites.

In our robes and other drapes of holiness we are always something of a clown. Our shabbiness is comic, but on liturgical occasions it is typically overpowered by finery; so the comedy is seldom evident. But somewhere there is a summersault and a grin – detached from us while playing with us. Imperceptibly, liturgy begins to shift toward celebration.

However serious our stride and tone, however fundamental our rhythms and ultimate meanings, we are pretenders to office; our work is dramatic and therefore fictional. Our robes are always too big; the pleats are a stylized cover-up for our under-size. We are incapable of absolute belief and total sincerity, and holiness does not need our struttings and smoke. So liturgical 'work' transcends itself, becomes its own opposite, in moments of play and performance. Despite the obvious opposition of holy work and holy play, in all liturgy a note (often obscured) of playfulness, fictionality, and drama arises.

When this note is fully sounded I call the ritual a 'celebration'. A celebration rite is one in which there is no bargaining, no gain, no pursued result, no magic. Celebration is expressive play. Celebration takes a variety of forms: carnivals, birthdays, feasting, pretending, gambolling, gaming, dancing, singing, music-making. Whenever we begin to detach ourselves from ordinary matters requiring pragmatic modes of participation so we may toy with forms themselves, we are beginning to play. Since ritual itself is a mode of formalization, it is inescapably connected to the ludic impulse. Play is at once a root of ritual and a fruit of the same. The imagining we do as-our-bodies, which is what play is, is a culturally creative moment. Celebration rites arise from expressive culture; hence, their link to the arts. They are subjunctive, and their 'as if' quality, like that of good fiction, must be at once convincing and specially framed. They evoke feelings, but the feelings are formalized (see Moore, Myerhoff, 1975:27–32). They are at once spontaneous and gamelike. So a celebration, we must say, is 'spontaneous'. The quotation marks are essential, because a celebration's basic mood is one of formalized feeling. Ritual expressivity is expected, cultivated, self-aware. These traits differentiate celebration from ritualization, which is not so reflexive or socially buttressed.

I need not be embroiled in theological controversies about the righteousness of good works versus the imputed righteousness of grace to know that something is drastically wrong with an understanding of ritual which can only apprehend it in terms of work. If ritual freezes into a structure of liturgical work alone, it becomes not celebration, but magic, that form of ritual preoccupied with results and accomplishments. I do not want to suggest that there is something wrong with magic; rituals do, in fact, sometimes accomplish empirical ends, for example, healing. I do, however, think such ritual 'results' are the issue of dramatic and symbolic means, not causal ones. Every religion has both magical (achievement-oriented) and celebrative (expressive or ludic) processes deeply imbedded in its ritual system. Celebration is ritualized play. It is the inverse of magic, ritualized work, as Callois (1961), Neale (1969), and others have recognized. In celebration we do what we do to achieve no external end. Celebration tends toward pure expressivity and response. While playing a celebration (as we might a game or a drama), we are, for the moment, utterly disinterested and yet fully engaged in the act at hand.

Festive occasions cannot be commemorative without lapsing into ritual work. Festivity revels in the presence and power of what is transpiring and cannot be reduced to the mere fulfilment of theological, ritual, or moral obligation without becoming holy busy work again.

Celebrative rites do not have the monotonous characteristics of liturgy. They are ritually polychromatic. They are events, transitions rather than structures. In liturgy we work to prepare for metamorphosis, for ritual transformation. All liturgy, then, is structurally parallel to rehearsal. Liturgy is ritual practice. It is a necessary but insufficient condition for celebration. When celebration occurs, we are whole and without need of what is conventionally expected. Such ritual play occurs in a moment, in the twinkling of an eye, between two beats of the heart, and it is gone.

Celebration is social and metaphysical fiction. When we are in the midst of it, questions about the reality of its characters (gods, heroes, tutelary spirits, incarnations), along with questions about its continuation, authenticity, and origin are irrelevant. When celebration occurs, theology as a separate, critically reflective discipline, is not needed. When that action which is whole arrives, partial acts are included. Whereas in liturgy I am afraid that I might be duped into confusing a mask or icon with what it symbolizes, in ritual play I celebrate the coincidence of my knowledge that a craftsman carved the thing with my experience of the thing as a power lending me its rhythms, shape, and life. I do not care to protest. I am little interested in what is merely fictional, playful, dramatic, and imaginative, on the one hand, and what is metaphysical, real, and eternal, on the other, because in festivity I know there is no difference in value (though there may be in form) between what is utterly serious and what is playful.

Celebration is not to be identified with Western optimism; it is not mere yes-saying. It is a mode of embracing the present which draws future and past into itself. But that embrace may take many forms – a Christian kiss of peace or Zen swat with the *kyosaku* stick, for example. Celebration can take the form of a Christian 'Yes!' or a Buddhist '*Mu!*' ('Nothing'). The Christian's politically and theologically critical Yes or the Zen Buddhist's humorously serious No are equally capable of cutting attachments to rewards, goals, the status quo, and even spiritual accomplishments by dramatizing their irrelevance in rites of celebration.

References

Robert Bellah, 'Civil Religion in America', in *American Civil Religion*, ed. Russell E. Richey and Donald G. Jones (New York: Harper and Row 1974).

Gotthard Booth, *The Cancer Epidemic: Shadow of the Conquest of Nature* (New York: Edwin Mellen 1979).

Roger Callois, *Men, Play and Games* (New York: Schocken 1961).

Fritjof Capra, *The Tao of Physics* (Boulder, CO: Shambhala 1975).

Rand Castile, *The Way of Tea* (Tokyo: Weatherhill 1971).

Max Gluckman, *Order and Rebellion in Tribal Africa* (London: Cohen and West 1963).

Erving Goffman, *The Presentation of Self in Everyday Life* (Garden City, NY: Doubleday 1959).

Erving Goffman, *Interaction Ritual: Essays on Face-to-Face Behavior* (Chicago: Aldine 1967).

Edward T. Hall, *Beyond Culture* (Garden City, NY: Doubleday 1976).

Julian Huxley, 'A Discussion on Ritualization of Behaviour in Animals and Man', *Philosophical Transactions of the Royal Society of London*, Series B (1966) 251:247–526.

Cornelius T. Kane, *Habit: A Theological and Psychological Analysis* (Washington, DC: University Press of America 1978).

Ari Kiev, *Magic, Faith and Healing: Studies in Primitive Psychiatry Today* (New York: Free Press 1964).

J. S. La Fontaine, ed., *The Interpretation of Ritual: Essays in Honour of A. I. Richards* (London: Tavistock 1972).

Konrad Lorenz, *On Aggression* (London: Methuen 1966).

Bronislaw Malinowski, *Magic, Science, and Religion and Other Essays* (Garden City, NY: Doubleday 1954).

Leonel L. Mitchell, *The Meaning of Ritual* (New York: Paulist 1977).

Sally Falk Moore and Barbara G. Myerhoff, eds, *Secular Ritual* (Amsterdam: Van Gorcum 1975).

Robert E. Neale, *In Praise of Play: Toward a Psychology of Religion* (New York: Harper and Row 1969).

Kakuzo Okakura, *The Way of Tea* (New York: Dover 1964).

Alfonso Ortiz, *The Tewa World: Space, Time and Becoming in a Pueblo Society* (Chicago: University of Chicago Press 1969).

Roy Rappaport, 'Ritual, Sanctity, and Cybernetics', *American Anthropologist* 73 (1971), 59–76.

Carl Simonton, 'Belief Systems and Management of the Emotional Aspects of Malignancy', *The Journal of Transpersonal Psychology* 7/1 (1975), 29–47.

Victor Turner, *Drama, Fields and Metaphors: Symbolic Actions in Human Society* (Ithaca, NY: Cornell University Press 1974).

★★★

Liturgical supinity, liturgical erectitude: on the embodiment of ritual authority

[handwritten annotations: Not a liturgical posture. Lay down on back. Vulnerable posture → Feminine]

Two postures, two attitudes

A central theme in ritual studies, at least as practised in the field of religious studies, is embodiment. When embodiment is given a position of theoretical primacy, posture and gesture emerge as crucial considerations in the interpretation of a rite. Posture and gesture, though micro-units in a ritual enactment or ritual tradition, assume considerable importance, because they encode both intended and unintended meanings – meanings 'transmitted' as well as meanings 'given off'. We use the term 'posture' in two ways. On the one hand, it refers to one's physical posture (as in, 'That child has poor posture'). On the other, when we speak of 'political posturing', the phrase refers to one's ideological commitments and ways of displaying them. A posture is not only one's manner of physical comportment (how one parks the body, so to speak) but also one's attitude – one's manner or style in the world. 'Attitude' denotes the spiritual counterpart of posture, though even this term has both psychological and physiological connotations. We speak of 'mental attitudes' but also of the attitude, or tilt, of a sailboat. A mental or spiritual attitude is indicated by our tilt or cant – that is, the way we sit, walk, or move. The terms 'attitude' and 'posture', then, refer to the same thing, except that 'attitude' emphasizes the psychological and spiritual dimensions, while 'posture' connotes the physiological and ideological dimensions.

In liturgies participants assume postures that both reflect and cultivate attitudes. When deeply embodied, these attitudes become determinative metaphors that permeate the intellectual, social, and spiritual lives of those who practise them. Here, I want to consider two liturgical postures and their corresponding implications for our understanding of ritual authority. I am being both playful and polemical when I dub them 'erectitude' and 'supinity'. Liturgical erectitude is a style typified by poise and verticality. When we embody it, we stand up straight; we process with a noble simplicity. We rise above our surroundings with a quiet and confident dignity – the fruit of age, tradition, and reflection. Liturgical supinity, on the other hand, is characterized by its flexibility and its closeness to the ground. Supine, the

148

spine hugs the earth. Supine, we are integrated with our surroundings. We are attuned to them, but our openness leaves us in danger of violation.

Described in this general and abstract manner, neither posture is particular to a specific person, gender, or tradition. Buddhists may assume either or both attitudes; so may Jews or Christians, though a given tradition may cultivate one of the attitudes more deeply than the other. All of us can probably imagine persons who more obviously typify either erectitude or supinity, and we may suppose that one is more characteristic than the other of a specified gender, but in theory no person, gender, or tradition 'owns' either posture.

However, my reflections on the two attitudes did not arise in the abstract, so, lest these characterizations seem disembodied in the very moment that I propose to discuss embodiment, I will situate them more concretely. Recently, two queries regarding ritual authority arrived at my desk. The first came in the proposal for this symposium, which bears the title, 'Reclaiming Our Rites', and which originally bore the subtitle 'Reasserting Ritual's Authority in a Pluralistic, Privatized Culture'. This proposal embodies the posture that I am calling liturgical erectitude, so I will spend most of my energies considering it.

The proposal asks specific questions and assigns me the task of addressing them from the point of view of ritual studies. I was given the tentative title (and implicit question): 'What "ritualizing" can teach "rites" and "liturgies".' My job description implicitly calls these terms into question by framing them with quotation marks, and yet it elevates 'ritualizing' (which I suspect is associated with my own writing) to authoritative status by assuming that it has something to 'teach' rites and liturgies (which, I assume, is associated largely with Christian, perhaps even Roman Catholic, liturgy).

The proposal for the symposium contained these two paragraphs:

> The liturgy is no longer seen as an established pattern of invariable words, music, and gestures, but as a freely improvised service that varies enormously from parish to parish – or from Mass to Mass within the same parish. While such innovation may showcase the skills of some parish members (e.g., the presiding priest, the musicians), it also risks subverting the larger community's participation in the ritual action. For a primary purpose of ritual is surely to enable the participation of everyone by creating a pattern of familiar, repeated actions that can be 'done by heart', without artifice or self-conscious display.
>
> This rather widespread disregard for the integrity and authority of ritual is a principal reason why the Center for Pastoral Liturgy has chosen to host this symposium on the problem of ritual's declining authority in both church and society. It is not so much that our churches – or our cultures –

lack rituals, but that these rituals lack authority. Unlike those of archaic peoples, our rituals (whether those of the rock concert, the football stadium, or the church) seem quite improvisatory and provisional. We often 'make them up' at will, without invoking ancestral precedent or tradition, and we just as often discard them in favor of 'new and improved rites'.[1]

The second query, which I will use to illustrate the posture of liturgical supinity, arrived in the form of a phone call from a woman I had not met and whom I will call 'Renata'. She is, let us say, from Tucson. Renata wanted some advice about an initiation rite that she was constructing for half a dozen girls between the ages of twelve and fourteen. She had roughly the month of August during which to construct the rite, prepare the girls and their mothers, and perform the ceremony. She had been reading books on women and ritual having to do with menstruation, female body imagery, 'croning', and other such matters of ceremonial importance to contemporary North American women, and she wanted my reactions to the scenario for the ceremony. Clearly an intelligent and articulate woman with considerable initiative, she had made phone calls to adults actively involved in creative forms of initiating adolescents into adulthood. Unfortunately, they were all men. Even though she knew many ritualizing women, she could find no groups of women who were designing rites for groups of girls.

In talking with me she was obviously not escaping her dilemma, so I put her in touch with the only local woman I knew who had any experience with initiating girls. For the duration of our first conversation I mostly asked questions, for example: What was the sequence of actions? Her plan, still in very provisional form, was to have several discussion meetings in town. After that she, the girls, and their mothers would go on a brief retreat to the mountains, where they would 'die' by entering a darkened sweat lodge and then 'rise' into womanhood by coming out into the light. This was to be the central ritual act. All the other gestures would be tributaries to this paradigmatic ritual act.

> I asked more questions: What was her goal?
> To initiate the girls into adulthood.
> Who would effect this transition?
> She would, assisted by the girls' mothers.
> What had been the role of the mothers so far – were they
>   actively involved in the planning?

---

[1] Notre Dame Center for Pastoral Liturgy, 'Proposal for a Symposium on "Reclaiming our Rites".' The version printed in the actual symposium program differs slightly from this one.

No, not really.
Was she a mother of one of the girls?
No.
Was this initiation authorized by the church in which the discussions would occur?
No.

The question of ritual authority

These two queries were the sources of the two polarized voices I heard as I began to reflect on the question of ritual authority. When I was feeling playful and a bit perverse, I sometimes reduced each inquiry to a single question. The question for this symposium became: How can a massive, centuries-old, multi-national religious institution maintain its ritual authority among highly pluralistic, materialistic, individualistic, mobile parishioners living in a racist, militaristic, deeply psychologized society? And I rendered Renata's inquiry this way: How can a young adult woman with few degrees, no children, no formal religious sanction, and no 'grandmothers' successfully initiate half a dozen girls in the four weeks that compose the month of August?

Despite my hyperbolic reframing of the essential questions, I take both queries with equal seriousness. I probably do what the symposium organizers suspected I would do, since, in describing my task, they posed this question: 'To what degree – and in what ways – does the field of ritual studies (with its habit of "phenomenological levelling", its penchant for taking the Tennessee snakehandler's ritual as seriously as the bishop's solemn ministrations) challenge the (Christian) liturgist's affection for norms, paradigms, and "privileged moments" of history?'

The question of religious authority is a classical western one, and it has traditionally been framed in ways that are not only culture-specific but androcentric. I am referring not only to the obvious historic exclusion of women from positions of liturgical authority, but to the inscription of masculine postures and attitudes in liturgical practice and theology. For instance, I cannot imagine Renata being the least interested in a liturgy whose symbols and gestures (as described by the symposium organizers) are 'hearty' and 'robust'. Not only would she question whether the liturgy is, in fact, hearty and robust, but she would probably hear in both adjectives an old-boys'-club rhetoric that fails to grasp the tenor of her aspirations. Heartiness and robustness are among the virtues of liturgical erectitude. In the current North American cultural situation, they are expressions of an androcentric liturgy. Even more directly to the point, I cannot imagine Renata agreeing with the claim that when a 'liturgical order' is enacted, those who engage in it indicate – to themselves and to others – that they *accept* whatever is encoded in the canons of the liturgy they are performing. In short, they accede to the liturgical rite's *authority*, an authority that yet remains independent of those who participate in it.[2]

> For what gives liturgical rites their authoritativeness is not, ultimately, the participants' approval or fidelity. What makes the liturgy *socially and morally binding* is not the participants' private, prayerful sentiments (however worthy these may be), but *the visible, explicit, public act of acceptance itself.*[3]

These two statements seem to me a fundamental premise and under-girding value of this symposium. It is the tip of an iceberg, a flag signalling a view that is gaining momentum in the wake of post-Vatican II disenchantment and the waning authority of traditional Euro-American masculinity. It is a very Catholic view (though, of course, there are other Catholic views), and it is set squarely against the individualistic 'habits of the heart' (that Robert Bellah and his colleagues have criticized). I am intrigued by the fact that the claim is buttressed not by arguments from scripture or Catholic theologians but by anthropological theory, especially that of Roy Rappaport. My objection is not to the use of anthropological theory as such but to the uncritical appropriation of it. Rappaport's work seems to me fundamentally descriptive and analytical in intent, whereas this use of it is undeniably normative. The logic seems to be: 'Ritual is like this, therefore liturgy *must be* like that.' Rappaport says ritual insulates 'public orders from private vagaries', and thus the proposal for this symposium concludes that the liturgy is inherently superior to personal prayer, popular devotions, and made-up rites.

I am sympathetic with the insistence that Christian liturgy ought to assume a critical, prophetic posture toward middle-class American popular culture. Certain aspects of American culture certainly deserve sustained spiritual critique, and liturgical enactments have on historic occasion provided an effective platform from which to launch such an attack: 'The liturgy of the Christian assembly stubbornly resists the manipulations of both politics and civil religion.'[4] No doubt, it sometimes does. However, no doubt, it sometimes does not. My claim that it sometimes does not is central to a deep disagreement with the aim of this symposium: 'reclaiming our rites' understood as a re-assertion of liturgical authority. Who are numbered among the 'our'? Christians, clearly. Catholics, clearly. But how can women, who have

---

[2] Nathan Mitchell, 'Americans at Prayer', *Worship* 66 (1992), 181.
[3] Ibid., 182.
[4] Ibid., 180.

been systematically denied liturgical authority, be counted among those privileged with inclusion in the first person plural? Women can hardly be imagined as wanting to reclaim what they have seldom had. So I confess that, whatever the intentions of the title of this symposium, I cannot help hearing in such words a nostalgia for pre-Vatican II days when the liturgy was the liturgy and lay people knew their place. Neither can I help hearing it as a parallel to complaints by men that their authority in families and jobs has been eroded by women, particularly feminists. Perhaps it is the 're-' in 'reclaiming' and 'reassertion' that conjures such connotations. In any case, I first coined the term 'liturgical erectitude' after I read the symposium proposal, because in the current cultural and ecclesiastical climate liturgical authority is largely and obviously masculine.

Many who assume the posture of liturgical erectitude are busy appropriating a host of allied theological and anthropological notions, for instance, tradition. Liturgical erectitude maintains a proper relation to tradition:

> Understood correctly, tradition is a word denoting those aspects of a group's social compact which have managed to survive the traumas of history *because they work in maintaining the social group as a whole.* It is by this compact that the group coheres and is thus able to survive. Because of this, the social compact – however it is stated or left unstated – is the result of the entire group and its deliberative processes. Responsibility lies with the group itself and cannot be appealed to anyone's private 'revelation', nor ought it to be taken from the group and handed over to anyone less than the total body politic.
>
> Thus differing from mere custom and convention, tradition frees from the tyranny of the present: it also protects against aggression by the compulsively articulate, as well as against opportunism by unchecked authority.[5]

I hear such claims as aspirations rather than descriptions, and so I would have to shift into the subjunctive in order to affirm them: 'Oh, *if* liturgical tradition were consistent in delivering us from the tyranny of the present! Oh, *if it were only true* that liturgical tradition represented the total body politic! *Don't we all wish* we could be sure that structures which have enabled us to survive would continue to do so?'

If we couple unquestioning trust of liturgical tradition with this symposium's statements about ritual authority, Renata's kind of ritualizing is reduced to caricature and made a symbol of the 'tyranny of the present'. As a middle-class woman she becomes an example

---

[5] Aidan Kavanagh, *The Shape of Baptism* (Collegeville MN: Liturgical Press 1978), 146.

of *embourgeoisement*.[6] She is taken to be an instance of 'private ritual vagaries'.[7] If one adds to this multi-layered critique a definition of ritual that takes it to be 'the performance of more or less invariant sequences of formal acts and utterances not encoded by the performers', Renata's ritualizing is not only caricatured and devalued but defined out of existence, a situation all too familiar to women and one that I find both morally and theoretically intolerable.[8]

Though it may hope to claim anthropological support, a liturgical theology which holds that a rite's authority transcends its ambient culture and the social relationships on which it is based is not likely to receive much support from anthropologists themselves. Such a theology probably derives from buttressing theological images and ideas, such as that of a god who transcends the land. This god, of course, is metaphorically male. This 'god of the gaps' (to appropriate Dietrich Bonhoeffer's well-worn term) will be increasingly relegated to the edges of the cosmos, not so much because he is male but because he is fundamentally removed and essentially unrelated. My prediction is that in North America a ritual authority that is not grounded in the social relationships on which it depends will suffer the same fate as the god of the gaps, and not at the hands of feminists alone. Renata, along with many other women and a growing number of men, would insist that the authority (if they would even use such a term) of ritual is *dependent* on – in fact, ought to grow organically out of – those who participate in it. This view is not without its difficulties, but is a cogent option.

Another feature of liturgical erectitude is what we might call 'liturgiocentrism', by which I mean theological ideologies that treat 'the' liturgy as both the single centre of the ritual tradition in which it is embedded and as the norm for judging its ambient culture. Several assumptions and axioms are regularly associated with liturgiocentric theologies and implicitly present in the proposal for this symposium: (1) that 'public orders', such as the liturgy, are by their very nature superior to personal or private ones; (2) that Christian liturgy is somehow above its ambient culture (called in the proposal for this symposium, 'the social contract'); (3) that the fundamental shape of

[6] The term was used by Aidan Kavanagh in *Studia Liturgica* 20 (1990), 102, and quoted by Nathan Mitchell in 'Americans at Prayer', 180.
[7] The term was originally Roy Rappaport's, *Ecology, Meaning, and Religion* (Richmond CA: North Atlantic Press 1979), 197. It is used by Nathan Mitchell in 'Americans at Prayer', 182.
[8] Rappaport, *Ecology*, 175. In my *Ritual Criticism: Case Studies in Its Practice, Essays on Its Theory* (Columbia SC: University of South Carolina Press 1990), 9–14, I have argued against such exclusion by definition.

Christian liturgy is 'invariable';[9] (4) that ritual invariance (if there were such a thing) is one important factor that helps to guarantee the authority of the liturgy.

The fact that Christian liturgy has a history at all means that it is variable, changing, fluid. Even if it is a stream that flows more slowly than all others, it nevertheless changes, and its changes are often consonant with other cultural and historical changes. Though a liturgy may criticize and judge social structures, it also reflects them. In short, the liturgy is a cultural process, itself in need of constant reformation and revision. The liturgy, like persons, can err. It can and does embody oppressive structures. If in aspiration it has overcome racism and nationalism, it has not in fact. And it has not overcome sexism even in aspiration, except on rare occasion. The liturgy is not, at least in moral terms, superior to some of the private, invented rites celebrated in homes, convents, forests, and urban work places. Some of these kinds of ritualizing judge the liturgy. Renata's attempt to initiate six girls into the mysteries of menstruation and womanhood, flawed though it may be, judges the baptismal rites of a church in which there are no huts, no nests, to which women may have repose in order to bleed, write theology, weave, or draft resolutions. Nothing guarantees that '*Liturgy* is what underwrites [that is, is the standard for] the social contract.'[10] Sometimes the social contract functions as a standard for evaluating liturgy. One ought only to decide which underwrites which after observing actual instances of liturgy/culture interaction. One ought not assume, for theological or other reasons, the priority of public liturgy, since it has at times in its history proved itself culture- and gender-bound. It has proved itself faithless for the same reason that any rite does: because it does *not* transcend the people who engage in its performance.

If my language seems too strong and too theological, then let us at least admit that the process of ritual revision, in which many, if not all, religious groups engage, implies the necessity of ritual criticism and the possibility of ritual infelicity. And let us recognize that, even though liturgy sometimes earns the right to be the 'model for' a culture, it is also a 'model of'[11] culture, and thus it participates in the foibles, injustices, and contradictions of culture.

In 1990 Helen Ebaugh delivered a presidential address called, 'The Revitalization Movement in the Catholic Church: The Institutional

---

[9] Mitchell, 'Americans at Prayer', 183.
[10] Ibid., 184.
[11] The terms belong to Clifford Geertz, *The Interpretation of Cultures* (New York: Basic Books 1973).

Dilemma of Power'.[12] Her address is about the dilemma of hierarchical authority precipitated by Vatican II. Though the article says little about ritual, some of its conclusions are germane to our consideration of ritual authority. Ebaugh's argument is that personalized religious individualism was one of the *results* of Vatican II, this 'revitalization movement'.[13] Far from setting Catholic liturgy with its collective sensibility against or above American cultural individualism, she sees the church and its liturgy as one of the *sources* of that individualism. The relationship is not antithetical but circular; there is no pure or simple division between liturgy and culture, religion and society. In Ebaugh's view, 'selective Catholicism' (picking and choosing which aspects of Catholicism one will participate in) is another *result* of Vatican II. I mention Ebaugh's argument because we are so used to hearing accounts that blame these qualities on American culture rather than the church.[14] I do not intend simply to reverse the causal sequence by blaming the church rather than the culture but rather to argue against any dualistic understanding of liturgy and culture.

Vatican II left largely untouched the gender arrangements that underwrite Roman liturgy. Insofar as the church has begun to challenge such arrangements, it has, by and large, followed the lead of culturally informed critics. Joan Laird, for instance, has mounted a powerful critique of the gender arrangements presupposed by most traditional ritual systems, among which we must count Roman Catholic liturgy as well as much that remains of Protestant and Jewish liturgy. She argues that these arrangements 'leave men free to design rituals of authority that define themselves as superior, as special, and as separate', and 'because men can be separate, they can be "sacred"'.[15] Thus, she concludes that, 'since rites of passage are important facilitators in the definition of self in relation to society, there is clearly a need for women to reclaim, redesign, or create anew rituals that will facilitate life transitions and allow more meaningful and clear incorporation of both familial and public roles.'[16]

I believe Laird's conclusion is essentially correct. I see no way to refute the core of feminist critique of ritual authority and no reason

---

[12] Helen Ebaugh, 'The Revitalization Movement in the Catholic Church: The Institutional Dilemma of Power', *Sociological Analysis* 52 (1991), 1–12.

[13] The idea is borrowed from anthropologist Anthony Wallace.

[14] This rhetorical strategy parallels the strategy of the 1992 Republican convention in the United States, namely, blaming all moral ills on 'the culture' while maintaining that 'America' (the country) is unblemished. I am indebted to S. L. Scott for pointing out this parallel.

[15] Joan Laird, 'Women and Ritual in Family Therapy', in Evan Imber-Black et al., eds, *Rituals in Families and Family Therapy* (New York: Norton 1988), 337.

[16] Ibid., 338.

to obstruct women's attempt to claim (or re-claim, if they ever had control of) their rites. In fact, liturgy, liturgical theology, and ritual theory ought to be put in the service of this critique rather than having to be the repeated objects of it. There is a tacit but fundamental conflict between the project to 'reclaim our rites', the stated aim of this symposium, and the feminist attempt to reclaim ritual, so let us not pretend this is not a power struggle.

So far I have not engaged in critique of the assumptions about authority implicit in the ritualizing represented by Renata. If she were in attendance at this symposium, I would do so, but its presuppositions exclude her. If I were addressing, say, a New Age convention in Boulder, Colorado, at which she might be present, I would challenge at the least following problematic assumptions: (1) that personal insight and private passion, such as one finds in contemporary Anglo-American ritual groups, are by their very nature more authentic than public liturgical orders; (2) that women's concerns, merely because they are rooted in women's bodies (or men's concerns merely because they are rooted in men's bodies), are universal and timeless – the same now as in ages past and in other cultures; and (3) that ritual creativity or authenticity displaces the need for ritual authority in the more public or conventional sense; (4) that all ancient or Native American symbols are available for mining by the White middle class for use in its ritualizing. I will not argue each of these points here. My aim is simply to illustrate that I am not uncritical of contemporary ritualizing and its assumptions about authority.

In Christian history the usual sources of authorization for anything, liturgy included, have been the Bible, tradition, and the hierarchy (pastoral as well as papal, and gender-based ones as well as ecclesiastical ones). But I have not yet tackled directly the evasive theoretical question: What is ritual authority? There are multiple candidates for an answer to it. Ritual authority might be, for example, whatever

1 is *endorsed* (by the gods, elders, officiants, or other kinds of participants);
2 is *traditional* (usually done, done for generations);
3 is *performed according to the rules* (contained in sacred and/or liturgical texts);
4 *functions* (that is, fits the social context) or *works* (to achieve explicit goals);
5 is *just* (according to moral criteria).

Distinguishing kinds or levels of authority at least would enable us to notice that the symposium organizers emphasize 1 and 2 (what is endorsed and traditional), whereas Renata is more interested in 4 (what functions or works), and feminist critiques of mainline liturgy often question its moral authority (5). Such emphases are, of course, not mutually exclusive, so there is no *necessary or logical* conflict between the three positions (that of established liturgiology, that of feminist liturgical theology, and that of private ritualizing outside the ecclesiastical context). The very complexity of ritual precludes any simple answer to the question, What is ritual authority? But we will do much talking past each other if we do not distinguish at least among these sorts of authority. Furthermore, there are different kinds of ritual, and these probably entail different sorts of ritual authority.

The notion of ritual authority conceals at least two, circularly related questions. The first is this: What authorizes ritual? – by which is meant: Where does it come from, how does it arise, who warrants it? The stated intention of this symposium seems to emphasize this aspect of current liturgical difficulties in North America. The organizers appear interested in fostering a liturgy that has public, not merely private, validity and that arises out of time-tested, ecclesiastically grounded tradition. The second question is this: What does ritual authorize? – by which is meant: What does it do, achieve, or enable? Renata is primarily interested in this question. She wants to construct a rite that will, in fact, enable girls to become women. A serious problem, as I see it, is the divorce between these questions that ought to be dialectically related. If we make the mistake of focusing entirely on the first one (what ritual authorizes), treating ritual solely as a pragmatic tool, we are tempted to ransack the world's ritual traditions for symbolic goods, much as we once plundered the globe for spices and gold. If we over-emphasize the second one (what authorizes ritual), treating liturgy solely as a paradigm or norm (with authority over participants and culture), we attribute to it a false, heteronomous transcendence removed from criticism but also from relevance and cultural roots. So in my view those who practise liturgical supinity (a posture emphasizing attunement to cultural currents and ecological realities) as a way of fostering ritual creativity need to attend to ritual traditions, especially their own. Those who defend liturgical erectitude (a posture emphasizing public accountability and traditional integrity) as a way of consolidating ritual authority need to attend to ritual generation, especially that of women and other groups marginalized by mainline liturgical activity.

Reframing the question of authority

I am calling, then, for a reframing of the question of ritual authority. Since the notion of authority is so contaminated with androcentrism, I prefer to change the terms of reference altogether. We might, for instance, speak of 'felicitous' and 'infelicitous' rather than authorized (or authoritative) and unauthorized (or 'unauthoritative') ritual.[17] This strategy does not get rid of the authority question, but it does put it in a larger context. We need to know how and in what respects liturgies lapse into infelicity. Are, for example, non-feminist liturgies and baptisms guilty of 'glossing', that is, of using ritual procedures to cover up social problems? Do they commit ritual 'violations', actions that are effective but demeaning?

If my budding glossary of ritual infelicities seems cumbersome, there are others in the making. William Seth Adams,[18] for instance, criticizes Episcopalian baptism on two accounts: its ritual incongruence and its ritual incoherence. Both of his judgments are made on the basis of observations and descriptions of that rite's handling of ritual space and action.

The temptation in trying to develop a vocabulary of ritual infelicity is that it could degenerate into mere academic name-calling. If so, it would, of course, be useless. But if it forced us to be more precise in identifying the level on which criticism of a liturgical rite is being levied, it might actually help the antagonists engage one another more fully and fairly. What worries me is the lack of sustained and direct public debate between male theologians who want to reassert liturgical authority and feminist ones who want to challenge or undermine it. What little debate there is, is far too circumlocutious and private.

Whether my terms are the best ones or not, the implication I want to press is this: liturgy's felicitousness does not arise from ecclesiastical, biblical, conciliar, or traditional warrant alone but also on the basis of a rite's ability to meet fundamental human need. Liturgy is as essentially cultural as it is religious. Consequently, it ought to be subjected not just to theological criticism but to ritual, ethical, and other sorts of criticism that proceed on anthropological, ecological, and psychological grounds.

If we were to be successful in reframing the question of ritual authority, our view of initiation, for example, might be different. In my view the attempt to re-imagine Christian baptism as an *initiation rite* has been a largely felicitous step in baptismal history, and the church ought to go further with this experiment, not retrench on it. From the point of view of liturgical erectitude, however, the step is an infelicitous one, making baptism too generic, too cultural. A

---

[17] See my *Ritual Criticism*, ch. 9, on ritual infelicity.
[18] William Seth Adams, 'De-coding the Obvious: Reflections on Baptismal Ministry in the Episcopal Church', *Worship* 66 (1992), 327–38.

cross-cultural perspective, however, has helped provide a critical edge
for assessing liturgy.

For example, Marjorie Procter-Smith in her critique of Christian
baptism lays out several criteria for judging rites: the centrality of
women's bodies, naming the sources of oppression, baptism's connectedness with the everyday, dependence on relationships among
women, and ritual empowerment.[19] These are dependent in part on
cross-cultural research mediated through feminist theological scholarship. Procter-Smith is, at least indirectly, indebted to the notion of
initiation or some equivalent, culturally-grounded idea. Her sources
are not *only* theological or narrowly Christian but broadly cultural, even
cross-cultural. Initiation understood as a bodily, social, and political
phenomenon is a product of cross-cultural research. Some of the
grounds for liturgical critique, such as those launched by feminist and
Marxist critics of so-called 'gender ritual',[20] have their roots outside
Christian theology. They have been more attuned to ritual infelicities,
especially the abuse of ritual authority, than most liturgical theologies
have. Both feminist ritualizing (like that of Renata) and feminist liturgical rites (like those proposed by Procter-Smith) are more consistently open to, and dependent upon, cross-cultural research, because
they do not construe the authority of ritual as derivative from either
its distinctiveness or its exclusivity.

Whatever may be lost by considering baptism an initiation rite,
the gain has been considerable. If Christian baptism seems to lose its
uniqueness, and therefore authority, by being assimilated to a cross-
cultural model, it gains connectedness, not only with women but
with other cultures and classes and with human ordinariness. I am not
suggesting that some generic initiation rite is necessarily less sexist
or more humane than Christian baptism. And I am not arguing for
the moral or ritual superiority of other kinds of initiation, but for
the value of continuing to imagine baptism pluralistically, as just one
(not 'the') version of human initiatory activity. Christian baptism, I
believe, is more, not less felicitous, if it remains permeable to cross-
culturally informed initiation rites – if those who conduct and the-
ologize about baptism do so in the light of non-Christian as well as
Christian data.

I do not mean to imply that liturgical theologians need authoritative 'correction' from anthropologists and historians of religion who

---

[19] Marjorie Procter-Smith, *In Her Own Rite: Constructing Feminist Liturgical Tradition* (New
York: Abingdon 1990).
[20] See, for example, Karen Ericksen Paige and Jeffery M. Paige, *The Politics of Reproductive
Ritual* (Berkeley CA: University of California Press 1981).

work on rites of passage, but rather that mutual critique and collaborative reimagining of ritual processes should be our aim. We in the humanities and social sciences need critique as surely as liturgical theologians need ours. For example, a recurrent assumption of rites of passage theorists is that rites of passage have their proper home in pre-industrial cultures. Victor Turner represents a widespread anthropological view when he says, '*Rites de passage* are found in all societies but tend to reach their maximal expression in small-scale, relatively stable and cyclical societies, where change is bound up with biological and meteorological rhythms and recurrences rather than with technological innovations.'[21] Is this claim true? No anthropologist that I know has presented data that demonstrates that it is. Perhaps the problem is rather a failure of the theoretical imagination – this time among secular academics rather than liturgists or liturgiologists. If baptism is, in fact, an initiation rite, is it not evidence that rites of passage continue in industrial cultures? Is not Christian baptism an example of a kind of initiation that continues, recast and re-imagined, into industrial and post-modern society? I do not claim that the example of Christian baptism disproves Turner's assumption, but only that it makes it questionable.

In *Rites of Passage Theory*, which is not yet published, I am currently struggling with the history of rites of passage theory, which is indebted largely to van Gennep and Turner. Turner's theory of ritual is constructed around the cornerstone of liminality, the second phase in the rites of passage model. But rites of passage theorizing from van Gennep (its originator) to Turner (in whom it culminates) is determined mainly by one kind of rite of passage, namely, initiation; initiation has been regarded as the paradigm for the other rites of passage such as those surrounding birth, marriage, and death.[22] In turn, the examples of initiation are, in almost every instance, those of male initiation. So ritual theory itself is not immune from the kinds of critique I have levelled at liturgical theology, because the theorizing itself is contaminated by androcentrism and colonialism.

But so what? What difference does such a conclusion make? It makes little if we imagine that theory has no life beyond the halls of academe. However, I know people who design initiations in three phases (separation, transition, incorporation), the classical threefold pattern formulated by van Gennep. I know feminist ritualizers who

---

[21] Victor Turner, *The Forest of Symbols: Aspects of Ndembu Ritual* (Ithaca NY: Cornell University Press 1967), 93.

[22] William Seth Adams (op. cit., 332), who advocates a 'baptismal paradigm', ought to take this bias in rites of passage theory into account, since he makes explicit use of the theory.

set out deliberately to foment liminality, a notion borrowed from Turner, who borrowed it from van Gennep, who borrowed it from . . . Ritual theory itself is currently inspiring and permeating North American ritual practices, both ecclesiastical and self-generated. Whether or not van Gennep and Turner would have approved of such a use of their ideas, they (like Jung and Eliade), nevertheless, have fed the initiatory fantasies that have been with us since at least the origins of romance in the Middle Ages and the revival of romanticism in the nineteenth century.

I do not want to privilege ritual studies, religious studies, anthropology, or any other discipline, making it some new arbiter in the clash between ecclesiastical liturgiology and private ritualizing. Each of these is in need of critique. However, liturgical theologians need to stop uncritically appropriating and start questioning their anthropological (largely white male) authorities[23] and begin listening to their female ritual critics.[24] The opening of liturgy and liturgical theology to the cross-cultural resources provided by anthropology and religious studies, though not without its problems, is nevertheless essential to the felicitous functioning of a liturgy that must negotiate its position in what we all hope is a decreasingly androcentric and increasingly pluralistic world. It is also essential for debunking liturgical or theological claims to a false transcendence over culture. When culture is construed as the bipolar opposite of a male-engendered and male-controlled liturgy, it necessarily becomes the overcrowded home of women and 'others'.

So, what am I actually recommending? I hope for continued, strengthened moral and cultural pressure on Christian liturgies in the direction of a more collaborative, less hierarchical, less androcentric sensibility for handling ritual power. I would like to see a sustained reconsideration of certain key notions – among them: authority, power, order, and tradition. The view of tradition, for example, that identifies its authority with rule-like order or maintains that tradition stands above culture should not be regarded as sacrosanct. There are other ways to understand tradition.[25] It is time we admitted that the reigning definitions of such notions are themselves both andro- and ethno-centric and thus in need of theological critique. When I hear calls for liturgical order and pleas for enhanced ritual authority, I cannot help thinking of Huntington and Metcalf's compelling

---

[23] Such as Victor Turner, Clifford Geertz, and Roy Rappaport.
[24] Such as Rosemary Radford Ruether, Marjorie Procter-Smith, Janet Walton, Mary Collins, Kathleen Hughes, and the many unknown Renatas.
[25] I have considered some of them in 'Reinventing Ritual', *Soundings* 75 (1992), 21–41.

interpretation of Bara funerals. For these Madagascar islanders death is 'an overdose of order', and thus funerals are necessary injections of chaos to revitalize and re-balance the socially generated cosmos.[26]

The Christian liturgical imagination can no longer afford the luxury of reasserting ritual authority on the basis of rules assumed to be unchanging and universal. Participants can begin to create the conditions for nurturing the liturgical imagination by refusing to reassert the authority of liturgy (or ritual theory) *over* those who participate in it, for the simple reason that many of us who exercise such authority are white middle-class, middle-aged Euro-American males, who present addresses at symposia like this one. If such a divestment of ritual authority means that one can no longer do the liturgy 'by heart' and 'without artifice' (two aspirations specified in the symposium proposal), so be it. Let us learn to ritualize our self-consciousness and our lack of authority.

In my view the feminist critique and environmental crisis require of us men who hold various kinds of ritual authority that we drop our preoccupation with ritual *authorization* so that we have the energy to follow the leads of others who know more than we about ritual *generation*. The former is typical of the posture of liturgical erectitude; the latter, of liturgical supinity. The difference between the two emphases is that the authority question (at least as posed for this gathering) starts at the top (the head) rather than the bottom (the roots). The question we should be asking, then, is not what stands above ritual to authorize it, but what lies below it. The best position from which to answer the question is supine. So if I were forced to answer the question, What constitutes ritual authority, without arguing against the question itself, I would have to say something like this: Ritual has (or ought to have) authority only insofar as it is rooted in, generated by, and answerable to its infrastructures – bodily, cultural, ecological, and spiritual.

I might have approached the topic of ritual authority in a variety of ways, for example, theoretically or practically, theologically or social scientifically. I have done so ritologically, thereby assuming a position between these two sets of alternatives. My aim in doing so, however, has not been to pretend that I am neutral or to escape critique. I am not neutral, and I am well aware of the dangers of assuming mediating positions in disputes where dividing lines are deeply inscribed. In the present circumstances my own position is largely that of an advocate of the virtues of liturgical supinity (even though

---

[26] Richard Huntington and Peter Metcalf, *Celebrations of Death: The Anthropology of Mortuary Ritual* (Cambridge: Cambridge University Press 1979).

I know I have argued for it with considerable erectitude). I am not recommending it for women, who have known the posture for generations, but for men occupying positions of power and authority. From a supine position, into which many women have been forced both literally and metaphorically (but which I as a man have been able to imagine that I can assume by choice), one has to 'overcome from underneath', to borrow a Taoist phrase. One has to employ cultural and religious refuse, that is, the symbols our culture would prefer to bury or forget, recycling and transforming them into tools useful for liberation of a captive liturgy.

Before I conclude, I must confess to a trick I have been playing. The image of a 'supine liturgy' is not my invention. It belongs to Aidan Kavanagh,[27] from whom I have pilfered it. I have inverted it, using it in ways quite contrary to his original intentions. Liturgical supinity is not a posture to which he aspires but rather one he fears and deplores. He uses the phrase to characterize the plight of a liturgy that capitulates to middle-class American culture. To quote him, 'Liturgy is not [I think he means, "ought not be"] adapted to culture, but culture to the liturgy.'[28]

When I first encountered the image, it stopped me flat and stole my breath. It provoked an imagined scenario: Liturgy was lying on its back, its spine following the curvature of the ground. It was, if you will, in missionary position. I imagined (my imagination being more perverse than Kavanagh's) a very tall, very threatening, not very trustworthy Mr Culture. He was standing over Supine Liturgy, whose gender I leave to your imagination.

This scenario is one Kavanagh rejects. He would have us reverse the polarities; so I inverted the imagery and ran out another scenario: Now, Liturgy is vertical, male, and standing erect; liturgical authority walks tall. Culture, now obviously female, is supine and vulnerable. To be lying on one's back is dangerous, not to mention bad liturgical style. It is an invitation to abuse.

I do not like either scenario; I mistrust them both. By teasing out the images of erectitude and supinity, I am not suggesting that liturgical issues are really sexual ones. Instead, I am using the sexual images as metaphors for understanding the relations between liturgy and culture. I do mean, however, to imply that gender issues (as distinct from

---

27 Aidan Kavanagh, *Elements of Rite: A Handbook of Liturgical Style* (New York: Pueblo 1982), 56.

28 Ibid., 55. This statement is softened considerably by one that follows: 'The liturgical assembly is normally always in the business of absorbing cultural elements into itself in a rich diversity of ways and over long periods of time' (57). Clearly, Kavanagh is aware that the liturgy/culture relation is not a one-way street.

sexual issues)[29] are more fully determinative of both liturgical practice and liturgical theology than most white male theologians readily recognize or openly admit. I am also arguing that the middle-class culture before which liturgy is not supposed to be supine includes some of the most articulate, critical, and creative women in the church. Thus, I question both the wisdom and morality of a liturgy-vs.-culture model. I am defending liturgical supinity not because I believe that the church ought to lie prostrate before culture, but because I believe the supine position best symbolizes what men presently prefer to ignore. Men, largely Euro-American males, have been the inventors of most Christian liturgical traditions, and so I believe that we should practise the posture we have assigned women as a way of educating ourselves ritually. We ought not pretend that the Renatas of our time merely invent their rites, while assuming that ours were 'somehow given' to us.

American culture can be rapacious. We all know this. I certainly do not want to be seduced, much less raped, by a rapacious American culture. I am wary of it. But I am just as wary of canonized posturing and liturgical displays of the feathers of erectitude. I do not believe that a more prophetic liturgy needs to assume the form of liturgical erectitude or remain impervious to the supine virtues. I believe that Christianity, both Catholic and Protestant, is much in need of liturgical supinity. A more supine liturgy, which I am espousing for white, Euro-American men, would, of course, be perpetually endangered, a rare species. It would be a liturgy whose authority consists of the act (at once both real and ritualistic) of divesting itself of power. We men who organize and speak at symposia such as this need to meditate upon – or within – the vision of a supine liturgy, one that teases the spines of its practitioners into parallel alignment to, and contact with, the earth.

I conclude, then, by commending the metaphor of supinity to you. If you choose to embody and practise it, it will stretch muscles you did not know you have. And you may be sure that you will be sore the day after.

---

[29] The usual distinction is that sexuality is biologically given, whereas gender is socially constructed.

8

Catherine Bell

Introduction

Part of the dilemma of ritual change lies in the simple fact that rituals tend to present themselves as the unchanging, time-honored customs of an enduring community. Even when no such claims are explicitly made within or outside the rite, a variety of cultural dynamics tend to make us take it for granted that rituals are old in some way. (Catherine Bell, *Ritual, Perspectives and Dimensions*, 210)

In her article, 'Ritual, Change, and Changing Rituals', originally published in *Worship* 63 (1989), 31–41, Catherine Bell deals with the difficult topic of ritual change, implicitly challenging those who would assert the absolute invariability of rites. Hers is a solidly grounded approach which would neutralize the opinions of critics of modern liturgical change who would claim validity for only, for example, the Tridentine Mass, the 1662 *Book of Common Prayer* or the 1526 *Deutsche Messe*.

Since people need to express their social dependence through ritual, political forces that have control over community rites are in a good position to have their authority legitimized. Through such rituals, authority is dramatized and thereby glamorized. This dramatization not only establishes who has authority and who does not; it also defines the degrees of relative authority among the politically influential. (David I. Kertzer, *Ritual, Politics, Power*, 104)

Catherine Bell's paper, 'The Authority of Ritual Experts', was delivered at the same symposium as that by Ronald Grimes entitled 'Liturgical Supinity, Liturgical Erectitude', reproduced earlier in this book. It was originally published in *Studia Liturgica* 23 (1993), 98–120. The roles of ritual experts in defining, shaping, and magnifying ritual, in establishing the authority of ritual itself, and in orchestrating relationships between liturgical and social change are the issues which she explores here. She wisely suggests that rather than seeking theoretical models, interested scholars would do well to consider framing a theological consensus and only then re-examine questions of authority as well as change.

Catherine Bell teaches in the Department of Religious Studies at Santa Clara University in California.

For further reading

Catherine Bell, *Ritual. Perspectives and Dimensions* (New York: Oxford University Press 1999).

David I. Kertzer, *Ritual, Politics, Power* (New Haven: Yale University Press 1988), Chapter 6, 'Rite Makes Might: Struggling for Power through Ritual'.

★★★

Ritual, change, and changing rituals

Liturgical reform has not been well received by some cultural anthropologists and sociologists of religion. Most of course, have ignored this quiet revolution and its ramifications, but a few have reacted strongly. In this very journal, for example, the justly renowned anthropologist Victor Turner lamented the loss of the dignified pre-Conciliar Mass and the emergence of 'relevant' liturgical experimentation.[1] Turner's reaction is not an isolated case among scholars, although it may be the most direct.[2] Such opinions clearly suggest the dangers of forsaking scholarly distance or appealing to a professional 'expertise' to decide what is proper ritual and what is not. It is doubtful, for example, that Turner would have so harshly judged ritual reforms carefully deliberated and implemented by the Ndembu. Yet with regard to Catholic ritual, he even backed his critique with the credentials of 'science'.[3] The root of such reactions, however, is not simply a loss of objectivity or a display of scientific aggrandizement. Rather, self-consciously changing ritual presents scholars with a major conundrum, a contradiction of sorts that is rooted in the history of approaches to the study of ritual.

Since the turn of the century, the study of ritual has been closely tied to issues of social change. Two general approaches have predominated. The first, rooted in W. Robertson Smith's study of Semitic sacrifice,[4] has been developed with great sophistication by Turner and

---

[1] Victor Turner, 'Ritual, Tribal and Catholic', *Worship* 50 (November 1976), 504–26.

[2] Mary Douglas presents a more historically nuanced critique of recent liturgical changes in general in *Natural Symbols* (New York: Random House/Vintage 1973), 19ff. David Martin has also published several critiques of changes in the Anglican *Book of Common Prayer*, speaking both as a sociologist of religion and as a deacon in the Church of England. See David Martin and Peter Mullen, eds, *No Alternative: The Prayer Book Controversy* (Oxford: Basil Blackwell 1981) and D. Martin, *The Breaking of the Image* (New York: St Martin's Press 1979). The ambiguities of Martin's position have been criticized in Jonathan D. Harrop, 'The Limits of Sociology in the Work of David Martin', *Religion* 17 (April 1987), 173–92.

[3] 'I do not wish to sound uncharitable towards sincere and devout individuals but science must have a say, and the comparative study of cultures has already some valid findings to its credit.' Turner, 525.

[4] W. Robertson Smith, *The Religion of the Semites* (New York: Meridian 1956). Originally published in 1889.

Mary Douglas among others. This approach has focused on the role of ritual in the maintenance of social groups. It therefore tends to analyze ritual as the expressive deployment of the symbolic structures that undergird a group's common world view. In this way ritual is seen to act as a mechanism of continuity to resist forces that could fray the fabric of the community.

A second approach has focused on how groups change through ritual. Within this perspective, ritual is seen as integral to the way in which the ideals and traditions of the social group are adapted to changing circumstances. This approach is probably rooted in Durkheim's analysis of cult, but articulated most recently and persuasively in the work of Clifford Geertz.[5] According to this perspective, ritual is seen to facilitate meaningful social change by fusing a community's 'general conceptions of the order of existence' with the actual circumstances of its daily life.[6]

The first approach casts ritual as a mechanism of continuity, a way of countering change. The second approach regards ritual as affording change via adaptation or integration. Examples abound to support both approaches, but as theoretical formulations of the basic dynamics of ritual can both approaches be correct? Of course, the apparent contradiction between these approaches is largely a matter of emphasis. Yet their stark polarization highlights the fact that our most influential theories of ritual use it to solve *other* questions, particularly those raised by bifurcations of culture and society, and stasis and change.[7] One result of this orientation is the relatively little attention paid to how rituals themselves change or to why a community's sense of appropriate ritual changes. When these questions are discussed, the results are often rather strained.

Indeed, Turner was led to characterize the post-Vatican II Catholic Mass as a 'hackwork of contemporaneous improvisation' in contrast to 'authentic ritual', which he defined as the 'outcome of . . . generations of shared and directly transmitted social life'.[8] Certainly Turner's tendency to see authentic ritual as 'liberated from historical determinations' left him little methodological room for analyzing how and why Catholic liturgy has changed today.[9] Yet much the same can also

---

[5] Emile Durkheim, *The Elementary Structures of the Religious Life*, tr. J. W. Swain (New York: Free Press 1965). Originally published in 1912.

[6] Clifford Geertz, *The Interpretation of Cultures* (New York: Basic Books 1973), 44–45, 48, 89, 113, 127, etc.

[7] Catherine Bell, 'Discourse and Dichotomies: The Structure of Ritual Theory', *Religion* 17 (1987), 95–118.

[8] Victor Turner, 'Ritual, Tribal and Catholic', *Worship* 50 (November 1976), 507, 523–24.

[9] Ibid., 524.

be said of Clifford Geertz's famous analysis of another equally 'modern' ritual scenario, the Javanese funeral ritual that 'failed to function properly'.[10] Indeed, with an initial definition of ritual as integrating cultural values and social ethos so as to bring about personal detachment and communal harmony, Geertz is forced to imply that this funeral, which failed to do just that, barely qualifies as ritual – despite the fact that things were done and words were said by which a child was buried and formalities of mourning were observed. In both cases, Turner and Geertz bypass analysis of that which constituted effective ritual for the people involved in favour of illustrating what ritual should be.

Turner and Geertz portray modern modifications of older ritual traditions as chaotic and unsatisfactory at least in part, I would suggest, because such modifications violate reigning scholarly assumptions about ritual and its social role, according to which ritual functions either to transcend historical change or as a medium for the smooth, ongoing and unconscious accommodation of change. It is possible, however, that ritual is not intrinsically concerned with resisting or embracing change. Although ritual may be mobilized for either purpose, a focus on ritual and change will be of little use when it comes to analyzing how and why rituals themselves change. A more useful approach would incorporate the many insights of Turner's and Geertz's work, while not similarly restricting ritual's social role. Such an approach would attempt to identify dynamics intrinsic to ritual that, on the one hand, enable it to serve unchanging tradition *or* cultural adaptation, while on the other also make apparent the logic by which rituals are altered. Recent scholarship provides many resources for just such a social-analytical approach to ritual dynamics. While a complete development of this theory is beyond the scope of this paper, its basic principles can be sketched out briefly.

First of all, observers of the social performance of ritual often point out that rites are not composed of unique acts that occur only in the context of rite. Rather, ritual is a *way* of acting. As a way of acting, however, ritual is intrinsically concerned with distinguishing itself from other ways of acting. Thus, it is probably more appropriate to use the term 'ritualization' to refer to a way of doing certain activities that differentiates those activities from other, more conventional ones. The ritualized activities gain a special status by this type of contrast. For example, distinctions between eating a regular meal and participating in the Christian eucharistic meal are drawn in numerous ways in

---

[10] Clifford Geertz, 'Ritual and Social Change: A Javanese Example', in *The Interpretation of Cultures*, 146.

nearly every aspect of the ritualized meal. Some of the most obvious social strategies for distinguishing a special eucharistic meal involve gathering a larger community to participate in it, establishing a distinctive periodicity for repetition of the rite, highlighting the insufficiency of the food for physical nourishment, and so on. However, theoretically, ritualization of the meal could employ a different set of strategies to differentiate it from conventional eating – holding the meal only once in a lifetime or with too much food for normal nourishment, and so on. Which strategies are used would depend on which could most effectively render the meal distinct from and symbolically dominant to its conventional counterparts. Given this analysis, ritualization could involve the exact repetition of a centuries-old tradition or deliberately radical innovation and improvisation.

It is in the orchestration of such strategic schemes that ritualization distinguishes certain things from others, attests to values inherent in such distinctions, and affords participants an experience of these distinctions as grounded in the nature of reality. Yet the strategies of ritualization themselves are little more than the production of a series of weighted oppositions in which one side of the opposition quietly dominates the other side – as 'spiritual' nourishment, for example, dominates 'physical' nourishment. Through their orchestration in the course of the rite, whole sets of these oppositions will also come to dominate other sets.[11] For example, in the traditional Catholic Mass discussed by Turner, the scheme of a 'centred' community versus a dispersed one is generated as people congregate together at a specific place and time. When assembled, this scheme is overlaid with a higher versus lower opposition in which a raised altar and host, lifting and lowering voices and eyes, standing and kneeling, and so on, all generate a contrast between a higher reality and a lower one. This scheme is overlaid in turn by an inner versus outer opposition when that higher reality is internalized through the food shared by participants. Ultimately, inner/outer will nuance the oppositions of higher/lower and centred/dispersed to generate an experience of spiritual authority as an internalized reality.

The basic dynamics of ritual, therefore, can be seen to involve two processes. First, ritualization is itself a matter of drawing strategic contrasts between the acts being performed and those being contrasted or mimed. Second, the schemes established by ritualization are impressed upon participants as deriving from a reality beyond the activities of the group. Participants embody these schemes of

---

[11] See Pierre Bourdieu, *Outline of a Theory of Practice*, tr. R. Nice (Cambridge: Cambridge University Press 1977), 114–30, for a discussion of ritual strategies.

perception and interpretation and deploy them in their social world. Such embodied schemes enable ritual participants to perceive and interpret their world in ways that facilitate the domination and validation of the values attested in the rite. Ritualization is, therefore, a type of creative socialization. It is most effective and most heavily used in communities that differentiate themselves from other groups on the basis of distinctions ascribed to the very nature of reality. Hence, some ritualization will attend the activities of a board of trustees, more ritualization will attend the activities of a national community, even more the activities of a sectarian community claiming a unique revelation.

This approach to ritual activities suggests that an ethos of timeless continuity based on the exact repetition of unchanging tradition is only one strategy of ritualization – one that creates a particular contrast between eternity and truth on the one hand and the daily, provisional and false on the other. Likewise, ritual activities that orchestrate an integration of tradition and historically new circumstances may equip the ritualized actor with other schemes, ones more effective perhaps for an individual negotiation of religion in pluralist communities. Finally, this approach also suggests that when the strategic schemes of the ritual can no longer effectively interpret and dominate the social milieu, then these schemes will shift.

There is no better way to illustrate these conclusions than by turning again to the Roman Catholic Mass. It is an excellent 'test' for a comprehensive analysis of ritual and social change, since it has demonstrated both exemplary stability and sudden and radical innovation. In addition, our relative familiarity with the historical contexts of Christian liturgy makes it possible to analyze a succession of ways in which the forms of this rite interacted with their socio-historical contexts. It is no less pertinent as well that the field of ritual studies has been at something of a loss in addressing recent developments – opting, in the main, to judge the liturgical revolution of the last twenty years as an aberration of sorts, a symptom perhaps of religion's feeble and undignified disarray in the face of the forces of secularity. However, even a cursory analysis of the schemes of these new ritual formulations within the context of the history of the Christian Mass reveals something more vital.

Indeed, various historical formulations of the Mass reveal quite different relations to the historical moment or its transcendence. For example, the eucharistic rites of the first few centuries of the Christian era appear to have involved a conscious sense of historicity that does not fit neatly with either Turner's or Geertz's approaches. These rites celebrated an event that occurred in time, occasioned the historical establishment of a community of the faithful, and anticipated a further historical agenda for the world. According to Dix, the emphasis within these rites was on the *doing* of certain actions, those thought to have been done before by Christ.[12] There was no equal importance to what was said, nor was the invocation of devout feelings thought necessary. This ritual meal was, above all, an *anamnesis*, a reappropriated enactment of the passion of Christ that simultaneously gave thanks for the events themselves, handed the story on to others, and grounded the particular community in the lived example of Christ.[13]

On the other hand, the strictly standardized Tridentine liturgy formulated in the 1570 Roman Missal systematically invoked that transcendence of time which Turner saw as a feature of all authentic ritual. In that Mass, the historicity of Christ and his community of the faithful gave way to the eternity of the church and the miracle of 'transubstantiation'.[14] The emphasis was not so much on what was done as on what was *said* – the words that made this miracle occur. The dramatic words of consecration and adoration became the new crescendo, while the communal consumption of the consecrated food fell into a longer concluding sequence. Theologically as well, history became allegory, while the laity became passive witnesses to the drama unfolding in the often incomprehensible cadences of the priest's Latin.[15]

A few scholars have attempted to illustrate how the form and activities of this Mass both reflected and affected its social milieu. John Bossy, for example, finds the expression of a particular social doctrine in the medieval Mass by its representation of major social groups and their access to sources of power. Through the orchestration of components of sacrifice and sacrament, entreaties for the living and the dead, and distinctions between 'friends' and 'enemies', the medieval Mass impressed upon participants a variety of schemes and values, such as strategies for avenging oneself on enemies, channelling social violence, legitimating social hierarchies, and acknowledging a transcendently unified community. Bossy goes on to contrast this Mass with those of the Reformers, whose theological objections were inseparable from new social demands.[16] Keith Thomas has also

---

[12] Gregory Dix, *The Shape of the Liturgy* (New York: Seabury 1983; first edition 1945), 12–15.

[13] Bard Thompson, *Liturgies of the Western Church* (New York: New American Library 1961), 17.

[14] Thompson, 42–43.

[15] Thompson, 46–49.

[16] John Bossy, 'Essai de sociographie de la messe, 1200–1700', *Annales, Economies, Sociétés, Civilisations* 36 (Jan.–Feb. 1981), 16–25.

demonstrated the social role of the medieval liturgy, noting its need to compete with surprisingly resilient rival systems of belief and practice. In the total organization of its ritual corpus, he finds, late medieval Christianity claimed both the transcendent identity of church and society and the impregnable hold of the official church on the here and now of local affairs.[17]

The ritual schemes embodied by participants in these two types of liturgies certainly differed as dramatically as the social circumstances of the church in these two periods in history. The same is true of the Mass after the liturgical reforms of this century.

Some observers at Vatican II were surprised that the opening sessions addressed matters of liturgical reform. It is now widely recognized, however, that the guidelines issued by the Council for 'a general restoration of the liturgy' did more to change the face of the church and individual experience within it than any other resolutions.[18] Even while the Council portrayed the liturgy as 'the summit toward which the activity of the Church is directed', it was actually dismantling a towering mountain of centuries of unified worship.[19] Indeed, the central liturgical issue facing the Council – universal unity of practice versus the need for cultural adaptation to local communities – fundamentally challenged the theology and tradition of the Roman liturgy.[20] What have emerged from local applications of the conciliar guidelines appear to be very distinctive strategies of ritualization.

Most dramatically, the communal aspects of the liturgy were again strongly emphasized in the prominence given to lay understanding and participation, but also in the recognition of a place for local cultural traditions within the liturgy. This was not a return to the ethos of the early church, however. The Council had reasoned that there were parts of the rite instituted by Christ himself that could not be changed; yet those considered to have been instituted by the church might be.[21] Thus, the Council recognized both unchanging and changing aspects of the liturgy in a way that would recognize the historical and particular only in relation to the eternal and the

---

[17] Keith Thomas, *Religion and the Decline of Magic* (New York: Scribner's 1971), 151–53. Also see Natalie Zemon Davis, 'From "Popular Religion" to Religious Cultures', in Steven Ozment, ed., *Reformation Europe: A Guide to Research* (St Louis: Center for Reformation Research 1982), 321–43.

[18] Constitution on the Sacred Liturgy, no. 21.

[19] Ibid., no. 3.

[20] A. Bugnini and C. Braga, eds, *The Commentary on the Constitution and on the Instruction of the Sacred Liturgy*, tr. V. P. Mallon (New York: Benziger Brothers 1965), 13, 100. Also see Godfrey L. Diekmann, 'Is there a Distinct American Contribution to the Liturgical Renewal?', *Worship* 45 (November 1971), 578–87.

[21] Bugnini and Braga, 84.

universal. Indeed, the interplay of these two aspects of the rite depicts a *proper* relation between the universal, unchanging church and the particular community. The postconciliar Mass frequently presents itself as a 'celebration' of the particular community that is constituted in the ritual. As such, the Mass is an act of self-recognition by which the assembled group experiences itself as 'the church'. The accompanying ethos may be the quiet orchestration of symbols of the group's identity or the over-enthusiastic outpouring of idiomatic self-assertion that offended Turner.

The 'medium' of this expression of communal ritual emphasizes neither what is 'done' nor what is 'said' – despite a high degree of performance and very explicit dialogue. Rather, the emphasis is on 'expression'. In the postconciliar Mass Catholics 'express' themselves.[22] The ritual schemes implicitly foster participants' expression of themselves both as a community and as 'the church' by assuming that the basis for any and all community resides within each person. That is, the basis for liturgical community is not ascribed to anything in the social, historical or cultural environment, nor to simple obedience to traditional church authority and custom. Rather, a basis for community within each person is evoked, expressed and experienced in this form of ritualization.

The language of this type of liturgical community was particularly apparent in the self-presentation of American Catholics to Pope John Paul II during his 1987 visit. Lay spokespersons in particular made it clear that their identities as Catholics were based on the recognition that Rome rules not from without but from within – by virtue of the inner respect and humility that each Catholic willingly finds in him or herself, and which they need to have recognized.[23] Yet at times the Pope appeared to be on the other side of the gap that has opened between Roman ecclesiastical structure and the results of a new liturgical logic. No longer does Catholic identity reside in specific acts and verbalizations, in obedience to ecclesiastic authority, or in affiliation with a universal church. Rather, Catholic identity now lies in dynamics of self-expression instituted and nourished in a liturgical medium by which a group of individuals is empowered to experience themselves as a particular manifestation of the church. Indeed,

---

[22] Many have noted the prominence of 'self-expression' in various aspects of modern life in general. In particular, see the discussions of 'expressive individualism', in Robert Bellah et al., *Habits of the Heart: Individualism and Commitment in American Life* (New York: Harper and Row 1985), 32–35 and 333–34.

[23] See the remarks of Donna Hanson, chairwoman of the US Bishops' National Advisory Council, in her address to the Pope on September 18 in San Francisco, printed in 'Meeting US Laity', *Origins* 17 (15 October 1987), 320–21.

this liturgically forged and promoted identity may well be the basis for the further emergence of lay challenges to the local leadership of bishops that was laid out in the Constitution on the Liturgy.

Turner continued his critique of liturgical change in Catholicism by decrying 'the tendentious manipulation of particular interest groups', the abandonment of 'the spiritual for the material', and the use of 'jaunty verbal formulations' to 'express' the 'relevancy' of the sacred in its latest secular wrappings. All this, he maintained, was 'clean counter to all anthropological experience'.[24] Hardly! Rather, we can observe strategies in these liturgies that imbue participants with the sense that as persons in community they can orchestrate this rite and their relation to God. The immediate participants may not share common traditions, political consensus, or social values, but through this new means of ritualizing the traditional eucharistic meal they can embody schemes that render such assumptions unnecessary in establishing a modern and effective religious community.

The Mass as it emerges in these three formulations is significantly different in each case because of the great shifts in the political, social and institutional status of the church and its members. In each case the particular ritual schemes of the Mass functioned in their specific socio-historical milieu to make strategic distinctions that defined both community and personal identity in effective ways. At times the repetition of an unchanging rite was such a strategy. In other times, the freedom to innovate and adapt will be an appropriate and effective way of ritualizing. While the foregoing examples have been too brief to do full justice to the social dynamics of these three examples of the Mass, they suggest that such dynamics were both socially direct and complex. They also suggest that with regard to accommodating or transcending historical change, the Mass has not functioned in any one way. Thus, the intrinsic purpose of ritual is too narrowly conceived if it is tied simply to the issue of social change – a problem that may loom unnaturally large to sociologists of religion due to the historical peculiarities of how the study of religion has differentiated itself from the practice of religion. Ritualization can function either to accommodate history or to deny it. Moreover, in those circumstances in which the 'proper' rite cannot be performed or an improvised ritual fails to evoke the expected ethos – as in the muddled Javanese funeral witnessed by Geertz – the participants still possess and re-embody strategies with which to express an adequate or potentially powerful articulation of the values by which the community orders and reorders the events and emotions of their lives.

---

[24] Turner, 24–26.

Liturgical renewal illuminates the poverty of traditional ritual theory. The phenomenon of the liturgical movement as well as the scholarship that it has generated challenges nonsectarian scholars of ritual to be both better historians of the traditions within their own cultures and better sociologists of the impact of 'relevant' ritual on modern life.

★★★

The authority of ritual experts

It should give us pause that representatives of so many different fields can gather to discuss issues of ritual and liturgy, with liturgical scholars joined by anthropologists, sociologists, historians, and historians of religions. Not only is it interesting that there is sufficient consensus to pull us all into the same room to listen to each other, it is also remarkable that there now exist so many different types of professional expertise on ritual issues. I am not content simply to marvel at this state of affairs. Instead I would like to take this convergence of different ritual experts as *data* for analysis and as evidence of certain developments in the way we are all thinking about ritual. Hence, instead of simply reflecting on ritual issues, I want to reflect on our conjoined efforts of reflection. While this will directly invoke the problem of 'authority' that has been an explicit focus for this conference, we shall first have to deal with the authority of ritual experts before addressing the authority of ritual. I hope to show how closely intertwined these authorities can be.

Questions and issues

The issue of authoritative ritual has been distilled into the three specific questions that I was asked to address. Allow me to lay these questions out and then suggest how I would like to approach them.

The first question asked if it is not possible to generate a theoretical model of ritual that simultaneously respects the rites, the participants in those rites, and the social scientists analyzing them. Certainly there are good reasons for wanting such a theory. Yet social scientists – by whom I simply mean anthropologists, sociologists, and historians of religions among others – are more clearly aware than ever before that there is no single, total, and true-for-everyone view of things. Not only are the goals of ritual participants and ritual scholars quite different, but their medium is vastly different. I have always been suspicious when the scholarly enterprise is readily analogized with the ritual one. Can ritual replace scholarship or scholarship substitute for ritual? As I have argued elsewhere, much modern scholarship rests on a *very* fundamental, if contrived, distinction between observers and doers; when observers claim to have transcended this difference, I wonder whether the so-called doers would really agree with them.[25]

Nonetheless, we are not totally without some form of common ground. The notion of ritual itself has emerged as a relatively neutral theoretical construct, more or less acceptable to a variety of parties: spokespersons of liturgical traditions, ritual participants, and social scientists. As such, the notion of ritual directly facilitates gatherings such as this one. Yet the reality behind the term still means different things to all of us, and those meanings are often much more determined than we recognize.

The second question asked how one goes about analyzing both the internal dynamics intrinsic to ritual and the external pressures to which rituals respond. Clearly one of the underlying issues here is change: does ritual mirror social change, resist it, follow it, or lead it? How do we reconcile expectations of authoritative ritual as stable and consistent with what appear to be real social needs for constant adaptation and transformation? And ultimately there is concern that the current changes in ritual life seem so much more chaotic than the smooth dynamics suggested by anthropological models.

The third question concerned evaluation of post-Vatican II liturgical reforms, especially in terms of the power of ritual to shape modern Catholic identity and to affect the relationship between the historically defined centralized tradition on the one hand and plural forms of cultural adaptation and ritual expression on the other. I am insufficiently knowledgeable, both formally and practically, to offer any substantive observations about post-Vatican II liturgies. However, I would like to refer to some critiques that have been made within liturgical studies, as well as the whole issue of evaluation – the criteria, goals, expectations, idiom, and, of course, the experts who do the evaluating.

In order to develop responses to these three questions – I will not commit myself to answers – it is necessary to re-contextualize them. At bottom, I want to show that they are questions that emerge in a particular social and historical situation vis-à-vis ritual. They are, that is, the questions of a specific class of ritual experts. I want to explore various types of ritual experts and their roles in defining, shaping, and sometimes magnifying ritual, in establishing the authority of ritual

---

[25] See Catherine Bell, *Ritual Theory, Ritual Practice* (New York: Oxford University Press 1992). For the opposite point of view, one that attempts to synthesize sociology and theology, see Kieran Flanagan, *Sociology and Liturgy: Re-presentations of the Holy* (New York: St Martin's Press 1991).

and diagnosing its problems, and in orchestrating specific relationships between liturgical and social change. To do this is to reconstruct the particular perspective on ritual that has generated these questions. An appreciation of some of the contingent forces that have shaped this perspective may help put questions and answers in a new light.

Alternative model of the ritual expert

What are ritual experts? A number of ritual experts are familiar from well-known ethnographies, though primarily in their role as informants – figures such as the blind Ogotemmeli of the Dogon described by Marcel Griaule, or Muchona the Hornet, the Ndembu healer described by Victor Turner. Yet aside from suggestions here and there, no one has systematically probed the relationships among classes of ritual experts, ritual practices, and corresponding views of what ritual activity is all about. Certainly, the general invisibility of professional ritualists helps to promote the old but still powerful model in which the only effective or authentic ritual is that which rises up spontaneously from the community by means of faceless social forces. Such a model presents problems for liturgical scholars dealing with the history and future of Christian ritual. Indeed, this model has led one liturgical scholar to observe: 'It is unheard of, say anthropologists, that rites expressing living belief should be devised and decreed by so-called ritual experts. I suspect they are right.'[26] If they are right, then liturgists will have a hard time understanding where they have come from and making sense of what they can actually do. But I don't think they are right. The role of ritual experts in devising and decreeing rites is in fact much more widespread, dynamic, and complicated than most current models would lead us to suppose.

It is useful to recount very briefly a specific historical scenario that for me has provided a useful counterpoint to many ahistorical ethnographic treatments of ritual. It is drawn from the history of Taoism in fifth-century China, a highly literate, stratified, and very ritualized society. The full story illustrates a variety of levels of ritual experts, texts, institutions, social movements, and changing definitions of authority, but a synopsis can focus simply on the figure of Lu

---

[26] Mary Collins, 'Liturgical Methodology and the Cultural Evolution of Worship in the United States', *Worship* 49 (1975), 87. Collins has noted that more recent sociological and anthropological models have begun to come to terms with ritual as a function of more complex social processes, as seen in the work of Clifford Geertz and Victor Turner: see Mary Collins, 'Critical Ritual Studies: Examining an Intersection of Theology and Culture', in *The Bent World: Essays on Religion and Culture,* ed. John R. May (Chico, CA: Scholars Press 1981), 132. Yet I find these very popular models still somewhat misleading when used in liturgical studies.

Hsiu-ching.[27] In the middle of the fifth century Master Lu began to gather up and edit a set of scriptures that claimed to have been revealed the century before. In fact two major sets of scriptures appeared in the fourth century, the first predicting the end of the world, the other appearing after the predicted date of destruction had passed by uneventfully.

In sorting through these texts and the various imitations of them that had proliferated, Master Lu found that '[true] scriptures and worldly writings have become mixed up . . . the pure and the vulgar are confused, the true and the false are practiced together'.[28] He concluded that the second set of revelations were the final, culminating revelation of the Tao in human history, and he gave them a special place in the first Taoist canon. Master Lu also drew on these revelations to compose an important set of liturgical manuals that would be the basis for much of the subsequent tradition of Taoist ritual.

An interesting unity underlies Lu's projects. His canonization of the scriptures closed off any further revelations, at least any authentic ones. And Taoist practice, which had depended to a great extent on securing and venerating these scriptural texts, was put on a new footing, a specifically liturgical footing. 'In this generation', wrote Master Lu, 'devotees are both numerous and widespread. They cannot all be given scriptures.'[29] Therefore, he concludes, they should perform the ritual of the Spiritual Treasures. This ritual was a modified version of an older rite to which Master Lu gave new scriptural legitimation. Before this, wealthy devotees sought to buy copies of the scriptures in order to acquire the celestial boons promised to those who venerated the texts; but Master Lu made these boons available to all in a liturgical format – freely, but indirectly available to all through the mediation of the ritual expert. For Master Lu everything was to be subordinated to this liturgical development, even study of the scriptures. 'Now in studying the Tao', he wrote, 'nothing comes before [the ritual of the Spiritual Treasures] . . . To study without cultivating [this ritual] is like travelling blindly at night without a burning lamp.' For Lu, performing this ritual was 'the first step in studying the Tao'.[30]

Master Lu can be said to have 'ritualized' the scriptural texts by making their promises and benefits accessible to all through the

---

[27] For the basic Chinese and Western sources, see Catherine Bell, 'Ritualization of Texts and Textualization of Ritual in the Codification of Taoist Liturgy', *History of Religions* 27 (1988), 366–92; also Isabelle Robinet, *Histoire du taoisme des origines au XIVe siècle* (Paris: Les Éditions du Cerf 1991), 151–81.

[28] Bell, 'Ritualization of Texts', 373.

[29] Ibid., 386.

[30] Ibid., 387.

performance of ritual. At the same time, however, he also 'textualized' these new rituals, synthesizing older and newer practices into a set of liturgical manuals that became the authoritative basis for the ordained Taoist ritual masters who would shape so much of the religious life of traditional China. This shift in the basis of Taoist practice from the somewhat chaotic transmission of revealed texts to liturgical practices and the organized transmission of liturgical manuals controlled by ordained priests was decisive in generating a coherent ritual tradition and enduring post-millennial Taoist institutions.

Experts and ritual change

The story of Master Lu illustrates a form of ritual change that is not often seen in the ethnographic literature – one person 'devising' a compelling synthesis of practices that successfully becomes the basis for an organized liturgical community. His work was not in a vacuum, of course. There were precursors and older ritual customs; there were current practices with which his rites competed and some of which they absorbed; and there were subsequent elaborations, modifications, and even major revisions. Yet the story of Master Lu demonstrates that under certain circumstances ritual experts exert considerable influence on the form and content of ritual life. And there are many other examples of ritual experts devising rites that subsequent history deemed legitimate and successful.

One Californian New Age movement, for example, appointed a few members to sit down and design a complete set of communal rituals that expressed their beliefs and ideals. Devised as a total package, these rites were regularly and effectively performed for about twenty years until the group changed in decisive ways for a host of other reasons.[31]

A recent study of men's fraternal organizations in the nineteenth and twentieth centuries describes the emergence of the elaborate rituals that were, the author argues, the main attraction of associations such as the Freemasons and the Odd Fellows. Before most of these groups shrank dramatically in the mid-twentieth century, some actively solicited members to submit plans for rituals with prize money for the 'best rite'.[32]

Particularly interesting is the development and introduction in the former USSR of a full system of socialist rituals beginning in the

[31] Steven M. Gelber and Martin L. Cook, *Saving the Earth: A History of a Middle-class Millenarian Movement* (Berkeley: University of California Press 1990).

[32] Mark C. Carnes, *Secret Ritual and Manhood in Victorian America* (New Haven: Yale University Press 1989).

early 1960s. Contrary to the views of some western interpreters at the time, these civic rites were generally well received and socially effective, even though they were designed and revised in government offices by various scholar-bureaucrats for the purpose of social control and political indoctrination.[33] Of course, despite the hopes of these ritual specialists, ritual alone could not maintain the unity of a complex entity like the Soviet empire.

Just as ritual experts can create rites or initiate major changes in their practice, they can also retard evolution and adaptation – the most famous example of this phenomenon being the Roman Rite codified in the sixteenth century by the Council of Trent and performed with little alteration until the twentieth century. Yet the rites to Confucius that are observed annually even today in government-supported temples in Taiwan and Singapore go back even further in time with even less overt change, thanks to the incredible conservatism of a long succession of ministers of the now-defunct imperial Board of Rites. For those mandarins and their modern successors, conserving is what ritual is all about.

Sometimes ritual experts have made significant innovations in content, form, or interpretation, while presenting their rites as immutably true to ancient precedents. A good illustration is the Shinto enthronement ceremony, especially the rite of the 'Great Harvest Offerings' (*daijosai*), most recently enacted in November 1990 when Akihito ascended the throne after the death of his father Hirohito. Although these rites go very far back in Japanese history, how they are done, what is left out and what is included, and above all the significance given to their symbolism have been quite differently nuanced over time. The rites for Akihito were 'traditional' in almost every way, but their significance for imperial divinity was construed quite differently.[34]

In other situations, however, long traditions of rituals and experts have been suddenly and painfully abandoned – as in the emergence of messianic and prophetic movements in Africa, cargo cults in New Guinea, or the inter-tribal Ghost Dance of the American Plains Indians. The anthropologist James Fernandez has described how younger members of the Bwiti cult, an African reform movement, kept suggesting modifications of the 'old-fashioned' symbols used by

---

[33] Christel Lane, *The Rites of Rulers: Ritual In Industrial Society – The Soviet Case* (Cambridge: Cambridge University Press 1981); Jennifer McDowell, 'Soviet Civil Ceremonies', *Journal for the Scientific Study of Religion* 13 (1974), 265–79.

[34] Steven R. Weisman, 'Emperor's Ritual Bed Keeps Secrets', *New York Times*, October 9, 1990; 'Japan Enthrones Emperor Today in Old Rite with New Twist', *New York Times*, November 12, 1990; 'Akihito Performs Solitary Rite as Some Question Its Meaning', *New York Times*, November 23, 1990.

their elderly leader. At first there was no open criticism and small changes were made; but eventually the old leader was publicly challenged and he angrily told the disputants they were free to go elsewhere. Three-quarters of the group immediately did so, and most of the others gradually drifted over to the new cult house that was started in the village. In the end, the old leader had to join them too, closing his own cult house and doing the rites their way, or else he would have been an expert without a clientele.[35]

In his well-known analysis of a Javanese funeral for a young boy, Clifford Geertz has described ritual change at one of its particularly awkward stages – when the traditional ritual leadership began to balk at new circumstances, thereby forcing a new and *ad hoc* form of leadership to emerge. The results were not very satisfactory to everyone, yet no one felt the rite had to be redone.[36]

In contrast to oversimplified models of ritual, all these examples demonstrate that various types of 'so-called ritual experts' – traditional ones, new ones, *ad hoc* ones, etc. – have routinely 'devised and decreed' ritual practices. These examples also illustrate what we already know but tend to keep forgetting: that ritual is no *one* thing, no *one* way of acting, no *one* socio-political scenario; that ritual is not intrinsically rigid and unchanging; that effective ritual need not spontaneously well up from grassroots communities; nor need it develop smoothly, invulnerable to social upheavals, political manipulation, or power relationships. Why are we so drawn to the opposite, highly romanticized view of ritual – that of authentic ritual as unchanging, spontaneous, and harmonious? Part of the answer may lie in styles of ritualization, but part of it may also lie in the various ways ritual experts shape the practice and understanding of ritual.

Oral and literate forms of ritual expertise

Most theories of ritual have been rooted in ethnographic observations of oral societies. While such ethnography underscores the fact that there is nothing *simple* about such ritual systems, it can be convincingly argued that the ritual life of oral societies differs in significant ways from that of societies in which writing, literacy, and the printing press have defined new forms of authority and community. It has been suggested, for example, that cultural change takes different forms in these two types of societies: the transmission of

---

[35] James Fernandez, 'Symbolic Consensus in a Fang Reformative Cult', *American Anthropologist* 67 (1965), 902–29, especially 914–15.

[36] Clifford Geertz, 'Ritual and Social Change: A Javanese Example', in *The Interpretation of Cultures* (New York: Basic Books 1973), 142–69.

myth in stable oral societies tends to involve constant adaptation that keeps the myth in a 'homeostatic' relationship with the concerns of the community. Written texts, on the other hand, introduce new problems with change, since variation from the text as well as variation among texts is readily apparent, producing conflict or contradiction.[37]

The oral process of change is seen in the way in which royal genealogies were transmitted in traditional Tahiti. Because the noble houses claimed direct descent from divine beings, genealogies were important to legitimate the reigning chief's claim to the throne. These genealogies were embedded in myths recited at important festivals, and it was understood that the recitation could not contain any errors or the priest who made the mistake could be executed. This implied that the oral genealogical record was protected from mistakes and manipulation. However, when the dynasty did change, the traditional myth had to be brought into accord with the new political situation. To do so, the priests made small unobtrusive errors every time they recited them, until it was fully adapted. Officially nothing changed; in actuality, it was changing almost all the time.[38]

As this story suggests, change is construed as a constant and relatively unproblematic occurrence in oral societies because the closest thing to an *Ur* myth, *Ur* genealogy, or *Ur* ritual resides only in people's memories, as competing variants, always embodied in a particular situation. Changes can be routinely made in ritual and yet, without records that cast one version as original or true, such changes can be denied, ignored, or easily rationalized. For example, among the Dayak of Borneo there was the custom of making a foundation sacrifice when erecting a building like a large longhouse. A slave was placed in the hole dug for the main pillar of the house, and killed when the pillar was pounded into place. Under Dutch colonial administration, however, this practice was prohibited. Hence, the ritual was modified: a water buffalo was sacrificed in the pit instead of a slave and the myth altered to explain that in the time of the ancestors a slave who had been thrown into the pit had turned into a water buffalo.[39] Of course this story does not mean that no one noticed

---

[37] See Jack Goody and Ian Watt, 'The Consequences of Literacy', in *Literacy in Traditional Societies*, ed. Jack R. Goody (Cambridge: Cambridge University Press 1968), 27–68.

[38] Th. P. van Baaren, 'The Flexibility of Myth' in *Sacred Narrative: Readings in the Theory of Myth*, ed. Alan Dundes (Berkeley: University of California 1984), 218, citing J. Guiart, *Les Religions de l'Océanie* (Paris: Presses Universitaires de France 1962), 100. For other manipulative genealogical practices that support Van Baaren's point, see Douglas L. Oliver, *Ancient Tahitian Society* (Honolulu: University of Hawaii Press 1974), 624–25, 1117, 1179–81.

[39] Van Baaren, 'The Flexibility of Myth', 219, citing Hans Sharer, 'Die Bedeutung des Menschenopfers im dajakischen Totenkult', *Mitteilungsblatt der deutschen Gesellschaft für Völkerkunde* (Hamburg 1940), 25.

or cared about the difference in the rites. It was probably a big problem requiring lots of discussion and disagreement. Eventually, however, a consensus was reached on how to amend the rite and the myth. Yet the issue of truthfulness as a matter of conforming to what exactly happened at some point in the past was probably not the issue that was most important for an oral community.

The role of myth and ritual in oral societies is to enhance, enforce, and codify cultural attitudes, something they can do best if they are continually brought into some sort of fit with the current circumstances of the community. How effective the ritual modifications will be depends on many other circumstances beyond the ritual arena *per se*. There is also evidence that not all components of a rite can change equally well or easily.[40] Moreover, the community can play an important role in maintaining adherence to remembered conventions or ratifying departures from custom.[41]

In this social context, the authority of the ritual expert and the authority of the ritual itself are rooted in tradition – yet tradition is something that exists nowhere but in its flexible embodiment in memory and in current cultural life. Ritual must have both a convincing continuity with remembered rites and a convincing coherence with community life. As one of the most visible embodiments of tradition in oral societies, ritual ratifies the traditional in general, even as it recreates it in the specifics of each performance.[42]

Research on the effects of writing and literacy suggest that the emergence of literate social classes has important ramifications for ritual practice, for the perceptions of tradition, and for the locus of ritual authority.[43] First of all, written records lead to what can be called an historical consciousness, the realization that today is different from yesterday, that life now differs significantly from what it was

---

[40] Despite such flexible mechanisms for adaptation, however, ritual practices in oral societies clearly demonstrate some fixity of structure, as Roy Rappaport's work on the 'canonical' and 'indexical' dimensions of ritual practices illustrates. See Roy A. Rappaport, 'The Obvious Aspects of Ritual', in *Ecology, Meaning, and Religion* (Richmond, CA: North Atlantic Books 1979), 179.

[41] Valerio Valeri, *Kingship and Sacrifice: Ritual and Society in Ancient Hawaii* (Chicago: University of Chicago Press 1985).

[42] Mary Douglas, *Natural Symbols* (New York: Random House 1973), 86–87, suggests that the number of ritual experts, their social importance and formality of office may be linked to degrees of social hierarchy and stratification. Valeri's study demonstrates that the power of their positions can be constrained by competing forms of ritual expertise (*Kingship and Sacrifice*, 135–40).

[43] According to Jack Goody, *The Interface between the Written and the Oral* (Cambridge: Cambridge University Press 1987), xii, it is a mistake to divide societies into oral and literate, since literacy never completely replaces orality. He makes the distinction nonetheless, and so will I, but the point is well taken and certainly has ramifications for ritual.

in the past. Writing opens a gap between the past and the present.[44] Secondly, writing down activity creates a prescriptive and normative account. As we saw with Master Lu's written codes for ritual activity, what I called 'the textualization of ritual', they shifted authority from those who received visions to those who controlled transmission and interpretation of the texts – from self-proclaimed visionaries and prophets to ordained priests and trained scholars.

Indeed, with the emergence of authoritative texts and the sense of an historical gap, tradition itself comes to be understood differently: no longer directly embodied in custom and actual practice, tradition is now that which is described in and represented by texts; it is something to be reproduced as stipulated, to preserve and protect from change. As the historical gap widens, the need to link immutable historical sources with very mutable living communities gives rise to complex institutions of interpretive experts mediating the past and present. Authority tends to reside in the written rules and, by extension, in those who know them and interpret them, like Master Lu, who claimed to differentiate the true from the false scriptures, the original revelations from the imitations. 'Once writing was introduced,' writes the anthropologist Jack Goody, 'the voice of God was supplemented by His hand; scriptural authority is the authority of the written (scripted) word, not the oral one.' Written religion, he continues, brings heightened stratification, differentiating the priest to whom the written word belongs from the rest of the people who receive instruction.[45]

As writing redefines a tradition's socio-religious authority, so ritual itself comes to be understood and even used differently. No longer is ritual a matter of doing what it seems people have always done; it becomes the correct performance or enactment of the textual script. The audience has little right or opportunity to approve or disapprove, since only those who have access to the texts know whether it is being done correctly or not. In this framework, prayers are 'recited' or 'repeated', the liturgy is 'followed' or 'read', and aging linguistic forms create a separate and professional liturgical language.

In an oral society, the embodiment of tradition can flexibly change to keep pace with the community and win its assent as true to tradition and appropriate to the current climate. Ritual changes without necessarily being very concerned with change as such. But in literate societies with written models, change easily becomes a

---

[44] Goody and Watt, 'The Consequences of Literacy', 27–68.
[45] Goody, *The Interface Between the Written and the Oral*, 161.

problem threatening to tradition and authority. On the one hand, textually based ritual traditions can more readily forestall and control change because of the power of the authoritative text to act as a measure of deviance. Yet on the other hand, the textual medium affords more open access to liturgical knowledge, more explicit challenges to its meaning, legitimacy, or originality, and ultimately helps promote the rise of contending factions of experts. In comparison to change in oral societies, that in literate societies is much more apt to be deliberate, debated, ridden with factions, explosive, and concerned with fundamentals. In other words, in literate societies change is usually experienced as a mess.[46]

In addition, the textualization of ritual – the emergence of authoritative textual guidelines – has been linked to other developments such as (a) the ascendancy of so-called universal values over more local and particularistic ones; (b) the organization of larger, more bureaucratic, and centralized institutions; and (c) the formation of notions of orthodoxy versus heterodoxy, codified doctrines and formal dogma. Hence, textual ritual inevitably leads to tensions between a centralized liturgical tradition and local ritual life. Moreover, since orality is never completely displaced by literacy and some parts of social life remain predominantly oral, there are contending levels and types of ritual experts: literate experts with official positions and local folk experts with closer ties to sub-communities.

It is important to note that we do not know nearly as much as we should about ritual in literate, stratified, industrial and post-industrial societies. While some aspects of ritual in modern America appear similar to some aspects of Ndembu ritual life, many other dimensions are very different – including the general place and style of ritual. While the far-ranging effects of literacy can explain some differences, the effects of very different economic and political structures are equally important and dramatic. Ethnographic models in which ritual is central to cultural production are ill-equipped to deal with the divisions of labour, class, and knowledge found in complex political economies.[47]

---

[46] These observations follow Goody's argument, although his contrast between oral and literate societies is often too simple and stark. There are many examples of disconcerting or faction-driven change in oral societies, even though most of these examples are linked to the effects of contact with foreign or colonial powers.

[47] For a general description of the problems of studying such cultures, see Ulf Hannerz, 'Theory in Anthropology: Small Is Beautiful? The Problem of Complex Cultures', *Comparative Studies in Society and History* 28 (1986), 362–67.

Secular experts and ritual

We do know, however, that modern industrial society has given rise to a new type of ritual expert, the secular scholar, usually a non-participant or outsider who controls a new body of textual knowledge about ritual life.[48] Such secular ritual experts contrast with indigenous participants and experts in oral and literate societies. Although these are contrasts that scholars can maximize or minimize, there are lots of stories that illustrate how critical this contrast is to the social scientist's claim to objective knowledge.

There is, for example, the story of Frank Cushing, the early Smithsonian ethnologist who went to study the Zuni Indians in 1879. Uncomfortable in many ways with being an outside observer, a scientist putting Indians under a microscope, Cushing wanted to learn about being Zuni from the inside. Living and working with the Zuni for many years, he became fluent in their language and so comfortable with their customs that he was eventually adopted into the tribe and initiated as a priest and war chief. He claimed to think like a Zuni. Yet his claims to be one of them were probably not perfectly echoed by the Zuni. Indeed, the Zuni appear to have noted some significant peculiarities about Cushing, as seen from a song they composed about him:

> Once they made a White man into a Priest of the Bow
> he was out there with the other Bow priests
> he had black stripes on his body
> the others said their prayers from their hearts
> but he read his from a piece of paper.[49]

Aside from the contrast between prayers said from the heart and those read from the paper, the song also refers to Cushing's striped body paint. The Zuni call paper with writing 'that which is striped'. So it seems that Cushing's reliance on texts and writing was so strong and distinctive that the Zuni made it his emblematic design – in other words, they painted him up as a walking piece of writing.[50] Cushing would have had to stop writing if he wanted to overcome one of the most significant differences between him and the Zuni, and it is

---

[48] For an overview of the ramifications of scholarly control of texts, see James Clifford and George E. Marcus, eds, *Writing Culture: The Poetics and Politics of Ethnography* (Berkeley: University of California Press 1986), 1–26.

[49] Sam D. Gill, 'Nonliterate Traditions and Holy Books: Toward a New Model', in *The Holy Book in Comparative Perspective*, ed. Frederick M. Denny and Rodney L. Taylor (Columbia, SC: University of South Carolina Press 1985), 225.

[50] Ibid.

said that in 'going native' he did stop writing about certain things, unwilling to relate information that had been transmitted to him in confidence.[51]

The story of the early sociologist William Robertson Smith demonstrates the opposite movement in the development of the secular scholar of ritual. Smith's argument for 'totemic sacrifice' among ancient Semitic tribes pioneered the theory of ritual's social role in establishing the unity and solidarity of the group. Yet when brought to bear indirectly on the Bible, it provoked a conflict with the Free Church, a branch of the Church of Scotland, in which he was an ordained minister. He was tried for heresy and in 1881 dismissed from his professorship at the Free Church Divinity College of the University of Aberdeen.[52] The full story of how Smith's scholarly research led to a recasting of his personal faith and a renegotiation of the relationship between the Bible of belief and the demands of objective scholarship illustrates the emergence of another form of the 'us/them' boundary that has come to define secular social scientific expertise.

This new form of text-based secular expertise emerged with its own distinct understanding of its object 'ritual'.[53] It is a perspective which attempts to transcend all confessional affiliations with particular groups and in doing so defines its object as something that transcends any particular liturgical act, theological intention, and religio–cultural organization. The near universality claimed for 'ritual' *per se* as a category of analysis has meant that scholars are particularly interested in determining what are the fundamental similarities among very different ritual practices and traditions. The medium for these theoretical exercises could never be oral; this is not the mode of communication of a face-to-face community. Rather, the production of texts about ritual is intrinsic to this social science discourse and thoroughly shapes it. As Clifford and Marcus have argued so well for anthropology, investigation begins 'not with participant-observation . . . , but with writing, the making of texts'.[54]

---

[51] There is some question as to why Cushing did not complete several of his ethnographic projects; the reasons may have had less to do with idealism and more to do with Cushing's general work habits. On this point, see Christopher Winters, ed., *International Dictionary of Anthropologists* (New York: Garland 1991), 132.

[52] T.O. Beidelman, *W. Robertson Smith and the Sociological Study of Religion* (Chicago: University of Chicago Press 1974), 13–22. As Beidelman notes, the trial was technically for libel, but widely understood to concern heresy (13, 17).

[53] For a critique of this term as a 'global construct', see Jack Goody, 'Against "Ritual": Loosely Structured Thoughts on a Loosely Defined Topic', in *Secular Ritual*, ed. Sally F. Moore and Barbara C. Myerhoff (Amsterdam: Van Gorcum 1977), 25–35.

[54] Clifford and Marcus, *Writing Culture*, 2.

The importance of texts and text-making in secular studies of ritual can be seen in the case of the Berkeley linguist Frits Staal and the Nambudiri Brahmins of southwest India. In 1975 Staal organized international funding to sponsor a major twelve-day Vedic ritual, the *Atiratna-Agnicayana*, which had not been performed in some twenty years, for the express purpose of having it 'filmed and recorded' – that is, to create a documentary record. This meant twenty hours of film, eighty hours of recordings, and a mammoth two-volume analysis of nearly every detail of the rite.[55] The author saw these documents as literally *continuing* the tradition: Staal writes that his book project was 'a unique opportunity, indeed a responsibility, to continue the oral tradition by means of a book' – *his* book.[56] One doubts that the Nambudiris would agree: continue *what* exactly – and for whom? They have carefully maintained a tradition of oral transmission of Vedic rituals distinct even from the indigenous Vedic textual tradition. Early on in the project in fact, Staal showed them the textual version of the rite that they were planning to perform and pointed out the differences and discrepancies. The Nambudiris merely said, 'Interesting', and continued to plan the ritual the way *they* knew it should be done, the way their teachers had taught them.[57]

As a postscript to these stories, it is interesting to note that the emphasis on texts that helped define Robertson Smith's enterprise of secular sociology also seriously misled him. An old and incomplete fifth-century text that vividly described an Arab tribe's slaughter and wild communal consumption of a camel was Smith's primary evidence for his theory of ritual sacrifice. However, that text has proven to be very unreliable: unknown to Smith, it turns out to have been a Persian novel of sorts, a type of fictional travelogue, in which a witty and sophisticated urban traveller details hair-raising adventures among the desert tribes.

I have suggested that the emergence of an indigenous literate priesthood that codifies correct ritual procedures brings with it the perspective that ritual is the enactment of beliefs and truths revealed in sacred sources; that it is a communal witness to an inner state of faith; and that proper performance means adherence to the written directives that are considered to be the tradition. Likewise, the emergence of an outsider, secular-scientific expertise based on texts that purport to record and promote objective knowledge also brings its

---

[55] Frito Staal, *Agni: The Vedic Ritual of the Fire Sacrifice* (Berkeley: Asian Humanities Press 1983), I:23.
[56] Ibid., I:xxii–xxiii, 2.
[57] Ibid., I:2.

own understanding of ritual. And quite apart from the merits of this perspective, the dominance of the scientific model of knowledge and the prestige of the academy insures the influence of this perspective. For their part, secular scholars set up an understanding of ritual that reflects their textual orientation and the social framework in which they operate. Hence, such scholarship is apt to talk of ritual in terms of functions, structures, or logic that define the phenomenon in cross-cultural abstractions. Often we specify a narrative or performative structure primarily concerned with communicating or composed of meanings that must be decoded. Social scientists are apt to describe ritual as a key social mechanism or process that provides them with an analytical entry into the explanation of culture.[58] Although it is the social science expert who gives us the relative neutrality of the category of 'ritual' – which *is* a significant development in the history of true and false rites, orthodox and heterodox liturgies, our sacraments and their magical superstitions – this is a view that claims an unprecedented inclusivity and firmly subordinates all other under-standings of ritual as partial, deluded, or creative solutions to cultur-ally bounded situations.

It is interesting to note that at a time in American life when the demise of traditional ritual communities is being mourned with a particular finality, the tendency among many social scientists is to cast ritual as good and healthy, somehow humanizing in its shared sym-bols and communal affirmations.[59] One wonders if scholars have been romanticizing ritual at just the point in American social history when the reality cannot really challenge the ideal. Romancing ritual may be serving to soften the observer–observed dichotomy, encourage more study of ritual practices within American and European cultures, and perhaps even legitimize scholarship of a less reductive style. However, such romancing may have also contributed to the popu-larity of oversimplified ethnographic models of ritual and the critical attitude of some social scientists to modern examples of ritual change at home.[60]

Elsewhere I have suggested some other reasons for the emergence of ritual as an important if value-laden focus for the social sciences that have to do with defining a specifically cultural level and style of

---

[58] Bell, *Ritual Theory, Ritual Practice*, 25–9.

[59] One of the main vehicles of this view is Robert N. Bellah et al., *Habits of the Heart* (New York: Harper and Row 1985).

[60] I am referring here to the critiques of Victor Turner, Mary Douglas, and David Martin, among others. See Victor Turner, 'Ritual, Tribal and Catholic', *Worship* 50 (1976), 504–26; and David Martin and Peter Mullen, eds, *No Alternative: The Prayer Book Controversy* (Oxford: Basil Blackwell 1981).

analysis.[61] Here I want simply to make the point that the perspective of social scientific theories of ritual is as socio-historically determined and self-legitimating as the interpretations of ritual given by experts like Ogotemmeli, Master Lu, and the Nambudiri Brahmins.

Liturgical experts

What about liturgical studies? Where does this group of experts fit in? The emergence of liturgical studies in the last century has yielded another type of ritual expertise, not without some historical predecessors, of course, but still relatively unprecedented. From my perspective one of the most interesting things about liturgical studies has been the obvious and hidden ramifications of its appeal to non-theological forms of scholarship, specifically social science. To a great extent, it is this appeal to social scientific scholarship that has differentiated the expertise of liturgical studies from that of more traditional church scholars and legitimated its relative authority. Early work in historical research went beyond preceding studies to recover a more truly historical understanding of the development of Christian liturgy, with the result that however the essential nature of Christian worship might be defined, much of its form and content were shown to be very human and historically contingent. What had been historically made, of course, could be legitimately re-made. So this scholarship directly facilitated ways to think about major liturgical reform. Further research, especially in some areas of comparative religions and anthropology, also began to develop a type of second-stage argument: namely, that the similarities of human worship across religions and cultures argue for the universality of ritual, its intrinsic importance for community and personhood, and thus the necessity of a primary focus on nurturing ritual life in the face of the so-called anti-ritualism of modern secular society. While at one time the work of the liturgical scholar could be envisioned as a major task that was nonetheless complete-able, it soon became clear that the liturgist's work could never be done. The talk has been of process, continual transformation, and naturally ever-new problems and obstacles.

Although liturgical studies has developed independent degree programs, journals, and publishing houses – all signalling a formidable control of texts and the power to define ritual – it continues to call for more extensive use of social science and enthusiastically appropriates many forms of secular research. An example noted by others is

---

[61] Bell, *Ritual Theory, Ritual Practice*, 47–54. Also see Catherine Bell, 'Discourse and Dichotomies: The Structure of Ritual Theory', *Religion* 17 (1987), 95–118.

the editorial statement from *Worship*: 'We want . . . to mine the resources of the modern behavioral sciences and arts in an effort to determine which cultural forms best express and communicate the sacred mysteries celebrated by worshipping assemblies.'[62] Another example suggests that following 'further the lead of the more disinterested theoreticians of ritual dynamic[s]' would help clarify the direction of liturgical studies.[63] I am struck by the faith liturgical studies has in social science. Why is it so willing to take social scientific expertise at its word and believe that social science really has a clue as to which cultural forms express what?

Certainly social science contributes the important if romantic notion that ritual is a central, transformative social process.[64] It also contributes, we have seen, the idea that rites rise up most effectively from the people. While the first idea directly validates liturgical studies and the use of non-theological resources, the second idea – which states that living rites cannot be effectively devised and decreed from on high – supports the argument advanced by liturgical studies that the central church administration should grant much more discretion and expressive freedom to local communities. This argument has been very important to the political empowerment and growth of liturgical studies. Yet at the same time, such a theory of ritual makes it very hard to understand exactly what role local liturgical experts should play. The result seems to be that liturgical studies is left with a somewhat confused sense of the place of authoritative ritual experts who have been rendered invisible in theory on the one hand, and perhaps an exaggerated sense of the social role of ritual on the other. And these ideas are, of course, interdependent.

Certainly liturgical studies has put together its own particular view of ritual – (i) as the central socio-cultural process, (ii) as the source and shaper of values and beliefs, and (iii) as authentic when of the people and inauthentic when decreed from on high. This perspective clearly legitimates the development of liturgical studies and its historical and social scientific research. On the other hand, this view also severely constrains liturgical studies, since it leaves liturgical experts no basis on which to exert the authority to devise and decree, or to judge the success or failure of ritual. Given such great expectations for ritual, moreover, it encourages the conclusion that liturgical reform has failed or been derailed.

---

[62] Ronald L. Grimes, *Ritual Criticism* (Columbia, SC: University of South Carolina Press 1990), 56, citing the editorial notice in *Worship* 61 (1987) 81.

[63] Collins, 'Liturgical Methodology', 97.

[64] Victor Turner has probably been the most powerful but not the sole proponent of this view.

Of course liturgical scholars and working liturgists have been exerting a great deal of practical authority in their communities; but the contradictions of their position have led, nearly thirty years after Vatican II, to shaken confidence and confusion about both the results and direction of liturgical reform. The church and society in general have not been transformed, although parishes and religious communities are changing willy-nilly in ways no one really expected. There is still a great deal of energy behind liturgical reflection and experimentation, of course, but the outlook seems less satisfying. And oddly enough, although liturgical authority, conformity, and dignity had been seen as obstacles thirty years ago, we are here formulating the problem of their absence. Ritual solutions that effectively balance local needs with participation in a centralized tradition have not clearly emerged; instead, liturgical developments seem to underscore the problem. Liturgical devising and decreeing, even with great local support, does not seem to convey the power and authority of the old traditional liturgy. What has happened?

The historical record has some suggestions. One seems to be a brute political fact: the weakening of strong central control in order to empower local communities always introduces more chaos than anyone expects. We hardly need refer to the political parallels that have dominated the news for the last two years. In addition, the historical record suggests that complaints about a lack of ritual authority, conformity, or dignity often accompany the increasing institutionalization of new ritual experts: after a period of breaking with older practices, often characterized as something of a free-for-all of the spirit, new organizational and authoritative structures begin to emerge. And the critique is then made that recent ritual changes have become too uncontrolled, idiosyncratic, and aesthetically quite vulgar and unrefined.[65] It is something of a cliché, in Chinese religious history at least, that popular cults and folk rituals that eluded the control of Taoist, Buddhist, or Confucian experts are routinely described as tasteless and unrestrained. Such criticism is usually a rationale and prelude to these experts attempting to regulate such goings-on. Whether they go ahead and exert such control, and what type of control it is, depends on what sort of community is envisioned.

Perhaps liturgical experts are at a juncture now where the romantic view of ritual and social science that helped to usher them in as experts and to develop their skills must be amended with a new pragmatism about populism, change, and institutional authority. The

---

[65] See Catherine Bell, 'Ritual, Change and Changing Rituals', *Worship* 63 (1989), 31–41.

three questions raised at the beginning of this paper implicitly invoke this spirit of retrenchment. They also borrow, I believe, some unnecessary confusion.

I would suggest that what is needed is not a theoretical model that attempts or pretends to unite rites, participants, and theorists. Liturgical scholars and social scientists both would find more complex models very useful, of course, and liturgical experts should be concerned to develop theoretical models that recognize the impact of their position. The history of forms of liturgical leadership is vast if unwritten. Greater analysis of the emergence and influence of ritual leadership, the concomitant shifts in the understanding of ritual, the divisions of spiritual labour and cosmological authority, etc. all could be usefully explored. But theoretical models cannot re-establish some supposed unity that has broken into rites, participants, and theorists. For unifying ritual traditions, participants, and experts, it may be more effective to seek a working theological consensus and new forms of ecclesiastical organization.

The second question concerning ritual and change should also be recast, I believe, in the light of how literate, plural, and industrial cultures work. I do not think that the very valuable work of Turner and Geertz, which may seem to depict relatively smooth processes of social change, can be used to conclude that liturgical change in the Catholic Church in the twentieth century has not been successful or authentic. First of all, social science cannot claim to generate normative guidelines for socio-cultural processes. It is descriptive and interpretive analysis; when feeling particularly self-confident, it might attempt to predict. It should not prescribe. Second, change in an institution like the Catholic Church seems necessarily messy and inevitably contentious; it always has been. As for the relationship between ritual and its social world, between ritual changes and social forces – that is perhaps the heart of the social chemistry of ritualized practices. Should ritual reflect what is out there in the world, or should it set up models for that world? My own preference on this issue is to recognize how ritual activity is neither a 'model of' nor a 'model for', but a strategic, partial, and usually not perfectly coherent, reinterpretation of the world; most important, it is a very physical – bodily – reinterpretation. In minimally effective ritual, actors come away having embodied interpretive schemes that are at least minimally adequate to the task of experiencing that world in constructive or redemptive ways. In this view ritual is *not* a fulcrum for change; it is one of the most conservative media for social action. Yet it is creative, adaptable, and resourceful: constructed with the categories people use to deal with the world, it can give these categories back in schemes more effective for construing the world in ways that envision and empower.[66]

The third question concerning evaluation of post-Vatican II ritual implied that Catholic identity is increasingly pulled between the two poles of local community and the larger trans-local church. As I suggested, there is historical evidence that such polarizations inevitably follow various social developments, such as literacy. It seems a cruel political fact that a strong centre in harmony with strong local communities is rather hard to find. There always seems to be a tension, and the advantage slips back and forth. There is no evidence that ritual can alleviate these tensions, though liturgical life can undoubtedly embody them and perhaps heighten or ease people's sense of the problem.[67] But to imagine that ritual alone can shape the proper alignment of centre and locality strikes me as a primarily political form of idealism, that is, a view rooted in a political vision or rhetoric, not in any pragmatic or scholarly assessment of ritual.

Let me convert these opinions into a little morality tale. I know a graduate student who served for several years as a part-time Anglican pastor for a small town in California. His community is notorious as an idiosyncratic bunch of ex-hippies, whose style was formed by the creeds of the late 1960s – resist authority, do your own thing, and the communal summer of love need never end. This student took up his work there armed with an incredible confidence in ritual that pretty much matched the expectations of this community. Instinctively, I would suggest, he and the community knew that a theological consensus was highly unlikely and a truly meaningful ecclesiastical reorganization had yet to be envisioned. My student found himself, however, in an increasingly complicated situation. Nothing he arranged liturgically was right. They were always complaining. He worked at getting them to take responsibility and express what they wanted to express; but what some wanted, others did not. They tried some tradition; they tried some innovation. They tried 'finding themselves'; they tried 'coming together'. My student eventually tried some heavy-handed authoritarianism, which he admitted became more attractive to him as time went on and no less successful than other strategies. Everyone half expected that if they could

---

[66] This view of ritual is developed at length in Bell, *Ritual Theory, Ritual Practice*, 69–117.

[67] For two interesting accounts of this type of tension in recent Chinese history, see P. Steven Sangren, *History and Magical Power in a Chinese Community* (Stanford: Stanford University Press 1987); and James L. Watson, 'Standardizing the Gods: The Promotion of T'ien lou ("Empress of Heaven") Along the South China Coast, 960–1960', in *Popular Culture in Late Imperial China*, ed. David Johnson, Andrew J. Nathan, and Evelyn S. Rawski (Berkeley: University of California Press 1985), 292–324.

find the right ritual orchestration, they would be united as a community in which each person would also feel individually affirmed and fulfilled. Without having to contribute any theological or institutional investment, they believed that ritual could function alone as a medium for realizing the social and spiritual fruits of their vague sense of religiosity. Do not misunderstand: I am *not* saying that my student or this community had a faulty or even naïve understanding of ritual. They had the understanding that they had, and they had it for a variety of social and historical reasons. But I would say that their problem did not lie in how to perform the liturgy. Given who they are, there is no 'right' ritual that holds the answer for them. As one of my colleagues has said, many liturgical problems are community problems.

Conclusion

The questions about ritual authority raised by this conference reflect, I believe, developments in liturgical studies akin to the situations of many other types of ritual expert. Ritual experts or professional ritualists who may often be invisible in ethnographic models of ritual are much more visible in the historical accounts of societies which have recorded ritual and used writing to affect how ritual is understood. Master Lu is just one example of how decisive a class of ritual experts can be in 'devising' and 'decreeing' living ritual practices and traditions. I think historical examples of such 'so-called ritual experts' are of particular interest to liturgical studies – first, because they provide a vindication of the existence and importance of a group or class of people who throughout history have tried to reform ritual for a variety of reasons, probably both good and bad; and second, because the ritual expert, by virtue of his or her professional authority, defines to a great extent how ritual is formally understood in the community, what its purposes are, and whether they are being realized or not. Hence, if liturgical studies, like any field that produces a group of experts, finds itself confronting particularly stubborn problems, it may well want to backtrack and explore how those problems may result in part from its own perspective on ritual.

Different cultures generate different understandings and uses of ritual. The differences between oral and literate cultures are an obvious sort of example. In contrast to oral societies, the emergence of texts that are deemed to embody sacred truth and tradition gives ritual a different social place and vocabulary: local traditions are forced to relate to more centralized ones, ritual spontaneity is devalued in favour of testifying to belief, reciting creeds, and performing choreographed mysteries in which hierarchies of official mediators dominate. In the modern industrial world, many of these same text-related tendencies have gone on to help differentiate the social scientific expert from the traditional ritual expert. And a new social scientific understanding of ritual follows, defining itself for the most part in terms of observation by cultural outsiders who are composing textual accounts that reveal the meaning of the strange activities of other cultures – the expert takes a position of deciphering, not participation or creative leadership. Ritual, defined as a type of universal category subsuming activities that participants would never lump together, comes to be seen in terms of social functions and cultural meanings unknown to participants themselves but elucidated by the secular expert. Liturgical studies has differentiated itself from traditional church experts on the one hand and secular scholarship on the other. Yet through its use of social science models that are ill-equipped, perhaps, to address important aspects of the Catholic liturgical tradition, and because of its political stake in aggrandizing the role of ritual and unending liturgical revolution, liturgical studies has created a view of ritual that has its share of contradictions. Clearly one of these is that the spontaneity, localness, and informality encouraged by many experiments in liturgical reform yield a diverse landscape of practices that may now seem to lack the old authority and dignity.

Ritual activities actually offer many ways of negotiating the source and degree of authority. Indeed, ritual is the medium people usually use to recognize and defer to the authority of tradition, supernatural beings, divine right, or even, as Freud suggested, obsessive compulsions. The logic of most post-Vatican II modifications has been, of course, to give more authority to the local community – who are made to say, in effect, that we have gathered not because we are supposed to, nor because the pastor expects us, but because we have chosen to come together to celebrate these things as a community. The weakness of this ritual logic is that in most cases the community so constituted really does not quite exist outside the ritual. Aside from their presence in the same place on a Sunday morning, a group of Catholics can often have very little else in common. Yet the tendency in many such liturgies is to emphasize community all the more, trying to enhance its tangible and authoritative presence. However, such exaggerations may actually undermine people's sense of what is real and fitting. In this way, many liturgies lose authority primarily from lack of modesty. They are trying too hard to be too much, to claim too much. Ritual alone cannot do all the things liturgists want it to do. I also doubt it can do all things social scientists are wont to see it do.

A social scientist should not even pretend to offer more than a particular analysis, certainly no prescriptions or suggestions on how to do ritual or even what to think about ritual. At best one might offer only some suggestions as to *how* thinking about ritual may become over-determined. Indeed, as a social scientist I have an amoral and perhaps apolitical faith in the data: you are doing what you are doing and I will find it very interesting to watch and analyze no matter what direction is taken. Yet in the end, I might offer this: based on the historical study of ritual, I find little justification for seeing ritual as a political medium for quiet revolution in the church or in society, and even less justification for any return to easy authoritarianism. I do find that there is great justification for liturgical experts to 'devise and decree' within the liturgical life of their communities, to seek better theoretical models for how experts shape ritual, and, most emphatically, to attempt to develop the theological and ecclesiastical supports needed to build coherent and authoritative liturgical *communities* – not just experts.

Part 4

METHOD

9

Margaret Mary Kelleher

Introduction

> Knowing, accordingly, is not just seeing; it is experiencing, understanding, judging, and believing. The criteria of objectivity are not just the criteria of ocular vision; they are the compounded criteria of experiencing, of understanding, of judging, and of believing. The reality known is not just looked at; it is given in experience, organized and extrapolated by understanding; posited by judgment and belief. (Bernard Lonergan, *Method in Theology* [New York: Herder & Herder 1972], 283)

In her article, 'Liturgical Theology: A Task and a Method', first published in *Worship* 62 (1988), 2–25, Margaret Mary Kelleher details a 'method' for doing what she considers to be the 'task' of liturgical theology. Relying on Bernard Lonergan and Victor Turner for founding her 'task', she describes the liturgical act as 'ecclesial ritual praxis' and considers how a constructed 'world of meaning' can not only be understood, but also examined and analysed. Ecclesial disclosure of common meanings and commitments can be interpreted, using the methodological tools proposed by Turner, who understands ritual to be a dynamic social process which is goal oriented.

Margaret Mary Kelleher, OSU, teaches in the Department of Theology and Religious Studies at The Catholic University of America, Washington, DC. Her dissertation, 'Liturgy as an Ecclesial Act of Meaning: Foundations and Methodological Consequences for Liturgical Spirituality', is available from the University of Michigan.

For further reading

Clifford Geertz, *The Interpretation of Cultures: Selected Essays* (BasicBooks 1973), Chapter 1, 'Thick Description: Toward an Interpretive Theory of Culture'.

Margaret Mary Kelleher, 'Ritual Studies and the Eucharist: Paying Attention to Performance', in *Eucharist: Toward the Third Millennium*, ed. Martin F. Connell (Chicago: Liturgical Training Publications 1997), 51–64.

Margaret Mary Kelleher, 'The Communion Rite: A Study of Roman Catholic Liturgical Performance', *Journal of Ritual Studies* 5 (1991), 99–122.

Penny Oldfather, 'Qualitative Research as Jazz', *Educational Researcher*, 23/8 (November 1994), 22–26.

★★★

Liturgical theology: a task and a method

In his *Introduction to Liturgical Theology* Alexander Schmemann identified the church's liturgical tradition as the subject matter of liturgical theology and indicated that the methods of historical analysis and theological interpretation should be employed in studying this tradition.[1] In the years since his book was published, the complexity of carrying out such a project has become apparent in the diverse tasks which have been identified within liturgical theology as well as in the methodological pluralism which necessarily accompanies such diversity.

This essay will address both the topics of task and method within liturgical theology and will proceed in several steps. First of all, Bernard Lonergan's distinction between generalized empirical method and particular methods will be presented as a way of understanding the methodological unity and diversity at work in liturgical theology. Second, one of the tasks of liturgical theology will be designated as that of critically reflecting on contemporary liturgical praxis for the purpose of objectifying the horizon or world of meaning made public in that praxis. Third, the schematic framework of a particular method designed to facilitate this task will be offered. The method is an interdisciplinary one which incorporates principles from the work of both Bernard Lonergan and Victor Turner. Finally, the significance of the theologian employing any method will be addressed.

A methodological distinction

Particular methods, whether they are found in the natural or social sciences, or within the various branches of theology, are constructed for the purpose of coming to know or discover something. The nature of the unknown in each case plays a major role in shaping the method. The diversity of things to be known and of particular methods designed to know them might well give one the impression that there is no basis for collaboration within or among various fields. Bernard Lonergan has made a significant contribution toward promoting both interdisciplinary work and collaboration among persons working in one discipline by calling attention to the common core of operations which is foundational to all particular methods.[2]

This common core consists in the operations employed by anyone who is pursuing knowledge. They are the operations associated with human experience, understanding, judgment and decision. Specifically,

---

[1] Alexander Schmemann, *Introduction to Liturgical Theology* (New York: St Vladimir's Seminary Press 1975 edition), 16–17.

[2] See Bernard J. F. Lonergan, SJ, *Method in Theology* (New York: Herder and Herder 1972), 23.

they include such activities as 'seeing, hearing, touching, smelling, tasting, inquiring, imagining, understanding, conceiving, formulating, reflecting, marshalling and weighing the evidence, judging, deliberating, evaluating, speaking, writing'.[3]

Lonergan came to name this pattern of operations which can be applied to both the data of sense and the data of consciousness and which is foundational to all particular methods 'generalized empirical method'.[4] He described the normative pattern that relates the operations to one another as 'the conscious dynamism of sensitive spontaneity, of intelligence raising questions and demanding satisfactory answers, of reasonableness insisting on sufficient evidence before it can assent yet compelled to assent when sufficient evidence is forthcoming, of conscience presiding over all and revealing to the subject his authenticity or his unauthenticity as he observes or violates the immanent norms of his own sensitivity, his own intelligence, his own reasonableness, his own freedom and responsibility'.[5] These immanent norms have been designated elsewhere by Lonergan as the transcendental precepts: be attentive, intelligent, reasonable and responsible, and he has suggested that it is the function of method to spell out the implications of these precepts for each discipline.[6]

This understanding of foundational method as a dynamic pattern of human operations guided by immanent norms must be distinguished from method understood as a normative set of rules or directions which could be followed by anyone and would be expected to yield the same results over and over. The latter is method viewed as technique, something which might appear in assembly lines or, as Lonergan says, at 'The New Method Laundry'.[7] In contrast with such a static view, method must be recognized as a dynamic process of questioning and answering which is carried out by individuals and communities of scholars. It is a 'framework for collaborative creativity'.[8] Method is progressive and cumulative. Instead of repeating the same results over and over it can produce new results which, although they grow out of the old, often correct or qualify previous answers.[9]

A particular method is a series of questions designed for the purpose of transforming something that is unknown into something

---

[3] Ibid., 6.
[4] See Lonergan, 'The Ongoing Genesis of Methods', in *A Third Collection*, ed. Frederick E. Crowe, SJ (New York/Mahweh: Paulist 1980), 150.
[5] Ibid.
[6] Lonergan, *Philosophy of God, and Theology* (Philadelphia: Westminster 1973), 48.
[7] Lonergan, *Method*, 5–6.
[8] Lonergan, 'A Post-Hegelian Philosophy of Religion', in *A Third Collection*, 204–205.
[9] Lonergan, 'Method: Trend and Variations', in *A Third Collection*, 15.

that is known. In constructing a particular method one must first designate the unknown and then begin to construct a heuristic framework of questions to promote the investigation. The series of questions is open-ended. Some are designed at the beginning of the study and are likely to be refined in the course of the investigation. Others emerge in the course of the methodical process. The questions shape the investigation. Since, of course, they are formulated and answered by the scholars engaged in the study, those persons have a critical role in directing the process.

A task for liturgical theology

Theology can be understood as an ongoing process of reflection on the significance and value of religion within a culture, a process which is guided by method.[10] It is not religion in the abstract which is the object of reflection but 'a concrete religion as it has been lived, as it is being lived, and as it is to be lived'.[11] Religion, method, and theology are all dynamic processes.

Liturgical theology reflects on religion as it appears in public corporate worship and there are many unknowns which can be designated as topics for exploration. There are questions to be asked about the foundations and possibility of such worship, questions about the dynamics of worship, questions about the history of worship within a community, questions about the social, cultural, and political contexts of worship, questions about liturgical sources, language, and symbols. In Christian liturgical theology there are questions to be asked about the anthropology, christology, pneumatology, ecclesiology, soteriology, sacramental theology, doctrine of God and so forth that have been or are being mediated in public corporate worship. Finally, there are questions to be asked about the shaping of liturgical celebrations, about cultural and liturgical pluralism, about the relationship between liturgical worship and life, and critical questions about the adequacy of what is or has been mediated in public corporate worship.[12]

---

[10] Lonergan, *Philosophy of God*, 56.

[11] Ibid.

[12] This list of questions is not meant to be exclusive. For some approaches to the task of liturgical theology see Mary Collins, 'Critical Questions for Liturgical Theology', *Worship* 53 (1979), 302–17; Theodore W. Jennings Jr, 'Ritual Studies and Liturgical Theology: An Invitation to Dialogue', *Journal of Ritual Studies* 1 (1987), 35–56; Aidan Kavanagh, *On Liturgical Theology* (New York: Pueblo 1984); David N. Power, 'Unripe Grapes: The Critical Function of Liturgical Theology', *Worship* 52 (1978), 386–99; Kevin Seasoltz, 'Anthropology and Liturgical Theology: Search for a Compatible Methodology', in *Liturgy and Human Passage*, ed. David Power and Luis Maldonado (New York: Seabury 1979), 3–13; Robert Taft, 'Liturgy as Theology', *Worship* 56 (1982), 113–17.

All of those engaged in exploring such significant questions will do so by carrying out the operations of generalized empirical method. However, the sources which receive attention, the questions asked for gathering, understanding, and judging data will all be specified by the focus of a particular study: What is it that you want to know and why do you want to know it?

Liturgy as ecclesial ritual praxis. The church can be understood as a community which is continually in the process of being constituted by the gift of God's Spirit and the proclamation of Christ's message.[13] This, of course, happens in diverse local communities where the handing on of the message from generation to generation is a form of 'praxis alive and active'.[14] Theology is done when that praxis is questioned, scrutinized, made explicit and thematic.[15]

As the action of Christian assemblies, liturgy can be understood as a form of ecclesial ritual praxis in which the church is continually mediating itself within particular local contexts.[16] In its liturgical ritual action an assembly performs its corporate meaning and contributes to the ongoing creation of itself as a collective subject, a community.[17] The performed meaning may also include new meanings which are being made available for a community's appropriation as well as some which are in the process of being criticized, rejected or transformed.

In its liturgical praxis an assembly mediates a public horizon, a world of meaning which provides a context for the assembly's worship. This public world of meaning must be distinguished from the meanings that are personally appropriated by members of the assembly as well as from the meanings identified in official texts or commentaries on a rite, since individuals may not appropriate all that is publicly mediated and liturgical praxis may mediate meanings that are not included in the official rite. Although public and private meanings must be distinguished, public horizons play a significant role in the ongoing mediation of both individual and collective subjects. In order to illustrate this, more must be said about the notion of horizon.

---

[13] See Lonergan, 'Ongoing Genesis', 161 and *Method*, 361–64.
[14] Lonergan, 'Ongoing Genesis', 161. See Lonergan, 'Theology and Praxis', *Proceedings of the Catholic Theological Society of America* 32 (1977), 1, for his description of praxis as action, conduct which is the result of deliberation and choice.
[15] Lonergan, 'Ongoing Genesis', 161.
[16] For a more complete presentation of this theory see Margaret Mary Kelleher, 'Liturgy: An Ecclesial Act of Meaning', *Worship* 59 (1985), 482–97.
[17] For an explanation of the church as a collective subject see Kelleher, 485–88. For an explanation of liturgy as ecclesial performative meaning in which the church is mediated see pp. 491–94.

Horizon: a world of meaning. Every person has a horizon which can be understood as the limit or boundary of the world within which that person lives.[18] A horizon is not to be thought of as a rigid boundary for it can be expanded, differentiated and transformed. This dynamic sense of horizon can be grasped more easily when one realizes that there are two poles to one's horizon and that they condition each other.[19] The subjective pole is the actual person involved in the drama of living and the objective pole refers to the limit of the world of meaning which is possible for that particular subject.[20] One's horizon includes all that is within that world of meaning.

The two poles can and do change. If one thinks of one's horizon as the 'limit of one's field of vision', one realizes that for different personal standpoints or viewpoints there will be different horizons.[21] If one thinks of one's personal horizon as the outer unit of one's world of meaning, then one soon realizes that the scope of that world will be shaped by such factors as 'the period in which one lives, one's social background and milieu, one's education and personal development'.[22] Such factors are part of one's standpoint and if they change there will be corresponding changes in the limit of one's world.

Upon reflection it becomes clear that much of one's horizon is a social product. It is received from others. As Lonergan has said: 'We are products of a process that in its several aspects is named socialization, acculturation, education. By that process there is formed our initial mind-set, world view, blik, horizon. On that basis and within its limitations we slowly become our own masters, think for ourselves, make our own decisions, exercise our own freedom and responsibility.'[23] The influence of social factors on one's personal horizon extends throughout one's life. As people relate with one another, share knowledge, interests and values, they come to participate in each other's horizons.[24]

An assembly engaged in the performance of liturgy acts as a collective subject and in its ritual praxis symbolically mediates a public horizon. One might refer to that public horizon as the limit of the assembly's imagination. It sets out a public spirituality, a vision of what

---

[18] Lonergan, 'The Subject', in A *Second Collection*, ed. William F. J. Ryan and Bernard J. Tyrell (Philadelphia: Westminster 1974), 69.
[19] Lonergan, 'Metaphysics as Horizon', in *Collection*, ed. F. E. Crowe (New York; Herder and Herder 1967), 213.
[20] Ibid., 215. See also David Tracy, *The Achievement of Bernard Lonergan* (New York: Herder and Herder 1979), 14.
[21] Lonergan, *Method*, 235.
[22] Ibid., 236.
[23] Lonergan, 'Ongoing Genesis', 156.
[24] See Lonergan, 'Pope John's Intention', in *A Third Collection*, 234.

it means to live as a member of the Christian community. It is a horizon handed on by others, one which offers challenges as well as sets limits for the assembly, and it is a horizon which may change as a result of decisions made within the collective subject.

Identifying the particular task. The significant role played by public horizons in the ongoing mediation of assemblies suggests a task for contemporary liturgical theology, that of scrutinizing these horizons, questioning them, making them explicit and thematic. It is a task of objectifying the horizons which are made public in ecclesial ritual praxis. The task can be elaborated further as one of thematizing the culture, common fund of knowledge, living tradition which is symbolically mediated in a local community's liturgical celebrations.

A collective subject engaged in the ritual mediation of its public horizon is mediating something of its culture. Lonergan has defined culture as 'the set of meanings and values that inform the way of life of a community'.[25] This is compatible with Clifford Geertz's concept of culture as 'an historically transmitted pattern of meanings embodied in symbols, a system of inherited conceptions expressed in symbolic forms by means of which men communicate, perpetuate, and develop their knowledge about and attitudes toward life'.[26] Culture consists of 'webs of significance' spun by humans.[27] Cultures are plural, diverse and historical, and 'it is the culture as it is historically available that provides the matrix within which persons develop'.[28] In other words, culture is the matrix or context for the construction of individual and corporate horizons.

Lonergan differentiates two aspects of culture. First of all, there are the meanings and values immanent in everyday life. Beyond this, there is the process of elaborating and discerning those meanings and values, a process which takes place in a more reflective, deliberate, critical fashion.[29] On the first level meaning is felt, intuited and enacted in rites, symbols, language and art. The second level is a cultural superstructure which is the reflective product of critics, historians, theologians and others.[30] An assembly engaged in liturgical praxis mediates culture in a spontaneous undifferentiated manner. Those who engage in an attempt to identify the meanings and values which are made public in that praxis are operating on the second level.

---

[25] Lonergan, 'Revolution in Catholic Theology', in *A Second Collection*, 232.

[26] Clifford Geertz, *The Interpretation of Cultures* (New York: Basic Books 1973), 89.

[27] Ibid., 5.

[28] Lonergan, 'Revolution', 233.

[29] Lonergan, 'Belief: Today's Issue', in *A Second Collection*, 91.

[30] Lonergan, 'The Absence of God in a Modern Culture', in *A Second Collection*, 102–103.

Among the significant contents of any community's horizon or world of meaning are its beliefs, its common fund of knowledge.[31] Lonergan has suggested that those who wish to understand belief might learn from the sociology of knowledge.[32] In *The Social Construction of Reality* Peter Berger and Thomas Luckmann refer to a 'social stock of knowledge' which is gradually accumulated within a society and transmitted from generation to generation.[33] The social stock of knowledge that is available within any society guides its members in their daily lives and offers them meaning.

Although individuals do contribute to a society's common fund of knowledge, it is largely through a process of belief that they appropriate their social, cultural, and religious heritage.[34] The beliefs of a religious community function in the same way as do the beliefs of any society. They carry and communicate the fund of religious knowledge that has been accumulated within that community.[35] The existence and identity of any religious community depends on the transmission of its common fund, for that fund provides a context of meaning within which people learn about themselves, God, relationships and expectations within the community. The appropriation of the common fund strengthens the community's corporate memory, something that is essential for communal identity.

Beliefs that are transmitted within a community in its stories, symbols, songs, rituals and creeds constitute part of that community's existential history, its living tradition.[36] This living tradition carries the totality of available common meanings, the world of meaning or horizon which is offered to individuals within the community.[37] Since the common fund which is handed on may suffer from blindspots, oversights, errors and biases, the authenticity of a tradition can never be taken for granted.[38] This calls for critical attention to the tradition as it is mediated within any community. It means that the task of objectifying the horizon made public in liturgical praxis must be followed by an attempt to judge the adequacy of that horizon.

---

[31] Lonergan, *Method*, 43.

[32] Lonergan, 'The Human God', in *Humanitas* 15 (1979), 121.

[33] Peter Berger and Thomas Luckmann, *The Social Construction of Reality* (New York: Doubleday 1966), 41.

[34] Lonergan, *Method*, 41. See pp. 45–46 for his description of the process of coming to believe.

[35] Lonergan makes an important distinction between faith and belief. Faith is not specific to a religious community. Religious belief is the acceptance of the judgments of a particular religion. Beliefs specify faith. See *Method*, 118.

[36] Lonergan, *Method*, 182.

[37] Ibid., 79–80.

[38] For decline in the common fund, see *Method*, 44. For decline in a tradition and the need to apply dialectical analysis when studying a tradition see 'Ongoing Genesis', 155–59.

What I have been suggesting in the previous pages is that an attempt to thematize or objectify the public horizon mediated by an assembly in its liturgical praxis is an attempt to mediate by interpretation some aspects of the assembly's shared world of meaning and value, public spirituality, culture, common fund of knowledge, living tradition, corporate memory, vision of reality. Since a community's living tradition can be placed within the category of 'existential history', some of Lonergan's remarks about the study of history may shed light on the task.

Lonergan makes a distinction between 'history that is written about' and 'history that is written'.[39] A community mediates itself, discloses its common meanings and commitments in the way it lives; this is the first mediation, the history that is written about.[40] A community's liturgical praxis would certainly be included within this kind of history. It is in such praxis that the first mediation of the public ecclesial horizon takes place with ritual symbols functioning as the mediators. History that is written is an attempt to express knowledge of the history that is written about. The historian is engaged in a twofold process of gathering data on historical experience and then engaging in an interpretative process for the purpose of 'determining what was going forward in the community'.[41] Although liturgical theologians who attempt to objectify horizons which are made public in contemporary liturgical praxis are not historians, there is a similarity with the historian's twofold process. They too must first go through a process of gathering data on liturgical experience and then engage in an interpretative process. The interpretation will be a second mediation of the horizon that was initially mediated symbolically in ritual praxis. In this second mediation, however, the mediator is method.

A method for liturgical theology

A particular method has been described as a series of questions designed to transform an unknown into a known. One of the tasks of liturgical theology has been designated as that of objectifying and judging the horizons that are made public in the church's liturgical praxis. Of course, any one study can only hope to focus on some dimension of that praxis and therefore will objectify part of an

---

[39] Lonergan, *Method*, 175.
[40] See Lonergan, 'The Mediation of Christ in Prayer', *Method: Journal of Lonergan Studies* 2 (March 1984), 11.
[41] Lonergan, *Method*, 189.

ecclesial horizon. The method to be proposed in the following pages will offer a series of general questions which have to be made specific with regard to a variety of unknowns. For example, one study might focus on the horizon made public in the communion rite of the Sunday eucharistic celebrations of one or several assemblies. Another might attempt to objectify some aspects of the horizon which is disclosed in the way the rite of Christian initiation of adults is implemented in a particular local community. The number of possible unknowns is vast and varied.

According to Lonergan, contemporary theology has become an empirical science which means that it begins with data and follows an inductive rather than a deductive approach.[42] The empirical nature of contemporary theology also is a dynamic process because new data are always being discovered.[43] What is the proper starting point in an empirical method designed to objectify the horizon that is made public in ecclesial ritual praxis? If one understands a particular method as a heuristic framework of questions intending progressive knowledge of a series of unknowns, with what questions does one begin? To what does one attend? What are one's sources of data?

The sources of data and the questions asked in the method proposed in this essay are based on an understanding of liturgy as a form of ritual action, a social symbolic process in which meaning is symbolically mediated.[44] Liturgy is social because it is produced within the ecclesial process, is performed by an assembly, and participates in the ongoing life of the church, a social reality. It is symbolic because its basic units are ritual symbols: objects, actions, relationships, words, gestures, and arrangements of space.[45] It is processual in three ways. First of all, every ritual can be understood as a dynamic process having an inner rhythm which may be described in terms of ultimate and intermediate goals which are either explicit or implicit.[46] Secondly, liturgy is processual because of its intimate relationship to and participation in the ecclesial process. Liturgy has a history which is intimately related to the history of the church. Finally, liturgy is processual because its symbolic units themselves are dynamic, gaining

[42] See Lonergan, 'Theology in Its New Context', in *A Second Collection*, 58.
[43] Ibid., 59.
[44] See Kelleher, 'Liturgy: An Ecclesial Act', 488–91.
[45] See Victor Turner, 'Process, System, and Symbol. A New Anthropological Synthesis', *Daedalus* 106 (1977), 77.
[46] Turner, *The Forest of Symbols. Aspects of Ndembu Ritual* (Ithaca: Cornell University Press 1967), 273.

and losing meaning in the course of their lives. Turner describes them as being 'semantically open'.[47]

In accord with the social, symbolic and processual nature of liturgy, a particular method constructed for the purpose of objectifying the public horizon that is mediated in liturgical praxis will have to include questions about the assembly or ritual subject, the ritual symbols, and the ritual process. Because ritual meaning is symbolically mediated the focus will be on ritual symbols. However, since the decisions and actions of persons involved in the ritual play an important role in the assignment of meaning, ritual symbols should not be studied in isolation from the assembly. Since the symbolic mediation of meaning actually occurs only within the performance of ritual, liturgical performance or praxis is identified as the primary source of data. Such a locus on performance is characteristic of an approach to the study of ritual which has been called 'processual symbolic analysis'.[48] Turner has described this kind of investigation as one which 'is concerned with the interpretation of the meaning of symbols considered as dynamic systems of signifiers, signifieds, and changing modes of signification in temporal sociocultural processes'.[49]

Gathering data from liturgical performance. Gathering data from liturgical performance obviously demands participation in and careful observation of that performance. One's task at this stage is that of attending to the ritual and recording data. One is aiming at a description of the assembly's liturgical praxis. Since assemblies are not static and liturgy itself is processual, the investigator must study a number of liturgical celebrations over a period of time in one place in order to be able to eventually move toward objectifying a public horizon. How many celebrations must be observed? This cannot be stated definitively at the beginning of a study. First of all, it takes time to train one's attention and to be able to answer all the questions one brings to the performance. Second, since other questions are likely to emerge as one participates and observes, there must be sufficient time to allow this to happen. Finally, one must continue to observe for as long as it takes to recognize a regular pattern in a particular

---

[47] Turner, 'Symbolic Studies', *Annual Review of Anthropology* 4 (1975), 154–55.

[48] Turner, 'Process, System', 77.

[49] Ibid. Turner identifies such a focus on process and performance as a characteristic of a 'postmodern' turn in anthropology. See 'The Anthropology of Performance', in *On the Edge of the Bush: Anthropology as Experience*, ed. Edith L. B. Turner (Tucson: The University of Arizona Press 1985), 181–82.

place or assembly, the variations which occur, and the factors which seem to be responsible for these variations.[50]

Questions to be asked of the liturgical performance can be gathered under the three categories of ritual subject, symbols, and process. Since liturgy is a product of the ecclesial process and participates in the dynamics of that process, questions about an assembly engaged in performing a ritual are apt to provide significant data toward disclosing some characteristics of that process. The following are examples of questions to be asked when observing an assembly as ritual subject: What is the general composition of the assembly? What distinguishing characteristics appear? How are roles distributed within the assembly? Is anyone excluded from certain roles? If so, who is excluded? What distinctions appear within the assembly during the celebration? What seems to be the basis for these distinctions? Are there any obvious expressions of feeling on the part of any members of the assembly? Questions such as these which attend to the composition, roles, and public reactions of ritual subjects attempt to isolate some aspects of what Turner identifies as the operational dimension of ritual meaning.[51]

Questions asked about ritual symbols continue to explore the operational dimension of meaning by focusing on what ritual participants do with or in relation to ritual symbols rather than on what is said about the symbols. There are also questions which attend to the positional dimension of ritual meaning, to relationships or associations established between or among symbols as the rite is performed. Still other questions attend to the exegetical dimension, to what is said about a symbol in a ritual, to explanations offered, to the names given to a symbol, the natural properties of a substance selected as a symbol, and the appearance of symbolic objects within a ritual. Questions which inquire about these three dimensions of meaning clearly disclose a position which believes that verbal or textual language, although a very significant mediator of meaning, is only one part of a complex system of meaning when it is employed in ritual. As Turner has said, 'texts not only animate and are animated by contexts but are processually inseverable from them'.[52]

---

[50] This is something I learned in my own first attempt to gather data as a participant-observer. Although my original plan was to observe two assemblies for three or four successive Sundays, questions which emerged in the experience of participating and observing led me to increase that number to eleven.

[51] For his presentation of the operational, positional, and exegetical dimensions of meaning see Turner, 'Forms of Symbolic Action: Introduction', in *Forms of Symbolic Action: Proceedings of the 1969 Annual Meeting, American Ethnological Society* (Seattle: University of Washington Press), 11–12.

[52] Turner, 'Process, System', 61.

Recalling that ritual symbols can be objects, actions, relationships, words, gestures or spatial arrangements, the following are examples of questions which might serve to focus the attention of one who is observing a particular ritual: Where does the ritual take place? How is the space organized? Are there any boundaries established? How is the place decorated? What symbolic objects appear? What symbolic actions take place? What relationships are established between and among persons, between persons and God, persons and objects, persons and actions, objects and actions? How are these relationships established? What dominant images are set out in prayers, readings, homily, song?[53]

Questions asked about the ritual process by a participant observer are of several types. First of all, one asks about the rhythm of the ritual itself. What is the order of events? Are there ever any variations? If so, what are they and who or what is responsible? Are there distinct phases within the ritual? If so, what are they and how are transitions made from one phase to another? Secondly, one must be concerned about the dynamics of the ritual symbols themselves. Here one might focus on one symbol and trace it through a single ritual celebration, continue to do this over the course of the study, and record any variations one notices as well as the occasion for such changes. Finally, one must attend to the relationship between the ritual process and the ecclesial process or the dynamics of the ritual in relation to the dynamics of the assembly. Are there changes in the ritual process associated with changes in the assembly? If so, what are they? The questions asked and answered during the period of participant observations provide one with data on the content and dynamics of liturgical performance. The data must then be subjected to a process of interpretation before one can answer any questions about the public horizon which was symbolically mediated in that performance. This is in accord with the approach of an empirical theology which moves beyond the data which are given in experience and tries to arrive at a satisfactory understanding of the data as an essential step toward establishing any facts.[54]

The process of interpretation. The task of interpretation which has been singled out in this essay is that of engaging in a second

---

[53] The use of such questions and discussion with others who have done so discloses a significant omission in the lack of attention given to the symbolism of music. The area of symbolic action also needs further attention.

[54] Lonergan contrasts this empirical approach with that of an empiricist who does not move beyond what is given in experience. See 'The Origins of Christian Realism', in *A Second Collection*, 241–43. For his distinction between data and facts see *Method*, 201–203.

mediation of the public horizon which was symbolically mediated within and by ecclesial ritual action. It engages one in an attempt to understand the liturgical performances one has experienced and in efforts to express that understanding.[55] This is not to suggest that there is no interpretation going on while one is gathering data from liturgical praxis. The questions which guide the data gathering are constructed on the basis of a particular theory about the ways in which meaning is mediated in ritual. Also, in the course of participating, observing, and gathering data one often formulates one or more hypotheses about the world of meaning that is being disclosed in the praxis. The difference between these two phases in the methodical process is one of focus. Whereas the focus of phase one is description, phase two is directed toward interpretation. Hypotheses generated in phase one will be accepted or rejected by the end of phase two.

In an attempt to understand the data from liturgical performance the process of interpretation formally begins with questions designed to provide more data about the ritual subject, symbols, and process under consideration. However, the source of the data is no longer liturgical performance. A number of sources are called upon: persons associated with the ritual and assembly, the official text of the rite being studied as well as the texts of other rites in the church's ritual system, other documents concerned with the rite, and historical and theological studies of the rite.

There are several reasons for consulting these sources, all of which are based on an understanding of liturgy as ecclesial ritual action and, therefore, a social symbolic process. First of all, the assembly which is being studied as a ritual subject is part of a larger ecclesial process, one which extends back as far as the first Christian communities and which includes the diverse communities which constitute the church today. In other words, the horizon which is disclosed in the liturgical worship of any particular assembly is part of a complex and dynamic ecclesial horizon, and any adequate interpretation must take this into consideration. Second, since ritual is intimately related to the dynamics of the social process within which it is celebrated, the history of the assembly along with its sociocultural context are significant sources of data. Third, since the particular rite which is being studied is only one part of a complex ritual system, any attempt

---

[55] For Lonergan's distinction between one's understanding and one's interpretation, which is the expression of one's understanding see 'Merging Horizons: System, Common Sense, Scholarship', *Cultural Hermeneutics* 1 (1973), 92. Although his treatment of interpretation is limited to texts here, the distinction can be more broadly applied.

to interpret ritual symbols must be carried out within this larger context. A rite as celebrated in a particular time and place is only one phase within a dynamic history of the rite, and that history provides a context for interpreting the contemporary celebration. Finally, all of the sources named above provide data on the exegetical and positional dimensions of ritual meaning and allow the theologian to make comparisons and contrasts with what has been disclosed in the actual performance of the rite.

Two types of question are asked of persons associated with the ritual and assembly. Questions are asked for the purpose of obtaining data on the parish or local community, information regarding size, membership, history, mode of organization, conflicts, significant events, and so forth. Such information provides the investigator with a 'social field' for the ritual performance.[56] Questions are also formulated for the purpose of discovering why certain choices were made in the ritual celebration, how long certain practices have been in operation, how people understand their roles, what changes have occurred in the community's history of celebrating the particular rite.

Questions asked of liturgical texts, official documents, historical theological studies are concerned with the dynamics of the ritual process, the ritual process in relation to the ecclesial process, and the dynamics of ritual symbols. Liturgical texts and official documents might be read with the following questions in mind: What order of events is set out? What rubrics, roles, and distinctions are established? What meanings are offered for ritual symbols? What choices are allowed? What restrictions are given? What ritual goals are identified? Do any of the symbols in the rite being studied appear elsewhere in the church's ritual system? What similarities and differences can be identified?

Historical and theological sources might be approached with such questions as: What meanings have been offered for the rite and its symbols? What changes have occurred in the names of ritual symbols, in the language used with regard to these symbols, in the substances used in the ritual, in the meanings offered for the symbolic objects and actions of the rite, in the division of roles within the assembly? What factors have been influential in bringing about all these changes? In answering historical questions the investigator must often rely on the work of historical scholars and this is a clear example of the collaboration that can take place within the field of liturgical studies.

---

[56] See Turner, *The Forest*, 47 and 264.

Objectifying the public ritual horizon. The information gathered from persons, liturgical texts, documents, theological commentaries and historical studies provides a context for interpreting the data gathered from liturgical performance. The theologian's task at this stage of the process is that of objectifying, expressing in words, some aspects of the horizon or world of meaning which was performed in ritual. It is an attempt to reconstruct some of the horizon which was symbolically mediated in liturgical praxis, to thematize what was unthematic, to make explicit what may have been only implicit.[57] It is important to recall that this is not an attempt to identify meanings which are personally appropriated by individuals within the assembly. Rather, it is an attempt to disclose something of the world of meaning that was made available in the ritual for their appropriation.

Once again, questions serve as the operators at this stage of methodical process. Questions which were asked about ritual subjects, symbols, and process in order to gather data from liturgical performance and other sources were based on a theoretical understanding of liturgy as a symbolic mediator of meaning within the church. Questions which are asked at this stage intend to disclose some of those meanings which are publicly mediated. Answering these questions requires the investigator to look for associations, patterns, relationships, conflicts and contradictions within the data.

The following are some questions which might be asked in the process of objectifying or thematizing an assembly's public ritual horizon: What information with regard to their identity is presented to members of the assembly in the ritual performance? What are they being taught to believe about themselves, God, Jesus Christ, life in a Christian community, salvation? What ecclesial self-image is mediated in the ritual performance? What beliefs, values, commitments are disclosed by the ritual symbols? What beliefs and values are censored out of the public fund? What beliefs and values are reinforced in the ritual? What beliefs and values are being criticized? What conflicts appear in the public horizon? What corporate memories are being evoked? What new meanings and values are emerging? What vision is held out for the assembly?

Obviously judgments made in answer to such questions have to be substantiated on the basis of data gathered from both liturgical performance and other sources. For example, the data from history should provide one with information on the multivocality and

---

[57] Lonergan's remarks about the intention of those who engage in cultural studies are pertinent here. See 'Ongoing Genesis' 154 and 'Aquinas Today: Tradition and Innovation', in *A Third Collection*, 44.

dynamics of ritual symbols, some of the meanings they have carried in the course of their lives. It is in the light of this knowledge that one can discern what potential meanings are being censored out of the horizon and what new meanings may be emerging. Data from official texts and documents provide a basis for comparison with data from liturgical performance and allow one to detect conflicts, variations and new meanings that are appearing in liturgical praxis.

Questions which intend to identify variations, conflicts, and new meanings recognize the significant role played by ritual in revealing, criticizing, and shaping the dynamics of the social process. The verbal and nonverbal components of ritual may serve as a 'metalanguage', a critical commentary on nonritual social processes.[58] As ecclesial ritual action, liturgical praxis may include elements of a critique of the ecclesial process itself and/or of the larger society within which the church is situated. In addition to providing a critique of present ecclesial or social norms or practices the strange and new elements which may appear in liturgical performance sometimes provide an image of alternative possibilities, suggestions in ritual action of 'what might be'.[59]

Because the horizon that is symbolically mediated in liturgical praxis is a dynamic or moving horizon, the product of an assembly which is itself in process, any judgments which are made in the process of objectifying that horizon are tentative ones. Assemblies and their horizons change. However, the tentative nature of such judgments does not excuse the interpreter from making as accurate a judgment as possible. Hypotheses that emerge in the course of the investigation must be subjected to certain conditions and it is only after those conditions have been met that one can make a probable judgment.[60] Conditions may appear in the form of questions that emerge in one's own mind or are asked by others. It is only after one has allowed all the relevant questions to emerge and has attempted to answer them that a probable judgment about a particular aspect

---

[58] See Turner, 'Dramatic Ritual/Ritual Drama: Performative and Reflexive Anthropology', *The Kenyon Review* New Series 1 (1979) 93; 'Process System', 70–71; 'Encounter with Freud: The Making of a Comparative Symbologist', in *The Making of Psychological Anthropology*, ed. George D. Spindler (Berkeley: University of California Press 1978) 578.

[59] Turner associates the critical and creative potential of ritual with liminality or, in certain situations, with the liminoid. See 'Process, System', 67–72 and 'Variations on a Theme of Liminality', in *Secular Ritual*, ed. Sally F. Moore and Barbara C. Myerhoff (Assen: Van Gorcum 1977), 43–46.

[60] For Lonergan's explanation of judgment as a virtually conditioned, a conditioned whose conditions are known and fulfilled see *Insight: A Study of Human Understanding* (London: Longmans, Green 1957), 280–83.

of the horizon can be made.[61] In fact, the context for each judgment may be a 'nest of interlocked or interwoven questions and answers' which is limited by the particular topic under consideration.[62]

Judging the public horizon. Judgments made about the content of the horizon made public in an assembly's liturgical praxis complete one part of the theologian's task, that of objectifying the horizon. A further dimension of the task is that of judging the adequacy or authenticity of the horizon that is being symbolically mediated in liturgy. Why is this necessary? Liturgy is one way in which the church's living tradition is handed on and shaped and, as was stated earlier in this essay, the authenticity of that tradition cannot be taken for granted. There is always the possibility that the tradition which is being mediated may suffer from devaluation, distortion, dilution, or corruption.[63] As ecclesial ritual action, liturgy can be viewed as a classic of the Christian tradition. Like any other Christian classic, liturgy bears the ambiguity that is associated with its creation and reception within the history of the ecclesial process.[64]

Lonergan describes an authentic tradition as one which is 'a long accumulation of insights, adjustments, re-interpretations, that repeats the original message afresh for each age' and an unauthentic tradition as one which 'may consist in a watering down of the original message, in recasting it into terms and meanings that fit into the assumptions and convictions of those that have dodged the issue of radical conversion'.[65] Since traditions are usually a complex mixture of authenticity and unauthenticity, of both creative progress and decline, attempts must be made to uncover what is not authentic, to detect seeds of aberration, bias, and decline.[66]

There is no easy way of making a judgment about the authenticity of a living tradition as it is being mediated in liturgical praxis. What takes place in liturgical performance is the outcome of any number of decisions made by a variety of persons including those who construct the official text of a rite and those who actually celebrate the

[61] See Lonergan, *Method*, 162–65.
[62] Ibid., 163. See also 'Merging Horizons', 96–97.
[63] See Lonergan, 'A Post-Hegelian Philosophy', 213.
[64] See David Tracy, *Plurality and Ambiguity: Hermeneutics, Religion, Hope* (San Francisco: Harper and Row 1987), 69. Tracy refers here to a classic text and most of his attention is directed to texts. However, he does include rituals within the category of classics. See, for example, pp. 15 and 36.
[65] Lonergan, 'Merging Horizons', 94–95.
[66] Lonergan recognized that a hermeneutic of suspicion and a hermeneutic of recovery must be applied to any tradition in order to detect distortions and retrieve what is good. See 'Ongoing Genesis', 161–64 and 'The Human Good', 125.

rite. All of these decisions are subject to the possibility of their being tainted by unauthenticity or bias.[67] One cannot make an appeal to authoritative norms as the only criteria for authenticity since persons in authority, as well as those subject to authority and the community, are all carriers of both authenticity and unauthenticity.[68] It is also possible that those handing on the tradition may themselves have authentically appropriated a tradition already infected with unauthenticity.[69]

The church is continually being constituted in various local communities by the combination of the gift of God's Spirit and the proclamation of Christ's message. That message is carried in the church's living tradition and is symbolically proclaimed in liturgical praxis. In trying to make a judgment about the authenticity of the horizon which is mediated in liturgical praxis one might ask: Are there any elements of Christ's message that are consistently censored out of the public horizon? Are there any elements of the horizon which seem to contradict or distort that message? Are there signs of symbolic impoverishment or collective amnesia in the horizon? Does the vision of reality that is ritually mediated address significant human questions in a way which is faithful to Christ's message? This is only a sample of the kinds of question one might ask.

Studies of actual liturgical performance will inevitably yield diverse horizons and this means that liturgical theologians will have to engage in a constructive use of dialogue and dialectic.[70] Pluralism among horizons is no indication of unauthenticity. Differences have to be identified and the roots of these differences ascertained before any judgment can be made as to whether the diverse horizons are complementary or contradictory.[71] Criteria must be developed for distinguishing between elements which contribute to the richness of the Christian tradition and those which impoverish or distort it. If, at any time, the world of meaning which is symbolically mediated in ecclesial liturgical praxis is judged to be seriously inadequate, then a final question for those involved in the study of such praxis may well be: What do we do to promote change?

---

[67] According to Lonergan, an authentic subject is one who is faithful to the transcendental precepts. See 'The Response of the Jesuit as Priest and Apostle in the Modern World', in *A Second Collection*, 169–70. Therefore, lack of authenticity would appear in a refusal to be attentive, intelligent, reasonable, and responsible. For Lonergan on bias see *Insight*, 191–206; 218–44.

[68] See Lonergan, 'Dialectic of Authority', in *A Third Collection*, 8.

[69] See Lonergan, 'Existenz and Aggiornamento', in *Collection*, 247.

[70] See Lonergan, 'Ongoing Genesis', 162.

[71] See Lonergan, *Method*, 235–37.

The theologian as mediator

Earlier in this essay the task of interpretation was described as that of performing a second mediation of the horizon which is symbolically mediated in liturgical praxis, and method was identified as the mediator. However, since all of the operations which constitute the method are carried out by a theologian, it is more accurate to recognize the fact that it is the theologian who executes the second mediation. Since this may raise a question about the possibility of objectivity in the process, this final section of the essay will briefly address the problem.

Some might think that an objective interpreter is one who drops all preconceived ideas and personal biases in an attempt to see only all that is 'out there' and nothing else. Lonergan has named this approach to objectivity 'the principle of the empty head' and has rejected it as an example of naive intuitionism.[72] His position is that, instead of an empty head, an investigator needs a mind well stocked with knowledge and questions, precise and detailed questions if possible.[73] Rather than trying to detach themselves from their own worlds, investigators need to attend to themselves, become aware of their own biases and strive to keep these biases from blocking their ability to learn about others.[74]

Although detachment has sometimes been proposed as the preferred stance for cultural anthropologists in their fieldwork, Victor Turner gradually came to recognize that such a stance was neither desirable nor adequate for one engaged in the study of human actions such as ritual. As he developed a more processual approach to ritual studies, he realized that the investigator has to become involved in the socio-cultural process being studied and attempt to account for any biases which may accompany this involvement.[75]

Those who gather data on liturgical praxis by acting as participant-observers and then proceed to interpret and judge that data must recognize the fact that their own horizons, perspectives, biases, knowledge, and so forth influence the whole process. Of course, this is also true of those who study liturgical texts. How can one become aware of one's biases? One step which may prove helpful is that of having participant-observers attend to and record their own personal reactions as they proceed through the process. If it is possible to have more than one person observe the same series of rituals, this can

---

[72] Ibid., 157.
[73] See Lonergan, 'Method: Trend and Variations', 17.
[74] Ibid., 19.
[75] See Turner, 'Process, System', 77–78.

provide a way of checking the accuracy of the data. In addition, those engaged in the process of interpretation should be critical of the traditions that have shaped their own minds.[76] Finally, persons who study a particular rite in the same or different locations should place their interpretations in dialogue with each other. Different persons may study and interpret liturgical praxis from a variety of perspectives. They are bound to ask different questions and may produce multiple interpretations. Serious conversations among such scholars should reveal the ways in which these interpretations complement or contradict each other. They should also help bring to light any basic differences which are the product of bias.[77]

In the final analysis, any interpretation is mediated by the experience, understanding, judgment and responsibility of the interpreter.[78] A method is only as good as the person who is carrying out the operations. Lonergan warns against deluding oneself with the belief 'that there is an island of safety called method', a set of rules which, if followed, can assure an objective interpretation which is independent of the person employing the method.[79] In the final analysis, 'objectivity is simply the consequence of authentic subjectivity, of genuine attention, genuine intelligence, genuine reasonableness, genuine responsibility'.[80]

Conclusion

A number of proposals have been made in this essay. Liturgical theology has been described in broad general terms as reflection on religion as it manifests itself in corporate public worship. The methodological pluralism associated with the diversity of tasks which can be identified within liturgical theology has been recognized. The suggestion has been made that this pluralism can find a source of unity in the foundational method which underlies all particular methods, the human operations carried out by anyone engaged in the pursuit of knowledge. Whether one is studying a third-century liturgical document or the ritual action of a twentieth-century assembly, one is carrying out the operations associated with being attentive, intelligent, reasonable, and responsible. Particular methods have been described as heuristic frameworks of questions which focus these

---

[76] See Lonergan, *Method*, 162.
[77] For Lonergan on perspectivism see *Method*, 214–20. For Tracy's position on pluralism of interpretations of religion see *Plurality and Ambiguity*, 91ff.
[78] See Lonergan, 'Merging Horizons', 91.
[79] Lonergan, 'The Human Good', 126.
[80] Lonergan, *Method*, 265.

operations with regard to particular unknowns. The ultimate dependence of particular methods on the persons who employ them and the consequent importance of collaboration and conversation among scholars have been stressed.

A proposal was made that one of the tasks within liturgical theology is that of critically reflecting on contemporary liturgical praxis for the purpose of objectifying and judging the horizon or world of meaning made public in that horizon. This was presented as a significant task because of the role liturgy plays in the church's self-mediation.

A method was proposed for facilitating this task. This method was initially constructed within a process which combined theory and praxis. A framework of questions was constructed on the basis of principles from Victor Turner's theory of ritual, but these questions were refined as they were used in an actual case study. Subsequent attempts to employ the method as well as conversations with others who have engaged in the study of liturgical performance have surfaced new questions and contributed to the process of refinement, a process that will continue.[81]

There are many unknowns which can be identified within the task of reflecting on liturgical praxis, and many particular methods which must be constructed in response to these unknowns. It is probable that such methods will be interdisciplinary in nature. The method proposed in this essay provides only one example of what is possible. Perhaps it can serve as an invitation to others to explore the various ways in which liturgical praxis can serve as a source for theological reflection.

---

[81] Parts of this method have been employed by some members of the Ritual/Social Science Study Group of the North American Academy of Liturgy.

Author index

Subject index